FIFTEENTH CENTURY
PROSE AND VERSE

AN ENGLISH GARNER

FIFTEENTH CENTURY
PROSE AND VERSE

WITH AN INTRODUCTION BY
ALFRED W. POLLARD

NEW YORK
COOPER SQUARE PUBLISHERS, INC.
1964

Published by
Cooper Square Publishers, Inc.
59 Fourth Avenue, New York, N. Y. 10003
Library of Congress Catalog Card No. 64-16741
Printed in the United States of America

PREFACE

OF the contents of the present volume about a half now appears in the ENGLISH GARNER for the first time. Professor Arber (whose ready acquiescence in my meddlings I wish cordially to acknowledge) had gathered his good corn wherever he could find it without concerning himself with the claims of the different centuries ; and his specimens of Lydgate and Hoccleve, Robin Hood Ballads, and trials for Lollardy, needed as much more added to them to make up a homogeneous volume in the arrangement now adopted. My additions consist of some Christmas Carols, a Miracle Play, a Morality, and a number of the interesting prologues and epilogues of William Caxton ; also two extracts on the art of translation and the need for its exercise, and some depositions in a theatrical lawsuit. The extracts are of the end of the fourteenth century, but are germane to our period as heralding the numerous translations by which it was distinguished ; the lawsuit is of the sixteenth century, but throws light on the transition from municipal to private enterprise in theatrical matters which had then been for some time in progress. As these pieces are included for their matter, not for their style, I hope they will not be considered intrusions in a volume essentially devoted to the fifteenth century, though the extracts on translation have led me in my Introduction to an excursus on the authorship of the Wycliffite translations of the Bible, which can only be excused on the pleas that Purvey and Trevisa both lived on into the fifteenth century, and that it was in the early years of that century that the Bibles were most in circulation.

In editing my texts I have availed myself of the help of the edition of the play of the Coventry Shearmen and Tailors in Professor Manly's *Specimens of the Pre-Shaksperean Drama* (Ginn, 1897), of Dr. Henri Logeman's *Elckerlijk and Everyman* (Librairie Clemm, Gand, 1892), of Professor Ewald Flügel's transcript of the Balliol College Carols published in the Festschrift presented to Professor Hildebrand in 1894, of the Caxton Prefaces printed in Blades's *Life of Caxton*, of Mr. Henry Plomer's transcript of the pleadings in Rastell *v.* Walton in vol. iv. of the Transactions of the Bibliographical Society, and of Forshall and Madden's Wyclif Bible. In Professor Arber's text of the Robin Hood Ballads I have ventured to make a few corrections by the light of the excellent edition (based on the work of Professor Child), printed by

Professor Gummere in his *Old English Ballads* (Ginn, 1894). That of Hoccleve's *Letter of Cupid*, originally printed from Urry's text, has been revised with the aid of the collations published by Professor Skeat in his *Chaucerian and Other Pieces*. Professor Arber's other texts are reprinted substantially as they stood.

In accordance with the plan adopted throughout the *English Garner*, the extracts in this volume are given in modern spelling. I should have preferred myself to re-write them in the educated spelling of their own period, which would offer no obstacle of any kind to a modern reader. Not only, however, for the sake of uniformity, but because I am so convinced that this is the right method of dealing with badly spelt texts that I wish the experiment to be made for the first time by a better philologist than myself, I have fallen back on modern spelling. Whatever its disadvantages, they seem to me as nothing compared with the absurdity of preserving in texts printed for the second, third, and fourth time the vagaries of grossly ignorant scribes. In the play of the Shearmen holiness is spelt *whollenes*, merry *myrre*, voice *woise*, signification *syngnefocacion*, celestial *seylesteall*, and so on. These spellings are as demonstrably wrong as those of *consepeet* (concipiet) and *Glorea in exselsis*, with which the scribe favours us. It is ungracious to find fault with Professor Manly after appropriating some of his stage directions and his identifications of some French words, but I cannot think an editor is right in reprinting a text of which he is obliged to confess 'in general, the sound will be a better guide to the meaning than the spelling.' In any case I am sure that this is not the way to win new readers for our earlier literature.

As a matter of literary honesty, as well as for my own comfort, I may be permitted to state that this is the only volume of the new edition of the *Garner* for which I am responsible or can take credit. I have eaten at least one dinner intended for my friend Mr. A. F. Pollard ; my wastepaper basket has received applications for subscriptions which prove his reputation for generosity ; I have even received a cheque, which the fact that it is reckoned forgery under some circumstances for a man to sign his own name forbade my cashing ; and I have recently been more congratulated as the author of his *Henry VIII.* than I have ever been on any book of my own. So far from being identical, I regret to say that we are not even related ; but as we seem to be as much mistaken as the two Dromios, I hope that our appearance side by side in this new edition of the *Garner* may help to distinguish rather than further confound us.

ALFRED W. POLLARD.

CONTENTS

INTRODUCTION

In the world of politics and statecraft a nation which has once begun to decline seldom, perhaps never, recovers itself. There are too many other dogs about for the bone which has once been relinquished to be resumed later on. It is luck, indeed, if there are any decent scraps to be found on the platter when it is revisited. In the world of literature and thought the dogs are better bred, showing each other new hunting-grounds, and by example and precept often helping to restore a famished comrade to sleekness and vigour. Political conditions may not be gainsaid. A nation which has once lost its ideals cannot again produce a fresh, strong, and manly literature. But the possibilities of literature remain immense, and we cannot foretell in what country it may not revive and win fresh triumphs. Hence it is that while the political fortunes of a nation seem to move mainly along the three straight lines of ascent, enjoyment, and fall, its literary fortunes express themselves, when we try to generalise, in a series of curves, alternate rises and declines, which may be repeated again and again. In English literature out of the unknown past rose the Anglo-Saxon lyric and epic, *Deor's Complaint*, *Beowulf*, and the poems of Cædmon and Cynewulf. From the death-like sleep of our language which followed the Norman Conquest rose the heights of thirteenth-century romance. From the dull poetic pedantries of the age which succeeded Chaucer rose the glittering pinnacles of Shakespeare and his fellows.

From the coldness and shallowness of the eighteenth century rose the rich and varied tableland of whose occupants Burns was one of the first and Tennyson and Browning perhaps the last. No other literature has shown such recuperative power, a thought full of hope and consolation in these days, for those who can take pleasure in the anticipated joys of their great-grandchildren.

If this philosophising be thought dull, we have only repaid popular estimates in their own coin; for these sweeping generalisations, which condemn whole centuries as periods of depression, have been largely made for us by popular opinion, and like all generalisations, they have to be very considerably whittled down as soon as we descend to particulars. On a nearer view we find that the curves of literary progress have not been rolled smooth by any steamroller, but that the great chain of hills is connected by numberless ridges, some of which are already rising, long ere others have touched the plain. A pleasant book by an American professor (the *History of Romanticism in the Eighteenth Century*, by Henry A. Beers) has helped to draw attention to many of these rising ridges of romance in the century which most people connect only with the name of Pope; and I hope in these few pages to show that the fifteenth century, of which we are so contemptuous, was at least not all flat country.

For the poor esteem into which this period has fallen we must lay some of the blame at the door of the literary historians who have, until recent days, placed the English Mandeville nearly half a century too early, postponed the consideration of the dramatic productions till they reached the middle of the sixteenth century, when they gave a meagre summary of 'earlier attempts,' and chronicled the

industry of translators, which had been in full swing ever
since about 1380, as a special feature of the sixteenth
century, helping thus to account for the great Elizabethan
outburst of original work.   No poor period of literature
was ever more mercilessly or wantonly plundered to enrich
its prosperous neighbours on either side ; and having thus
credited to other generations all its little claims to distinction, our literary historians fixed their glance sternly on the
court poetry, which is its weakest feature, and made the
case of Hoccleve and Lydgate more pitiful than it need be
by cruelly comparing them with Chaucer.   To be incon-
venient to historians is not perhaps of itself a mark of
greatness, but Chaucer's professed lovers may take pleasure
in observing how largely he shares this characteristic with
Shakespeare himself.   To give each of them a separate
chapter is but a respectful subterfuge, thinly concealing how
unconscionably these two sudden elevations interfere with
that orderly progression which the historian loves.   It would
be much easier to tell the story of the Elizabethan-Jacobean
drama from rise to fall if Shakespeare could be left out of
it ; and if there had been no Chaucer, how gentle, how almost
mathematical, would have been the progression from the
Cursor Mundi and the *Handlyng Synne* to Gower's *Confessio
Amantis*, from Gower to Lydgate and Hoccleve, and from
Lydgate and Hoccleve to Stephen Hawes!   The Italian
influence would have come in for the first time with Surrey
and Wyatt, and the whole sequence would have been just
what a plain man would expect.   Not only by his incon-
venient possession of genius, but also by his great, if fitful
industry, and by what we can hardly call by any name but
good luck, Chaucer shoots up suddenly between Gower and
his natural successors, and thus revolutionises the standard

of poetry by which the next century is inevitably judged. The effect of his sudden uprising is almost as confusing to our judgments of his own poetry as of that of his unhappy 'successors.' Brought up, as most of us poor middle-aged critics have been, on textbooks which grudgingly devoted a scanty thirty or forty pages to all that happened ere Surrey and Wyatt began to write an English which literary historians could read without taking any trouble, we inevitably got it into our heads that with Chaucer we were at the very beginning; that he was really, as he was called, the Father of English Poetry, and represented the first blossoming of its spring. The spring had come and was fast fading when Chaucer began to write. It had come with the first blossoming of the romances, and with such lyrics as

> ' Lenten [1] is come with love to town,
> With blossoms and with birdes rown'; [2]

or as

> ' Blow, northern wind,
> Send thou me my sweeting';

of which the lightness and spontaneity are represented in only a few snatches in Chaucer. Other touches of the spring he has, for no man better loved the merry month of May, and he has sung it until he has become for ever identified with it in our minds. All the same, he represents also a reaction which sees the humorous side of the lover's springtide longings, and views all things very much as they are, without illusion. Fortunately, in Chaucer's case this prosaic mood was raised and transfigured by the revelation of Italian poetry, which enabled him to give us in *Troilus and Cressida*, and the knight's tale of *Palamon and Arcite*,

[1] Spring.   [2] Whispering.

the most perfect harmony of humour and romance English
narrative poetry has produced. No other poet of his time
came under the same influences, and to this fact, as well as
to his possession of genius, he owes his unique position.

That the worthy Lydgate and Hoccleve, without any
of Chaucer's good luck, failed to tread in his footsteps, is
thus hardly surprising. They took from him as much of
his machinery as they could carry, wrote in his metres with
the aid of ears sadly confused by the rapidly weakening
pronunciation of final -*e* and -*es*, and began the attempt,
pursued all through the century, to make up by magnilo-
quence what they lacked in poetry. This attempt was not
confined to England. In France also there was the same
invasion of long words, and it took our fair neighbour much
longer to get rid of them. As the fifteenth century pro-
gressed and its successor began, it became more and more
the object of the poetaster to end his lines with sounding
polysyllables, and verse not written in this style was
regarded as uncourtly and undignified. When we once
realise that this particular experiment in language was
one which had to be made, and that our fifteenth-century
poets made it with all their might, we can understand how
Hawes could hail Lydgate as 'the most dulcet spring of
famous rhetoric' (this new poetry being essentially
rhetorical); how Skelton, after condescendingly praising
Chaucer for the 'pleasant, easy and plain' terms in which
he wrote, hastened to explain that Lydgate's efforts were
'after a higher rate'; and how the same Skelton thought
it necessary in his *Phylyp Sparowe* to make his 'young
maid' excuse herself for her ignorance of 'polished terms'
and 'English words elect.' Every one in these days was
searching anxiously for the right word, which is indeed

the most proper object of every versifier's search. Un-
luckily, they only looked for it among polysyllables.

It will be gathered by this time that I hold no brief for
what we must call the court poetry of the fifteenth century,
that is to say, the compositions by which poets from Lydgate to Skelton sought to ingratiate themselves with noble
patrons and to prove their title to immortality. When
they were off their guard they wrote much better. The
reminiscences of the gay days of his youth stirred Hoccleve's muse to unwonted vivacity. In the *London Lick-
penny* Lydgate, if Lydgate's it be, wrote humorous satire
with success. Skelton himself, though in his (much too
respectfully spoken of) play *Magnificence* he could
flounder with the worst of his predecessors, in his light and
railing rhymes was nimble enough, and ranged easily from
vigorous invective of Wolsey to pretty panegyrics of fair
ladies. Now and again also these good souls ceased their
search for polysyllables, looked at some fair face or pleasant
landscape, and came near to a natural description. Now
and again, too, when they were on their knees (it is only
in prayers intended for other people that long words seem
appropriate), they got down to a phrase of simple beauty.
And meanwhile in the country in general, we may be sure,
many simple rhymesters were keeping up old traditions;
and if some diligent student would begin gleaning from
the earlier miscellanies with the industry and insight by
which Mr. A. H. Bullen extracted so rich a harvest from
the Elizabethan song-books, surely he also would not go
unrewarded. That the touch which we find in the religious
poems of an earlier date in the Vernon MS. had not been
wholly lost is witnessed by some favourite lines of
mine from a book called *Speculum Christiani*, printed by

Machlinia about 1485, and sometimes attributed to John
Wotton—

> 'Mary mother, well thou be!
> Mary mother, think on me;
> Maiden and mother was never none
> Together, Lady, save thee alone.
> Sweet Lady, maiden clean,
> Shield me from ill, shame and teen;
> Out of sin, Lady, shield thou me.
> And out of debt for charity.
> Lady, for thy joyés five,
> Get me grace in this live,
> To know and keep over all thing,
> Christian faith and God's bidding.
> And truely win all that I need
> To me and mine clothe and feed.
> Help me, Lady, and all mine;
> Shield me, Lady, from hell pine;
> Shield me, Lady, from villainy
> And from all wicked company.'

By the side of this religious verse is there any need to
quote more than a stanza from the *Nut Brown Maid*
just to remind us what the secular poets could do?

> 'Be it right or wrong, these men among, on women do complain,
> Affirming this, how that it is a labour spent in vain
> To love them well; for never a del they love a man again;
> For let a man do what he can their favour to attain,
> Yet if a new to them pursue their first true lover than
> Laboureth for nought and from her thought he is a banished man.'

To say that English poetry was dead when verse like
this was being written is absurd. It was not dead, but
banished from court.

We may well grumble at the mischance which has pre-
served to us such quantities of the verse of men like
Lydgate and Hawes, with which, despite all the blandish-
ments of their editors, a not unwise world refuses to con-

cern itself, and on the other hand has permitted to perish, or scattered seemingly beyond retrieving, the humbler poetry which has much greater worth. In the Robin Hood Ballads which Professor Arber has printed from an edition by Wynkyn de Worde we have at least one piece of salvage. It must be owned, indeed, that to claim a ballad as the product of any one century is rather rash, and that in some form or another this cycle was probably in existence before Chaucer died. The 'Ballad of Otterburn,' again, is founded on an incident of border war which took place in 1388 when Chaucer had just begun work on the *Canterbury Tales,* and this also belongs to fourteenth-century tradition. But both the one and the other, and still more certainly 'Chevy Chace,' must be reckoned in their present form to the credit of our period, and form a notable reinforcement to it, though we must regret that the early transcribers and printers took so little trouble to preserve a correct text.

Christmas carols again, as likely to be handed down from mouth to mouth in the same way as ballads, can be assigned neither to any single author nor to any precise year or even decade of composition. But the charming examples which I have picked out from a number transcribed by Professor Flügel from a Balliol College manuscript of the middle of the sixteenth century, may all safely be attributed to a date earlier than 1500, though perhaps not very much earlier, and in their simple tenderness and mirth they are in strong contrast to the pretentious poetry of the court.[1]

As with the ballads and carols, so with miracle-plays : the fact that they were handed down from one generation to

---

[1] Printed by him in 1894 in a 'Festschrift' in honour of Professor Hildebrand.

another, and in each generation revised, altered, and added
to, makes assignment of dates almost impossible. The
play of the Shearmen and Tailors from the Coventry Gilds
cycle,[1] here printed, survived in a transcript dated 1534, and
it is probable that it was then copied out for the sake of
combining what must originally have been four or five
different plays into one. Some of these plays in their
separate form may have been first written in the fourteenth
century; they appear to have been added to in the fifteenth,
and (as we have seen) assumed their final form in the
sixteenth. The whole of the pseudo-Coventry cycle,[2] in
like manner, seems to have been revised and largely written
when it was last transcribed in 1468. But the supreme
example of fifteenth-century addition to an older cycle is
that of the Wakefield Plays, which early in the century
were taken in hand by a dramatist of extraordinary ability,
whose traceable contributions amount to over three thousand
lines, distributed among at least six, or quite probably as
many as nine different plays, of which five are homogeneous
and entirely from his hand. Among these five are the
well-known *Prima* and *Secunda Pastorum*, the two
Shepherds' Plays with which the history of English comedy
begins. The humours of the two shepherds who meet
on the moor and come to blows over the grazing of an
imaginary flock of sheep are good; the humours of the
Secunda Pastorum, of Mak the sheep-stealer, his clever wife
Gyll, the sheep that was passed off as a baby, and Mak's
well-deserved blanketing,—these surely are not only good,

---

[1] To be carefully distinguished from the so-called Coventry Plays of Cotton
MS., Vespasian, D. viii., whose highly doubtful connection with Coventry rests
solely on a note of Cotton's librarian.

[2] It would be convenient if they could be called the Cotton Plays, as the
Wakefield cycle has been called after the Towneley family.

but as good, of their kind, as they well can be. That I
have not printed this second Shepherds' Play here is due
partly to its being easily accessible in the Early English
Text Society's edition, but chiefly to the serious obstacles
its northern dialect presents to any attempt at transcribing
it in modern English. The play of the Shearmen and
Tailors of Coventry, on the other hand, as I have noted in
my preface, cries aloud for such transcription. The fact,
moreover, that in its present conglomerate condition, it
gives the whole history of the Divine Infancy from the
Annunciation to the Flight into Egypt makes it very
representative, even the humour of the Miracle Plays being
exemplified, though poorly and incongruously, in the attack
of the mothers of the Innocents on Herod's knights. The
different sections of the play, the work no doubt of different
authors, have varying values, that of the Prophets, never
very successfully handled, being much the weakest. On
the other hand, in the simple gifts of the shepherds to the
Holy Child we have a very fair representation of one of
the stock incidents of a Nativity Play in which free scope
was given to whatever tender and playful fancy the dramatist
possessed. It should be said that during the fifteenth century
the popularity of these plays increased enormously, records
of their performance being found in all parts of England,
including Cornwall and Wales, where they were acted in
the vernacular.

Starting not very much later than the Miracle Plays,
since we hear of them at York in the middle of the
fourteenth century, the Moralities also increased greatly
in popularity during our period, offering ample opportunity
for the allegorising and personifying tendency which was
one of its most prominent, and in many respects most

baneful, characteristics. Several plays of this kind of undoubted English origin have come down to us from the fifteenth century itself, and are well worth study. Chiefly because of the interest which has been aroused by its recent performance, I have preferred to give that of *The Summoning of Everyman*, which, while presenting much less variety than such plays as *The Castle of Perseverance*, or *Mind, Will, and Understanding*, has the merit of being in very easy English, short, impressive, and homogeneous. It is these latter merits, quite as much as the evidence which can be obtained by comparing the two texts, that offer the best reason for acquiescing in the verdict that the Dutch play of *Elckerlijk*, attributed to Petrus Dorlandus, a theological writer of Diest, who died in 1507, has a better claim than our English version to be considered the original. Strict adherence to propriety of form was not a characteristic of the dramatic literature of this period, and had the play been of native origin its uniform seriousness of tone would almost assuredly have been broken by some humorous, or semi-humorous, episodes. While the two plays, with the exception of the Prologue, which is not found in the Dutch, agree speech by speech from beginning to end, the English version is not a slavish translation; indeed, the ease and happiness of the diction, and the freedom with which it moves, give it, until the Dutch text is examined, the tone of an original work, and the translator must have been a man of no small ability to achieve such a success. It should be said that the oldest Dutch edition now extant appears to have been printed about 1495; but the play may have been written some years before this, though hardly as early as 'about 1477,' the date Professor Logeman proposes, if the author was only born in 1454,

for it does not read like the work of a very young man.
Professor Logeman was, perhaps, influenced in proposing
this date by a desire to get in front of the critics of English
literature (including ten Brink), who have assigned the
English play to the reign of Edward IV., *i.e.* not later than
1483. As in the Miracle Plays, so in the Moralities, an
original purely didactic purpose was gradually influenced
by a desire to render the didacticism more palatable to a
popular audience by the introduction of humorous incidents.
The complete absence of these from *Everyman* naturally
caused critics to assign it the earliest possible date, so long
as it was regarded as an original work. But there is
nothing in the language which precludes it from having
been written immediately after 1495, when we know that
a Dutch edition was in print, and in judging it as a
translation we may be content to assign it to the end of the
fifteenth century. It is worth noting that at that date there
must already have been considerable literary intercourse
between England and Holland, and that several popular
English books had already been printed at Antwerp for
the English market.

It would have been pleasant to me, as a lover of these
forerunners of the Elizabethan drama, to have advanced
from the Miracle Play and Morality, and have given
examples of the Moral-Interlude and Farce; but these
belong emphatically to the sixteenth century, and come
too near the drama itself for inclusion in a non-dramatic
'Garner.' But as a counterpart to Professor Arber's Trial
of William Thorpe for Heresy, I have ventured to reprint
here from the Transactions of the Bibliographical Society
some pleadings in a theatrical lawsuit of the reign of
Henry VIII., one of the many interesting discoveries pub-

lished by Mr. Henry Plomer. Mr. Plomer's own interest
in the pleadings, and the reason which made them suitable
for publication by a Society in no wise concerned with
the history of the drama, arose from the fact that the
plaintiff in the case, John Rastell, besides being a lawyer
and (it is believed) a writer of interludes, was also a
printer, details of any kind that can be gleaned about the
lives of early printers being always welcome to bookish
antiquaries. But these particular details about Rastell's
stage in his garden, the classes from which actors were
drawn, the value of the dresses they wore, the practice of
hiring the dresses out, and the rather puzzling distinction
made between stage-plays and interludes,[1] are all of considerable interest for our period of the drama, and it seemed
a good deed to give them wider publicity.

We pass now from a survey of its poetry, both non-
dramatic and dramatic, to the work done in the fifteenth
century for the development of English prose. Until
quite towards the close of the fourteenth century England
can hardly be said to have possessed any prose literature
not avowedly or practically of a didactic character. To
save some one's soul or to improve some one's morals were
seemingly the only motives which could suffice to persuade
an Englishman to write his native language except in verse.
The impulse towards prose-writing may perhaps be dated
from about 1380, the date of the first Wyclifite translation
of the Bible. Of this the books of the Old Testament, as

---

[1] See p. 316. Stage-plays were acted in the summer, interludes in the winter,
the cost of hiring dresses being apparently from three to five times as great for
a stage-play as for an interlude. My own interpretation is that the distinction
has nothing to do with the plays acted, but solely to the place of performance,
interludes being acted indoors and stage-plays in the open air, where the dresses
were exposed to greater damage.

far as Daniel, are stated on contemporary authority to
have been rendered by Nicholas Hereford; while historians,
after salving their conscience by confessing that there is
substantially no evidence for attributing the rest of the
work to Wyclif, wherever they have afterwards to mention
it, invariably connect it with his name. A revised edition,
usually assigned to Wyclif's friend, John Purvey, was
completed a few years later. It was about 1380 that
Chaucer was engaged in translating Boethius's *De Con-
solatione Philosophiæ*, and not long afterwards Usk wrote
his *Testament of Love*. The first really secular English
book of any importance, the translation of Mandeville's
Travels, which has come down to us in a Cotton manuscript,
was probably made about the end of the century, and was
quickly succeeded by two variant versions. John of Trevisa,
an Oxford scholar, was the first to English an important
historical work, and a book of popular science, the *Polychronicon* of Higden and the *De Proprietatibus Rerum* of
Bartholomew.

It was necessarily by the free use of translation that
an English secular prose literature had to be built
up. All the standard works hitherto had been written
in Latin, or in a few cases in French; and now that
English had been recognised, alike at court, in the law-
courts, and in the schools, as the natural language of the
inhabitants of England, the first thing which had to be
done was to provide Englishmen with the ordinary sources
of information in their own language. The need for
translation directed attention to its principles and canons,
and two interesting little essays on the subject are here
printed—the one from the preface, said to be by Purvey, to
the second Wyclifite Bible, and the other from that prefixed

by Trevisa to his translation of Higden's *Polychronicon*.
I have particular pleasure in placing these two prefaces
side by side, because, as far as I know, the really striking
resemblances between them, in their grammatical remarks,
in their survey of previous attempts at an English translation of the Bible, and in their attitude to such a translation,
have never been pointed out. Without wishing to intrude
myself into controversial matters on which no one is
entitled to speak who has not made a special study of
the subject, I would fain again draw attention to the fact
that whereas we have a definite statement by Caxton[1] that
the *Polychronicon* 'was englisshed by one Trevisa, vicarye
of barkley, which atte request of one Sir Thomas lord
barkley translated the sayd book [which we have], *the byble*,
and bartylmew *de proprietatibus rerum* [which we have] out
of latyn into englysshe,' in the case of Purvey his name was
first mentioned in connection with Bible translation in 1729
by Daniel Waterton, who 'guessed' and 'pitched upon' him
(Waterton's Works, vol. x. p. 361) as the author of the
second version, partly on the ground of his general pro-
minence as a Wyclifite, and also because of his ownership
of a Bible in Trinity College, Dublin, which Waterland
hoped would prove to be of that version. As it happens,
the text, which is only that of the New Testament, is,
apparently throughout, that of the earlier version, with
some of the Prologues of the later version to separate books
inserted. Inasmuch also as the manuscript was not completed till 1427 or later, its bearing on the question of the
authorship of a translation, which had then been in circulation for some thirty years, does not appear to be very
great. It was open to any one to combine the different

[1] Prohemye to *Polychronicon, ad fin.*

parts of the two versions in any way he pleased, and that
Purvey seems to have preferred the text of the earlier
version and the prologues of the later hardly proves that
the later version is due to him. If we must drag him in at
all, it would be much more reasonable to assign to him the
completion of Nicholas of Hereford's unfinished work.

Lightly arrived at as it was, Waterland's 'guess' was
adopted by Forshall and Madden in their fine edition of the
two versions published in 1850, and as buttressed up by
them with what seems to me a very weak additional argument, has ever since been repeated as an established fact.[1]
The readiness with which the conjecture was accepted can
only be accounted for by the desire to make the work of
translation centre at Lutterworth instead of, as I believe to
have been the case, at Oxford. It seems to be considered that
we shall be robbing Wyclif of his due unless the translations
are connected with him as closely as possible. Burdened as
he was in his last years with age and infirmities, it is surely

---

[1] The argument as I understand it runs as follows :—

    (i) The author of the Prologue is the author of the Translation of the
Bible (which may be granted, though not without the reservation that
the helpers to whom allusion is made may have written sections of the
Prologue, which would confuse any deductions).

    (ii) The Prologue has verbal resemblances to the treatise designated
Ecclesiæ Regimen (the instances quoted seem to me resemblances
merely of topics, and these not uncommon ones).

    (iii) The *Ecclesiæ Regimen* resembles Purvey's confession at his recantation
in 1400 (the previous criticism applies here much more strongly).

Therefore the translation of the Bible is by the author of the *Ecclesiæ Regimen*,
and the author of this is Purvey. I must repeat that the chain seems to me
lamentably weak, and that the resemblances which may be found between
Section xv. of the Prologue and Trevisa's Dialogue and Letter to Lord Berkeley
are stronger, because not arising out of quite such common topics. That they
are only to a slight extent verbal resemblances is no drawback. We do not
expect a man to repeat his own words exactly. What is interesting is to find
two translators both interested in their own methods, and these methods
similar.

enough if he inspired others to work at this great task; we
need not insist that he must have written at least part of the
first translation with his own hands, and that the second must
have begun under his immediate eye. I would submit, indeed,
that the tone of the second translator's reference to 'the
English Bible late translated' (p. 195) is quite incompatible
with any such theory. We know from the manuscript note
in the Bodleian MS. that Nicholas of Hereford began the
translation of the Old Testament; and when his work was
interrupted by the necessity for flight, it is far more likely
that it was taken up by some other of Wyclif's numerous
disciples at Oxford rather than by the master himself,
while the fact that it was the work of his disciples, urged no
doubt by his wish, would amply account for such references
as may be found to it under Wyclif's name. For the second
translation, it seems to me that the tone of the reference
already quoted, and the detailed account (see p. 194) which
the translator gives of the method in which he went to
work, compel us to seek an independent origin, and to look
for some other translator less immediately under Wyclif's
influence. The freedom with which the Bible admittedly
circulated for many years, and the well-known allusion by
Sir Thomas More to an English translation untouched by
any taint of heresy, point also in the same direction. That
the second version is really only a revision of the first can
hardly be adduced as a strong argument on the other side.
The ethics of literary acknowledgment were not appreciated
in Trevisa's days, and I believe that a very similar relation
can be found on comparison of what is known as the
'Vulgate' text of Mandeville with that of the Cotton
manuscript, which the second translator appears to have
used freely, though in this case without improving on it.

At any rate, William Caxton seems a better authority than
an eighteenth-century divine as to the authorship of a
translation made only a few years before he was born. We
know that Trevisa was what we may call a professional
translator, well equipped for his task; and we find him in
the preface to the *Polychronicon* discussing the translation of
the Bible in a strikingly similar spirit to that in which it is
discussed in the Prologue to one of the translations which
have come down to us. It is to be hoped that the subject
may receive further investigation, and that without the
importation of theological bias.

We meet with the name of John Purvey once more in
one of the longest and most interesting of the pieces here
printed, the Examination of William Thorpe before Archbishop Arundel, held at Saltwood Castle in Kent in 1407.
'I know none more covetous shrews,' said the Archbishop
to Thorpe in his railing way, 'than ye are when that ye
have a benefice. For, lo! I gave to John Purvey a benefice
(that of West Hythe, which Purvey held for fourteen
months from August 1401) but a mile out of this castle,
and I heard more complaints about his covetousness for
tithes and other misdoings than I did of all men that were
advanced within my diocese.' 'Sir,' replied Thorpe, 'Sir,
Purvey is neither with you now for the benefice ye gave
him, nor holdeth he faithfully with the learning that he
taught and writ beforetime; and thus he sheweth himself
neither to be hot nor cold; and therefore he and his fellows
may sore dread that if they turn not hastily to the way that
they have forsaken, peradventure they be put out of the
number of Christ's chosen people.'

The Archbishop's answer was to mutter threats against
Purvey as a 'false harlot'; and so the Bible-translator, if

such he were, was abused on both sides. The dialogue about him is a fair instance of the vividness with which Thorpe's account of his trial illustrates the fortunes of Wyclif's followers when they scattered before their persecutors without any leader to rally them. Thorpe was accused of holding all the chief tenets of Wyclif's which were condemned as contrary to the Church's order and teaching, and his answers, according to the account he gives of them, were at once bold and prudent. He seems, moreover, to have had a real gift as a reporter, and to have exercised it impartially enough, for not every Lollard would have put into his examiner's mouth that remarkably happy defence of taking a bagpipe on pilgrimage, which will be found on page 141. Thorpe, though he was sent back to prison, lived to write this account of his trial three-and-fifty years after it took place, but Sir John Oldcastle was burnt alive, despite all Prince Hal's efforts to win him to recant and save himself, and the short account of his trial, which follows that of Thorpe, has thus a more tragic interest.

The persecution of the Lollards was but an incident in the fifteenth century, little affecting its literature, though the burning of Oldcastle called forth a bad poem by Hoccleve. The wasteful wars in France, and the turmoil of the Roses, on the other hand, had a great and most disastrous influence. After Lydgate's death about 1447, Capgrave was our leading man of letters, and on his death in 1464 the post was left vacant, unless Master Bennet Burgh can be considered as having held it. The Paston Letters, which begin in 1422 and cover the rest of the century (till 1507), offer some consolation for the lack of more formal literature, but the lack is undeniable. Moreover, not only literature, but the bookish arts suffered terribly from this depression. The fine English illuminated manuscripts which at the beginning of the century had vied with those of France, ceased to be produced after about 1430 (the siege of Orleans was raised by Jeanne Darc in 1429, and the synchronism may be significant), and with the illuminations, the simpler art of penmanship declined also. It was thus small wonder that the art of printing was introduced but tardily to our country, more than twenty years after the first printed Bible had appeared at Mainz, and that, typographically, William Caxton, with no fine models in contemporary English manuscripts to guide him, produced no single book that can stand comparison with the best work of foreign printers. But if he was a poor printer, he was a most enterprising and skilful publisher, and in his homely way a genuine and most prolific journeyman of letters. As the word journeyman is written, shame bids us strike out the first half of it, lest we seem to cast a slight upon one who did so excellent a work for English literature, whose enthusiasm was so genuine and whose industry so great. But Caxton was always modest for himself, and we shall serve him best by not putting his claims too high. When he commenced author there is an ingenuity in the way he mixes his constructions, which, though it may delight his lovers, compels some little caution in introducing him, haply, to new readers, whom such a paragraph as that which begins 'When I remember' on page 213 might easily affront. But he certainly improved his style by constant practice, and the handful of his prefaces and epilogues here printed do not lack literary charm, while the information they give of the man, his character, his enthusiasms, and his business can hardly fail to please any reasonably sympathetic reader. Take, for instance, these delightful confidences as to the fears and hopes attendant on his translation and publication of that bulky work, the *Golden Legend* of Jacobus de Voragine, which might well daunt even an enterprising publisher :—

'And forasmuch as this said work was great and over chargeable to me to accomplish, I feared me in the beginning of the translation to have continued it, because of the long time of the translation and also in the imprinting of the same, and in manner half desperate to have accomplished it, was in purpose to have left it, after that I had begun to translate it, and to have laid it apart, ne had it been at the instance and request of the puissant, noble and virtuous Earl, my Lord William Earl of Arundel, which desired me to proceed and continue the said work, and promised me to take a reasonable quantity of them when they were achieved and accomplished, and sent to me a worshipful gentleman, a servant of his named John Stanney, which solicited me in my lord's name that I should in no wise leave it, but accomplish it, promising that my said lord should during his life give and grant to me a yearly fee, that is to wit a buck in summer and a doe in winter, with which fee I hold me well content. Then at the con templation and reverence of my said lord I have endeavoured me to make an end and finish this said translation and also have imprinted it in the most best wise that I have, could or might, and present this said book to his good and noble lordship, as chief causer of the achieving of it, praying him to take it in gree of me William Caxton, his poor servant, and that it like him to remember my fee, and I shall pray unto Almighty God for his long life and welfare, and after this short and transitory life to come into everlasting joy in heaven, the which he send to

him and to me and unto all them that shall read and hear
this said book, that for the love and faith of whom all these
holy saints hath suffered death and passion. Amen.'

Few publishers since Caxton's days have let us so far
into their secrets, and we can but hope that his patron
really took 'a reasonable quantity' of the edition (another
was published in a few years, so he probably did), and that
the bucks and the does furnished many jolly dinners.
Elsewhere in these prefaces Caxton tells us how he was
induced to take up the art of printing, narrates the trouble,
in which he has had successors, in getting a good text of
Chaucer's *Canterbury Tales*, pokes fun at English ladies
and at another of his patrons, the Earl of Rivers, and sets
down what is still one of the best criticisms ever penned
of Malory's *King Arthur*. With the mention of that noble
work it is well to finish this brief sketch of our fifteenth-
century literature. It is too well known, too easily accessible,
for any snippets to be quoted from it here. But with the
English version of Mandeville at the beginning of our
period, and Malory's *Arthur* completed in 1469 and published
in 1483, it is evident that we can lay claim to two master-
pieces which have not yet lost their hold on modern
readers. The simplicity and feeling of *Everyman* has
lately obtained recognition. I hope that, when boys and
girls are taught a little more of their own language, the
play of *Max the Sheepstealer* may win even greater
popularity, for it is an ideal play for children to act. If
we throw in 'Chevy Chace' and the 'Nut Brown Maid'
and the 'Robin Hood Ballads,' we shall not be lacking for
poetry. For the interest which we now seek in a realistic
novel we might well go to the Paston Letters. There are
not a few nations of Europe which might be well pleased

if they could show, century by century, as good a record
as this. It is only in fact the ill-fortune which placed it
midway between Chaucer and Shakespeare, and our own
perversity which persists in associating it mainly with
Lydgate and Hoccleve, that causes us to contemn this
particular century as dull.

JOHN LYDGATE (?).

The Siege of Harfleur and the Battle of Agincourt

1415.

Hereafter followeth the Battle of Agincourt and the great Siege of Rouen, by King HENRY of Monmouth, the Fifth of the name; that won Gascony, and Guienne, and Normandy.

[See Sir HARRIS NICOLAS'S *History of the Battle of Agincourt*, p. 301, 2nd Ed. 1832, 8vo.

OD, that all this world did make
And died for us upon a tree,
Save England, for MARY thy Mother's sake!
As Thou art steadfast GOD in Trinity.
And save King HENRY'S soul, I beseech thee!
That was full gracious and good withal;
A courteous Knight and King royal.
　　　Of HENRY the Fifth, noble man of war,
Thy deeds may never forgotten be!
Of Knighthood thou wert the very Loadstar!
In thy time England flowered in prosperity,
Thou mortal Mirror of all Chivalry!
Though thou be not set among the Worthies Nine;
Yet wast thou a Conqueror in thy time!

Our King sent into France full rath,
His Herald that was good and sure.
He desired his heritage for to have:
That is Gascony and Guienne and Normandy.
He bade the Dolphin [*Dauphin*] deliver. It should be his:
All that belonged to the first EDWARD
"And if he say me, Nay!; iwis
I will get it with dint of sword!"
But then answered the Dolphin bold,
By our ambassadors sending again,
"Methinks that your King is not so old,
Wars great for to maintain.
Greet well," he said, "your comely King
That is both gentle and small;
A ton full of tennis balls I will him send,
For to play him therewithal."

Then bethought our Lords all,
In France they would no longer abide:
They took their leave both great and small,
And home to England gan they ride.
To our King they told their tale to the end;
What that the Dolphin did to them say.
"I will him thank," then said the King,
"By the grace of GOD, if I may!"

Yet, by his own mind, this Dolphin bold,
To our King he sent again hastily;
And prayed him truce for to hold,
For JESUS' love that died on a tree.

"Nay," then said our comely King,
"For into France will I wind!
The Dolphin anger I trust I shall:
And such a tennis ball I shall him send,
That shall bear down the high roof of his hall.

The King at Westminster lay that time,
And all his Lords everych one;
And they did set them down to dine:
"Lordings," he saith, "by St. John!
To France I think to take my way:
Of good counsel I you pray,
What is your will that I shall do?
Shew me shortly without delay!"
The Duke of CLARENCE answered soon,
And said, "My Liege, I counsel you so!"
And other Lords said, "We think it for the best
With you to be ready for to go;
Whiles that our lives may endure and last."

"Grammercy, Sirs!" the King gan say,
"Our right, I trust, then shall be won;
And I will 'quite you if I may:
Therefore I warn you, both old and young,
To make you ready without delay
To Southampton to take your way
At St. Peter's tide at Lammas;   [1st August 1415.]
For by the grace of GOD, and if I may,
Over the salt sea I think to pass!"

Great ordnance of guns the King let make,
And shipped them at London all at once;
Bows and arrows in chests were take,
Spears and bills with iron gunstones,
And arming daggers made for the nonce:

With swords and bucklers that were full sure.
And harness bright that strokes would endure.

The King to Southampton then did ride
With his Lords ; for no longer would he dwell.
Fifteen hundred fair ships there did him abide,
With good sails and top-castle.
Lords of France our King they sold
For a million of gold as I heard say.
By England little price they told,
Therefore their song was "Well a way ! "

Between Hampton and the Isle of Wight,
These goodly ships lay there at road,
With mastyards across, full seemly of sight,
Over the haven spread abroad :
On every pavis [*target*] a cross red ;
The waists decked with serpentines [*cannon*] strong.
St. George's streamers spread overhead,
With the Arms of England hanging all along.

Our King fully hastily to his ship yede,
And all other Lords of every degree :
Every ship weighed his anchor in deed,
With the tide to haste them to the sea.
They hoisted their sails, sailed aloft :
A goodly sight it was to see.
The wind was good, and blew but soft :
And forth they went in the name of the Trinity. [7th August 1415.]

Their course they took toward Normandy,
And passed over in a day and a night.
So in the second morning early,
Of that country they had a sight :
And ever [as] they drew near the coast,
Of the day glad were they all ;
And when they were at the shore almost,
Every ship his anchor let fall,
With their tackles they launched many a long boat
And over ha[t]ch threw them into the stream ;

A thousand shortly they saw afloat,
With men of arms that light did leme.

Our king landed at Cottaunses [*Coutances*]   [*It should be* Clef
   without delay,   de Caus.]
On our Lady's Even [of] the Assumption ;   [14th August 1415.]
And to Harflete [*Harfleur*] they took the way
And mustered fair before the town.
Our King his banner there did 'splay,
With standards bright and many [a] pennon :
And there he pitched his tent adown ;
Full well broidered with armory gay.
First our comely King's tent with the crown,
And all other Lords in good array.

" My brother CLARENCE," the King did say,
" The towers of the town will I keep
With her daughters and her maidens gay,
To wake the Frenchmen of their sleep."
" ' London '," he said, " shall with him meet ;
And my guns that lieth fair upon the green ;
For they shall play with Harflete
A game of tennis as I ween.
Go we to game, for God's grace !
My children be ready everych one."

For every great gun that there was,
In his mouth he had a stone.
The Captain of Harflete soon anon
Unto our King he sent hastily
To know what his will was to be done,
For to come thither with such a meiny ?
" Deliver me the town ! " the King said.
" Nay ! " said the Captain, " by God and St DENIS !
" Then shall I win it," said our King,
" By the grace of GOD and his goodness,
Some hard tennis balls I have hither brought
Of marble and iron made full round.
I swear, by JESU that me dear bought,
They shall beat the walls to the ground."

Then said the great gun,
" Hold fellows, we go to game!"
Thanked be MARY and JESU her son,
They did the Frenchmen much shame.
" Fifteen afore," said " London " then ;
Her balls full fair she gan outthrow.
" Thirty " said the second gun, " I will win and I may."
There as the wall was most sure,
They bare it down without nay.
The " King's Daughter " said " Hearken this play !
Hearken Maidens now this tide !
Five and forty we have, it is no nay."
They beat down the walls on every side.

The Normands said, " Let us not abide !
But go we in haste, by one assent !
Wheresoever the gunstones do glide,
Our houses in Harfleet are all to rent :
The Englishmen our bulwarks have brent."
And women cried, " Alas that ever they were born !"
The Frenchmen said, " Now be we shent !
By us now the town is forlorn :
It is best now therefore
That we beseech this English King of grace,
For to assail us no more ;
Lest he destroy us in this place.
Then will we bid the Dolphin make him ready,
Or else this town delivered. must be."

Messengers went forth by and bye,   [10th September 1415.]
And to our King came they :
The Lord CORGRAUNT certainly,   [*It should be* Sir
For he was Captain of the place,   LIONEL BRAQUEMONT.]
And GELAM BOWSER with him did hie,
With other Lords more and less.
And when they to our King come where,
Full lowly set them on their knee :
" Hail, comely King !" gan they say
" CHRIST save thee from adversity !
Of truce we will beseech thee
Until that it be Sunday noon :   [22nd September 1415.]

And if we may not recovered be,
We will deliver the town."

Then said our King full soon,
" I grant you grace in this tide ;
One of you shall forth anon,
And the remnant shall with me abide ! "
Their Captain took his next way,
And to Rouen fast gan he ride.
The Dolphin he had thought there to find
But he was gone ; he durst not abide.

For help the Captain besought that tide
" Harflete is lost for ever and aye ;
The walls be beaten down on every side,
That we no longer keep it may."
Of counsel all he did them pray.
" What is your will that I may do ?
We must ordain the King battle by Sunday,
Or else deliver him the town ! "
The Lords of Rouen together did rown ;
And bade the town should openly yield.
The King of England fareth as a lion :
We will not meet with him in the field !
The Captain would then no longer abide,
And towards Harflete came he right ;
For so fast did he ride
That he was there the same night.

And when he to our King did come, [22nd September 1415.]
Lowly he set him on his knee :
" Hail, comely Prince ! " then did he say,
" The grace of GOD is with thee !
Here have I brought the keys all
Of Harflete that is so royal a city.
All is yours, both chamber and hall ;
And at your will for to be."

" Thanked be JESU ! " said our King,
" And MARY his mother truly !

My uncle DORSET, without letting,
Captain of Harflete shall he be.
And all that is within the city
Awhile yet they shall abide,
To amend the walls in every degree
That are beaten down on every side ı
And after that, they shall out ride
To other towns over all.
Wife nor child shall not there abide:
But have them forth, both great and small!"
One and twenty thousand, men might see,
When they went out, full sore did weep.

The great guns and ordnance truly
Were brought into Harflete.

Great sickness among our host was, in good fay,
Which killed many of our Englishmen:
There died beyond seven score upon a day;
Alive there was left but thousands ten.

Our King himself into the Castle yede,
And rest him there as long as his will was:
At the last he said, "Lords, so God me speed!
Towards Calais I think to pass."

After that Harflete was gotten, that royal city,
Through the grace of GOD omnipotent;
Our comely King made him ready soon,
And towards Calais forth he went.
"My brother GLOUCESTER *veramente*
Here will we no longer abide!
And Cousin of YORK, this is our intent:
With us forth ye shall, this tide!
My Cousin HUNTINGDON with us shall ride;
And the Earl of OXENFORD with you three!
The Duke of SOUTHFOLK [*SUFFOLK*] by our side
He shall come forth with his meiny!
And the Earl of DEVONSHIRE sikerly!

Sir THOMAS HARPING that never did fail;
The Lord BROKE that came heartily [*It should be Sir* THOMAS ERPINGHAM.]
And Sir JOHN of CORNWALL:
Sir GILBERT UMFREY that would us avail; [*It shonld be Sir* GILBERT UMFREVILLE.]
And the Lord CLIFFORD, so GOD me speed!
Sir WILLIAM BOWSER, that will not fail; [*It should be Sir* WILLIAM BOURCHIER.]
For all they will help, if it be need."

Our King rode forth, blessed might he be! [? 8th October 1415.]
He spared neither dale nor down;
By waters great fast rode he,
Till he came to the water of Seine. [*It should be* Somme.]

The Frenchmen threw the bridge adown
That over the water they might not pass.
Our King made him ready then;
And to the town of Turreyn went more and less.
The Frenchmen, our King about becast
With Battles strong on every side;
The Duke of ORLEANS said in haste
"The King of England shall abide.
Who gave him leave this way to pass?
I trust that I shall him beguile
Full long ere he come to Calais."
The Duke of BOURBON answered soon
And swore by God and by St. DENIS
"We will play them every each one,
These Lords of England at the tennis;
Their gentlemen, I swear by St. JOHN!
And archers we will sell them great plenty:
And so will we rid [of] them soon,
Six for a penny of our money."
Then answered the Duke of BAR,
Words that were of great pride:
"By God!" he said, "I will not spare
Over all the Englishmen for to ride,
If that they dare us abide:
We will overthrow them in fere [*company*],
And take them prisoners in this tide:
Then come home again to our dinner!"

HENRY our King that was so good ;
He prepared there full royally :
Stakes he let [*caused to*] hew in a wood,
And then set them before his archers verily.
The Frenchmen our ordnance gan espy.
They that we ordained for to ride
Lighted adown, with sorrow truly ;
So on their feet fast gan abide.

Our King went up upon a hill high
And looked down to the valleys low :
He saw where the Frenchmen came hastily
As thick as ever did hail or snow.
Then kneeled our King down, in that stound,
And all his men on every side :
Every man made a cross and kissed the ground,
And on their feet fast gan abide.
Our King said, " Sirs, what time of the day ? "
" My Liege," they said, " it is nigh Prime [9 *a.m.*] "
" Then go we to our journey,
By the grace of JESU, it is good time :
For saints that lie in their shrine,
To GOD for us be praying.
All the Religious of England, in this time,
Ora pro nobis for us they sing."

St. GEORGE was seen over the host :
Of very truth this sight men did see.
Down was he sent by the HOLY GHOST,
To give our King the victory.

Then blew the trumpets merrily,   [25th October 1415.]
These two Battles [*Armies*] together yede.
Our archers stood up full heartily,
And made the Frenchmen fast to bleed.
Their arrows went fast, without any let,
And many shot they throughout ;
Through habergeon, breastplate, and bassinet.
An eleven thousand were slain in that rout.

Our gracious King, as I well know,
That day he fought with his own hand.
He spared neither high ne low.
There was never King in no land,
That ever did better on a day.
Wherefore England may sing a song:
Laus DEO! may we say;
And other prayers ever among.
The Duke of ORLEANS, without nay,
That day was taken prisoner.
The Duke of BOURBON also in fere:
And also the Duke of BAR truly.
Sir BERGYGAUNTE he gan him yield;
And other Lords of France many.

Lo, thus our comely King conquered the field,
By the grace of God omnipotent,
He took his prisoners, both old and young,
And towards Calais forth he went.

He shipped there with good intent: [16th November 1415.]
To Canterbury full fair he passed,
And offered to St. THOMAS's shrine.
And through Kent he rode in haste;
To Eltham he came all in good time.   [22nd November 1415.]
And over Blackheath, as he was riding,   [23rd November 1415.]
Of the city of London he was ware.
"Hail, royal city!" said our King,
"CHRIST keep thee ever from sorrow and care!
And then he gave that noble city his blessing
He prayed JESU it might well fare!
To Westminster did he ride,
And the French prisoners with him also:
He ransomed them in that tide,
And again to their country he let them go.

Thus of this matter I make an end,
To th'effect of the Battle have I gone:
For in this book I cannot comprehend
The greatest battle of all, called the Siege of Rouen.

For that Siege lasted three years and more,
And there a rat was at forty pence
For in the city the people hungered sore.
Women and children, for fault of meat, were lore ;
And some for pain bare bones were gnawing,
That at their breasts had two children sucking.

Of the Siege of Rouen it to write were pity,
It is a thing so lamentable :
Yet every High Feast, our King, of his charity,
Gave them meat to their bodies comfortable ;
And at the last the town won, without fable.

Thus of all as now I make an end :
To the bliss of heaven, GOD our souls send !

Thus endeth the Battle of Agincourt.

Imprinted at London in Foster lane,
in Saint Leonard's parish,
by me JOHN SKOT.

F   I   N   I   S.

Thomas Occleve,

Clerk in the Office of the Privy Seal.

The Letter of Cupid.

[THOMAS OCCLEVE,

Clerk in the Office of the Privy Seal.]

The Letter of CUPID.

[Old forms like *serven*, serve ; *wollen*, will ; *tellen*, tell ; *doin*, done ;
and the Imperatives *bethe*, be ; *telleth*, tell ; occur in this Poem.]

UPIDO, (unto whose commandèment
    The gentle kindred of goddis on high
And people infernal be obedient ;
    And mortal folk all serven busily),
    Of the goddess son CYTHERA only ;
Unto all those that to our deity
Be subjects, heartly greeting, sendè we !

In general, we wollen that ye know
    That Ladies of honour and reverence,
And other Gentlewomen havin sow
    Such seed of complaint in our audience,
    Of men that do them outrage and offence ;
That it our earis grieveth for to hear,
So piteous is the effect of this matere.

Passing all landis, on the little isle
    That cleped is Albion, they most complain,
They say that there is crop and root of guile :
    So can those men dissimulen and feign,
    With standing dropis in their eyen twain ;
When that their heartis feeleth no distress,
To blinden women with their doubleness.

Their wordis, spoken be so sighingly,
  With so piteous a cheer and countenance
That every wight that meaneth truèly
  Deemeth that they in heart have such grievance.
  They say, "So importable is their penance,
    That but their lady lust to shew them grace
    They, right anon, must starven in the place."

"Ah, Lady mine!" they say, "I you ensure
  As doth me grace! and I shall ever be,
While that my life may laste and endure
  To you as humble and low in each degree
  As possible is, and keep all things secree
    Right as yourselven listé that I do!
    And elles must mine heartè burst in two."

Full hard it is, to know a manis heart
  For outward may no man the truthè deem,
When word out of his mouth may none astert
  But it by reason seemed a wight to queme,
  So it is said of heart, as it would seem.
    O faithful woman! full of innocence!
    Thou art deceivèd by false appearance!

By process moveth oft woman's pity.
  Weening all things were as these men ysay,
They grant them grace, of their benignity,
  For that men shoulden not, for their sake die,
  And with good hearte, set them in the way
    Of blissful lové: keep it, if they con!
    Thus, otherwhilé, women beth ywon.

And when this man the pan hath by the steel
And fully is in his possession;
With that woman keepeth he no more to deal
After, if he may finden in the town
Any woman, his blind affection
   On to bestow. But evil mote he preve!
   A man, for all his oaths, is hard to believe!

And for that every false Man hath a Make,
   (As unto every wight is light to know)
When this traitor, this woman hath forsake,
He fast him speedeth unto his fellow.
Till he be there, his heart is on a low;
   His false deceit ne may him not suffice,
   But of his treason telleth all the wise.

Is this a fair avaunt?   Is this honour?
   A man himself accuse thus and defame!
Is it good to confess himself a traitor?
   And bring a woman into slanderous name
   And tell how he her body hath do shame?
   No worship may he thus, to him conquer,
   But great dislander unto him and her!

To her! Nay! Yet ywas it no reprefe;
   For all for virtue was, that she ywrought!
But he that brewèd hath all this mischief,
   That spake so fair, and falsely inward thought;
   His be the slander! as it by reason ought
   And unto her be thank perpetual
   That, in such a neede helpen can so well.

Although through manis sleight and subtilty,
  A silly simple and innocent woman
Betrayed is : no wonder ! since the city
  Of Troy, as that the story tellen can,
  Betrayèd was, through the deceit of man,
    And set on fire, and all down overthrow ;
    And finally destroyèd, as men know.

Betrayen not men cities great and kings ?
  What wight is it that can shape remedy
Against these falsely proposèd things ?
  Who can the craft such craftés to espy
  But man ? whose wit is e'er ready to apply
    To thing that sowning is into falshede ?
    Woman ! beth'ware of false men ! I thee rede

And, furthermore, have these men in usage
  That where they not likely been to sped,
Such as they been with a double visage,
  They procuren, for to pursue their need ;
  He prayeth him, in his causé to proceed,
    And largely guerdoneth he his travail.
    Little wot women, how men them assail !

Another wretch, unto his fellow saith,
  " Thou fishest fair ! She which that thee hath fired
Is false, inconstant, and she hath no faith.
  She for the road of folk is so desired ;
  And, as an horse, from day to day she is hired !
    That when thou twinnest from her company,
    Cometh another ; and bleared is thine eye !

Now prick on faste! and ride thy journey
  While thou art there! For she, behind thy back,
So liberal is, she will nothing withsay,
  But smartly of another take a smack.
  And thus faren these women all the pack
    Whoso them trusteth, hanged mote he be!
    Ever they desire change and novelty."

Whereof proceedeth this, but of envy?
  For that he himselve her ne winnen may.
He speaketh her reprefe and villainy;
  As manis blabbing tongue is wont alway.
  Thus divers men full often make assay,
    For to disturben folk in sundry wise,
    For they may not acheven their emprise.

Many one eke would speaken for no good,
  That hath in love his timè spent and used.
Men wist, his Lady his asking withstood;
  Ere that he were of her, plainly refused.
  Or waste and vain were all that he had mused:
    Wherefore he can none other remedy,
    But on his Lady shapeth him to lie.

" Every woman," he saith, "is light to get,
  Can none say, ' Nay!' if she be well ysought;
Whoso may leisure have with her to treat
  Of his purpose ne shall be failen ought
  But he on madness be so deep ybrought
    That he shende all with open homeliness;
    That loven women not, as that I guess."

To slaunder women thus, what may profit
  To gentles? namely, that them armen should,
And in defence of women them delight
  As that the Order of Gentilesse would?
  If that a man list gentle to be held
    He must all flee that thereto is contrary.
    A slanderous tongue is his great adversary!

A foul vice is of tongue to be light.
  For *whoso mochil clappeth, gabbeth oft.*
The Tongue of Man so swift is, and so wight
  That when it is yraisèd up on loft,
  Reason it sueth so slowly and soft,
    That it him never overtaken may.
    Lord! so these men been trusty in assay!

Albeit that men find one woman nice,
  Inconstant, recheless, and variable,
Deignous and proud, full fillèd of malice,
  Withouten faith or love, and deceivable,
  Sly, quaint, false, in all untrust culpable,
    Wicked or fierce, or full of cruelty:
    Yet followeth not that such all women be!

When the high God angellis formèd had,
  Among them alle formed were there none
That founden were malicious and bad?
  Yes! all men wot that there were many one
  That for their pridé fell from heaven anon.
    Should we, forthy, give all angels proud name?
    Nay, he that that sustaineth, is to blame!

Of twelve Apostles, one a traitor was ;
　　The remenant yet good weren and true.
So if it happen men finden, percase,
　　A woman false ; such good is to eschew :
　　And deemé not that they be all untrue.
　　　　I see well, that men's owné falseness
　　　　Them causeth woman for to trust the less.

O, every man ought have a hearté tender
　　Unto woman, and deem her honourable ;
Whether her shape be thick, or else slender,
　　Or she be good or bad !　It is no fable.
　　Every wight wot, that wit hath reasonable,
　　　　That of a woman, he descendèd is :
　　　　Then is it shame of her to speak amiss !

A wicked tree good fruit may none forth bring ;
　　For such the fruit is aye as is the tree.
Take heed of whom thou took thy beginning !
　　Let thy mother be mirror unto thee !
　　Honour her, if thou wilt honoured be !
　　　　Despiseth her then not, in no manere !
　　　　Lest that thereby thy wickedness appear.

An old proverb there said is, in English,
　　That bird or fowl, soothly, is dishonest
What that he be, and holden full churlish
　　That useth to defoulen his own nest.
　　Men to say well of women, it is the best :
　　　　And naught for to despise them, ne deprave ;
　　　　If that they will their honour keep or save.

The Ladies ever complainen them on Clerks
That they have made bookis of their defame ;
In which they despise women and their works,
And speaken of them great reproof and shame :
And causèless give them a wicked name.
Thus they despisèd be, on every side,
Dislanderèd and blown upon full wide.

Those sorry bookes maken mention
How women betrayed in especial
ADAM, DAVID, SAMPSON, and SOLOMON,
And many one more ; who may rehearse them all,
The treasons that they havé done, and shall ?
The world their malice may not comprehend
(As Clerkis feign), for it ne hath none end.

OVID, in his book called *Remedy*
Of Lovè, great reproof of woman writeth,
Wherein, I know that he did great folly ;
And every wight who, in such case, him delighteth.
A Clerkis custom is, when he enditeth
Of women (be it prose, or rhyme, or verse)
Say, " They be wicked ! " all know he the reverse.

And the book Scholars learned in their childhead
For they of women beware should in age,
And for to love them ever be in dread.
Sith to deceive is set all their courage,
They say peril to cast is advantage,
Namely, of such as men have in been wrapped :
For many a man, by woman hath mishapped.

No charge is what so that these Clerkis sain
Of all their writing I ne do no cure
All their labour and travail is in vain
For between me and my Lady Nature
Shall not be suffred, while the world may 'dure.
Thus these Clerkis, by their cruel tyranny,
On silly women kithen their mastery.

Whilom full many of them were in my chain
Ytied ; and now, what for unwieldy age
And unlust, they may not to love attain :
And sain that "Love is but very dotage !"
Thus, for that they themself lacken courage,
They folk exciten by their wicked saws
For to rebell against me, and my laws !

But, maugre them that blamen women most,
Such is the force of mine impression
That, suddenly, I can fell all their boast,
And all their wrong imagination.
It shall not be in their election
The foulest slut in all the town to refuse ;
If that me list, for all that they can muse :

But her in heart as brenningly desire
As though she were a Duchess, or a Queen ;
So can I folkis heartis set on fire
And, as me list, them senden joy or teen.
They that to women ben ywhet so keen,
My sharpè piercing strokis, how they smite,
Shall feel and know, and how they kerve and bite !

Pardie! this Clerk, this subtle sly OVID
And many another have deceived be
Of women, as it knowen is full wide.
　What! no men more! and that is great dainty
　So excellent a Clerk as was he!
　　And other more, that coulde full well preach
　　Betrapped were, for aught that they could teach!

And trusteth well, that it is no marvail!
　For women knowen plainly their intent.
They wist how softily they could assail
　Them; and what falsehood they in hearte meant:
And thus they Clerkis in their danger hent,
　　With one venom, another is destroyed!
　　And thus these Clerkis often were annoyed.

These Ladies, ne these gentles ne'ertheless,
　Where none of those that wroughten in this wise;
But such women as weren vertueless
　They quittin thus these old Clerkis wise.
　To Clerkis muchil less ought to suffice
　　Than to dispraven women generally;
　　For worship shall they geten noon thereby.

If that these men, that lovers them pretend,
　To women weren faithful, good, and true,
And dread them to deceive, or to offend;
　Women, to love them woulde not eschew.
　But, every day hath man an harte new!
　　It upon one abiden can no while.
　　What force is it, such a wight to beguile?

Men bearen, eke, the women upon hand
    That lightly, and withouten any pain
They wonnen be ; they can no wight withstand
    That his disease list to them to complain !
    They be so frail, they may them not refrain !
        But whoso liketh them may lightly have ;
        So be their heartis easy in to grave.

To Master JEAN DE MEUN, as I suppose,
    Then, it is a lewd occupation,
In making of the *Romance of the Rose,*
    So many a sly imagination,
    And perils for to rollen up and down,
        So long process, so many a sly cautel
        For to deceive a silly damosel !

Nought can I see, ne my wit comprehend,
    That art, and pain, and subtilty should fail
For to conquer, and soon to make an end ;
    When men a feeble placé shall assail :
    And soon, also, to vanquish a battle
        Of which no wight shall maken resistance ;
        Ne heart hath none to stonden at defence.

Then mote it follow, of necessity,
    Sith art asketh so great engine and pain
A woman to deceive, what so she be ?
    Of constancy be they not so barren
    As that some of these subtle Clerkis feign ;
        But they be, as that women oughten be,
        Sad, constant, and fulfilled of pity.

How friendly was MEDEA to JASON
In his Conquering of the Fleece of Gold!
How falsely quit he her true affection,
By whom victory he gat as he would!
How may this man, for shame, be so bold
To falsen her, that, from his death and shame
Him kept, and gat him so great a prize and name?

Of Troy also, the traitor ÆNEAS,
The faithless wretch! how he himself forswor
To DIDO, which that Queen of Carthage was
That him relievèd of his smartis sore!
What gentilessè might she have doon more
Than she, with heart unfeigned, to him kidde?
And what mischief to her thereof betid!

In my *Legend of Martyrs* may men find
(Whoso that liketh therein for to read)
That oathis ne behest may man not bind
Of reprovable shame have they no dread
In manis hearte truth ne hath no stead.
The soil is naught; there may be no trothè grow!
To women, namely, it is not unknown.

Clerkis feign also there is no malice
Like unto woman's wicked crabbedness.
O Woman! how shalt thou thyself chevice;
Sith men of thee so mochil harm witness?
Beth ware! O Woman! of their fickleness.
Kepeth thine ownè! what men clap or crake!
And some of them shall smart, I undertake!

Malice of women! What is it to dread?
They slay no man, destroyen no cities,
Ne oppress people, ne them overlead,
Betray Empires, Realmes, or Duchies,
Nor bereaven men their landis, ne their mees,
Empoison folk, ne houses set on fire,
Ne false contractis maken for no hire.

Trust, Perfect Love, and Entire Charity,
Fervent Will, and Entalented Courage,
All thewis good, as sitteth well to be,
Have women ay, of custom and usage.
And well they can a manis ire assuage,
With softè wordis, discreet and benign.
What they be inward, they show outward by sign

Womanis heart unto no cruelty
Inclined is; but they be Charitable,
Piteous, Devout, Full of Humility,
Shamefastè, Debonaire, and Amiable,
Dread full, and of their wordis measurable:
What women, these have not, peradventure;
Followeth not the way of her nature.

Men sayen that our First Mother na'theless
Made all mankinde lose his liberty,
And nakid it of joyè, doubteless,
For Godis hestès disobeyed she,
When she presumed to taste of the tree,
That God forbade that she eat thereof should.
And ne had the Devil be, no more she would!

The envious swelling, that the Fiend our foe
    Had unto man in hertè, for his wealth,
Sent a serpent, and made her for to go
    To deceive EVE; and thus was manis health
    Bereft him by the Fiend, right in a stealth,
        The woman not knowing of the deceit,
        God wot! Full far was it from her conceit!

Wherefore I say, that this good woman EVE
    Our father ADAM, ne deceived nought.
There may no man for a deceit it preve
    Properly, but if that she, in heart and thought,
    Had it compassed first, ere she it wrought.
        And for such was not her impression,
        Men may it call no Deceit, by reason.

Ne no wight deceiveth, but he purpose!
    The fiend this deceit cast, and nothing she.
Then it is wrong to deemen or suppose
    That of this harm she should the causè be.
    Wytith the Fiend, and his be the maugree!
        And all excusèd have her innocence,
        Save only, that she brake obedience!

And touching this, full fewè men there be,
    Unnethis any, dare I safely say!
From day to day, as men may all day see,
    But that the hest of God they disobey.
    Have this in mindè, siris! I you pray.
        If that ye be discreet and reasonable;
        Ye will her holdè the more excusable!

And where men say, "In man is stedfastness;
  And woman is of her courage unstable."
Who may of ADAM bear such a witness?
  Tellith me this!   Was he not changeable?
  They bothè werin in one case semblable.
    Save that willing the Fiend deceived EVE;
    And so did she not ADAM, by your leave!

Yet was this sinnè happy to mankind,
  The Fiend deceivèd was, for all his sleight;
For aught he could him in his sleightis wind,
  God, to discharge man of the heavy weight
  Of his trespass, came down from heaven on height
    And flesh and blood he took of a Virgine,
    And suffered death, him to deliver of pine.

And God, to whom there may nothing hid be,
  If He in woman knowen had such malice,
As men record of them in generalty;
  Of our Lady, of Life Reparatrice
  Nold have been born: but for that she of vice
    Was void, and full of virtue, well He wist,
    Endowid! of her to be born Him list.

Her heapèd virtue hath such excellence
  That all too lean is manis faculty
To declare it; and therefore in suspense
  Her due praising put must needis be.
  But this we witen, verily, that she,
    Next God, the best friend is that to Man 'longeth.
    The Key of Mercy by her girdle hangeth!

And of mercy hath every man such need,
  That razing that, farewel the joy of man!
And of her power, now takith right good heed!
  She mercy may well and purchasen can.
  Depleasith her not! Honoureth that woman!
    And other women honour for her sake!
    And but ye do, your sorrow shall awake!

In any book also, where can ye find
  That of the workis, or the death or life,
Of JESU spelleth or maketh any mind,
  That women Him forsook, for woe or strife?
  Where was there any wight so ententife
    Abouten Him as woman? Proved none!
    The Apostles him forsooken everichone.

Woman forsook him not! For all the faith
  Of holy church in woman left only!
These are no lies, for Holy Writ thus saith,
  Look! and ye shall so find it hardily!
  And therefore I may well proven thereby
    That in woman reigneth stable constancy;
    And in men is change and variancy.

Thou Precious Gem of martyrs, Margarite!
  That of thy blood dreadest none effusion!
Thou Lover true! Thou Maiden mansuete!
  Thou, constant Woman! in thy passion
  Overcame the Fiendis temptation!
    And many a wight convertid thy doctrine,
    Unto the faith of God, holy Virgin!

But, understandeth this! I commend her nought,
By encheson of her virginity.
Trusteth, it came never into thought!
For ever werry against Chastity.
And ever shall. But, lo, this moveth me,
Her loving heart and constant to her lay
Drove out of my remembrance I ne may.

Now holdith this for firm, and for no lie!
That this true and just commendation
Of women tell I for no flattery;
Nor because of pride or elation:
But only, lo! for this intention
To give them courage of perseverance
In virtue, and their honour to advance.

The more the virtue, the less is the pride.
Virtue so digne is, and so noble in kind,
That Vice and he will not in fere abide.
He putteth vices clean out of his mind,
He flyeth from them, he leaveth them behind.
O, Woman! that of Virtue, art hostess;
Great is thy honour, and thy worthiness!

Then will I thus concluden and define.
We, you command! our ministers each one
That ready ye be our hestès to incline!
That of these falsè men, our rebell foon,
Ye do punishèment! and that, anon!
Void them our Court! and banish them for ever!
So that therein more comen may they never!

Fulfilled be it! Ceasing all delay,
  Look that there be none excusation!
Written in the air, the lusty month of May,
  In our Palace, where many a million
  Of lovers true, have habitation;
    In the year of grace, joyful and jocond,
    A thousand and four hundred and second.

Thus endeth
The letter of C U P I D.

The Ballad of

ROBIN HOOD.

The first printed edition by
WYNKYN DE WORDE,
about 1510.

❧ Here beginneth a little geste of Robin Hood and his meiny: and of the proud Sheriff of Nottingham.

ITHE and listen, Gentlemen
That be of free-born blood!
I shall you tell of a good yeoman;
His name was ROBIN HOOD.
ROBIN was a proud outlaw,
Whiles he walked on ground,
So courteous an outlaw as he was one,
Was never none yfound.
ROBIN stood in Bernysdale,
And leaned him to a tree;
And by him stood Little JOHN,
A good yeoman was he:
And also did good SCATHELOCK,
And MUCH the miller's son,
There was no inch of his body
But it was worth a groom.
Then bespake him Little JOHN,
All unto ROBIN HOOD,
  "Master, if ye would dine betime,
It would do you much good!"
  Then bespake good ROBIN,
"To dine I have no lust,
Till I have some bold Baron,
Or some unketh guest,
That may pay for the best,

Or some Knight or some Squire
That dwelleth here by West."
A good manner then had ROBIN,
In land where that he were,
Every day or he would dine,
Three *Masses* would he hear.
The one in the worship of the Father
The other of the Holy Ghost,
The third was of our dear Lady
That he loved, aldermost.
ROBIN loved our dear Lady ;
For doubt of deadly sin,
Would he never do company harm
That any woman was in.
    "Master!" then said Little JOHN,
" And we our board shall spread,
Tell us, Whither we shall gone,
And what life we shall lead ?
Where we shall take ?   Where we shall leave ?
Where we shall abide behind ?
Where shall we rob ?   where shall we 'reave ?
Where we shall beat and bind ? "
    "Thereof no force ! " said ROBIN,
" We shall do well enough !
But look, ye do no husband harm,
That tilleth with his plough !
No more ye shall no good yeoman
That walketh by green-wood shaw !
Ne no Knight, ne no Squire
That would be a good fellaw !
These Bishops and these Archbishops,
Ye shall them beat and bind !
The High Sheriff of NOTTINGHAM,
Him hold ye in your mind ! "
    "This word shall be held," saith Little JOHN,
" And this lesson shall we lere !
It is far day, God send us a guest,
That we were at our dinnèr ! "
    "Take thy good bow in thy hand," said ROBIN,
" Let MUCH wend with thee !
And so shall WILLIAM SCATHELOCK !

And no man abide with me.
And walk up to the Sayles,
And so to Watling street,
And wait after some unketh guest,
Upchance, ye may them meet:
Be he Earl or any Baron,
Abbot or any Knight,
Bring him to lodge to me!
His dinner shall be dight!"
They went unto the Sayles,
These yeomen all three;
They looked East, they looked West,
They might no man see.
But as they looked in Bernysdale,
By a derne street,
Then came there a Knight riding:
Full soon they 'gan him meet.
All dreary then was his semblante,
And little was his pride,
His one foot in the stirrup stood,
That other waved beside.
His hood hanged in his eyen two,
He rode in simple array;
A sorrier man than he was one,
Rode never in summer's day.
Little JOHN was full curteys,
And set him on his knee,
"Welcome be ye, gentle Knight!
Welcome are ye to me!
Welcome be thou to green wood,
Hende Knight and free!
My master hath abiden you fasting,
Sir! all these hours three!"
"Who is your master?" said the Knight.
JOHN said, "ROBIN HOOD!"
"He is a good yeoman," said the Knight;
"Of him I have heard much good!
I grant," he said, "with you to wend,
My brethren all in-fere:
My purpose was to have dined to-day
At Blyth or Doncaster."

Forth then went that gentle Knight,
With a careful cheer ;
The tears out of his eyen ran,
And fell down by his leer.
    They brought him unto the lodge door :
When ROBIN 'gan him see,
Full courteously did off his hood,
And set him on his knee.
    " Welcome, Sir Knight ! " then said ROBIN,
" Welcome thou art to me ;
I have abide you fasting, Sir,
All these hours three ! "
    Then answered the gentle Knight
With words fair and free,
" God thee save, good ROBIN !
And all thy fair meiny ! "
    They washed together, and wiped both ;
And set till their dinner :
Bread and wine they had enough,
And nombles of the deer ;
Swans and pheasants they had full good,
And fowls of the rivèr.
There failed never so little a bird
That ever was bred on brere.
    " Do gladly, Sir Knight ! " said ROBIN.
    " Grammercy, Sir ! " said he,
" Such a dinner had I not
Of all these weekes three :
If I come again, ROBIN,
Here by this country,
As good a dinner, I shall thee make
As thou hast made to me ! "
    " Grammercy, Knight ! " said ROBIN,
" My dinner when I have
I was never so greedy, by dear-worthy God !
My dinner for to crave :
But pay ere ye wend ! " said ROBIN ;
" Methinketh it is good right,
It was never the manner, by dear-worthy God !
A yeoman pay for a Knight ! "
    " I have nought in my coffers," said the Knight,

" That I may proffer, for shame ! "
　　" Little JOHN ! go look ! " said ROBIN HOOD,
" Ne let not, for no blame,
Tell me truth ! " said ROBIN,
" So God have part of thee ! "
　　" I have no more but ten shillings," said the Knight,
" So God have part of me ! "
　　" If thou have no more," said ROBIN,
" I will not one penny !
And if thou have need of any more ;
More shall I lend thee !
Go now forth, Little JOHN,
The truth, tell thou me !
If there be no more but ten shillings,
Not one penny that I see ! "
　　Little JOHN spread down his mantle
Full fair upon the ground ;
And there he found, in the Knight's coffer,
But even half a pound.
Little JOHN let it lie full still,
And went to his master full low.
　　" What tidings, JOHN ? " said ROBIN.
　　" Sir, the Knight is true enow ! '
" Fill of the best wine ! " said ROBIN,
" The Knight shall begin !
Much wonder thinketh me
Thy clothing is so thin !
Tell me one word," said ROBIN,
" And counsel shall it be :
I trow thou wert made a Knight, of force,
Or else of yeomanry !
Or else thou hast been a sorry husband
And lived in stroke and strife,
And okerer or else a lecher," said ROBIN,
" With wrong hast thou led thy life ! "
　　" I am none of them," said the Knight,
" By God that made me !
A hundred winters herebefore,
My ancestors Knights have be
But oft it hath befallen, ROBIN !
A man hath been disgrate,

But God that sitteth in heaven above,
May amend his state!
Within this two year, ROBIN!" he said,
"(My neighbours well it know!)
Four hundred pounds of good money
Full well then might I spend.
Now, have I no goods," said the Knight;
"God hath shapen such an end,—
But my children and my wife,
Till God it may amend!"

  "In what manner," said ROBIN,
"Hast thou lost thy riches?"

  "For my great folly," he said,
"And for my kindness!
I had a son, forsooth, ROBIN!
That should have been my heir:
When he was twenty winters old,
In field would joust full fair.
He slew a Knight of Lancashire
And a Squire bold.
For to save him in his right
My goods be set and sold,
My lands be set to wed, ROBIN!
Until a certain day
To a rich Abbot here besides,
Of Saint MARY's Abbey."

  "What is the sum?" said ROBIN;
"Truth then tell thou me!"

  "Sir," he said, "four hundred pounds,
The Abbot told it to me!"

  "Now, and thou lose thy land!" said ROBIN,
"What shall 'fall of thee?"

  "Hastily I will me busk," said the Knight,
"Over the salt sea,
And see where CHRIST was quick and dead
On the Mount of Calvary!
Farewell, friend! and have good day!
It may not better be!"
Tears fell out of his eyen two,
He would have gone his way.
  "Farewell, friends, and have good day!

I ne have more to pay ! "
" Where be thy friends ? " said ROBIN.
" Sir ! never one will know me !
While I was rich enough at home
Great boast then would they blow;
And now they run away from me
As beasts in a row,
They take no more heed of me
Than they me never saw ! "
 For ruth then wept Little JOHN,
SCATHELOCK and MUCH also.
 " Fill of the best wine ! " said ROBIN,
" For here is a simple cheer.
Hast thou any friends," said ROBIN,
" The borrows that will be ? "
 " I have none ! " then said the Knight,
" But God that died on the tree ! "
 " Do way thy japes ! " said ROBIN,
" Thereof will I right none !
Weenest thou I will have God to borrow,
PETER, PAUL, or JOHN ?
Nay, by Him that me made,
And shaped both sun and moon !
Find a better borrow," said ROBIN,
" Or money gettest thou none ! "
 " I have none other ! " said the Knight,
" The sooth for to say,
But if it be Our dear Lady
She failed me never or this day ! "
 " By dear worthy God ! " said ROBIN,
" To seek all England through,
Yet found I never to my pay
A much better borrow !
Come now forth, Little JOHN !
And go to my treasure !
And bring me four hundred pound,
And look that it well told be ! "
 Forth then went Little JOHN
And SCATHELOCK went before,
He told out four hundred pound
By eighteen [? *eight and twenty*] score.

" Is this well told ? " say Little MUCH.
JOHN said, " What grieveth thee ?
It is alms to help a gentle Knight
That is fallen in poverty ! "
" Master ! " then said Little JOHN,
" His clothing is full thin !
Ye must give the Knight a livery
To lap his body therein :
For ye have ꙅcarlet and green, Master !
And many a rich array ;
There is no merchant in merry England
So rich, I dare well say."
" Take him three yards of every colour,
And look it well meeted be ! "
Little JOHN took none other measure
But his bow tree ;
And of every handful that he met
He leapèd over feet three.
" What devilkins draper ! " said Little MUCH,
" Thinkst thou to be ? "
SCATHELOCK stood full still, and laughed,
And said " By God Almight !
JOHN may give him the better measure,
For it cost him but light ! "
" Master ! " said Little JOHN,
All unto ROBIN HOOD,
" Ye must give the Knight an horse
To lead home all this good."
" Take him a grey courser ! " said ROBIN,
" And a saddle new !
He is Our Lady's Messenger ;
God leve that he be true ! "
" And a good palfrey," said Little MUCH,
" To maintain him in his right ! "
" And a pair of boots," said SCATHELOCK,
" For he is a gentle Knight ! "
" What shalt thou give him, Little JOHN ? " said ROBIN,
" Sir ; a pair of gilt spurs clean,
To pray for all this company ;
God bring him out of teen ! "
" When shall my day be," said the Knight,

" Sir ! and your will be ? "
  " This day twelvemonth ! " said ROBIN,
" Under this green-wood tree.
It were great shame," said ROBIN,
" A Knight alone to ride ;
Without Squire, yeoman, or page,
To walk by his side !
I shall thee lend, Little JOHN, my man ;
For he shall be thy knave !
In a yeoman's stead, he may thee stand,
If thou great need have ! "

❧ The second fytte.

Ow is the Knight went on his way,
This game him thought full good,
When he looked on Bernysdale,
He blessèd ROBIN HOOD :
And when he bethought on Bernysdale,
On SCATHELOCK, MUCH, and JOHN ;
He blessed them for the best company
That ever he in come.
  Then spake that gentle Knight,
To Little JOHN 'gan he say,
" To-morrow, I must to York town,
To Saint Mary's Abbey,
And to the Abbot of that place
Four hundred pound I must pay :
And but I be there upon this night
My land is lost for aye ! "
  The Abbot said to his Convent,
There he stood on ground :
" This day twelve months came there a Knight,
And borrowed four hundred pound.
[He borrowed four hundred pound]
Upon his land and fee ;
But he come this ilk day
Disherited shall he be ! "
  " It is full early ! " said the Prior,

"The day is not yet far gone!
I had lever to pay an hundred pound
And lay [it] down anon.
The Knight is far beyond the sea
In England is his right,
And suffereth hunger and cold
And many a sorry night :
It were great pity," said the Prior,
" So to have his land :
And ye be so light of your conscience
Ye do to him much wrong !"

" Thou art ever in my beard," said the Abbot ;
" By God and Saint Richard ! "
With that came in, a fat-headed monk,
The High Cellarer.

" He is dead or hanged !" said the Monk,
" By God that bought me dear !
And we shall have to spend in this place,
Four hundred pounds by year ! "

The Abbot and High Cellarer
Start forth full bold :
The Justice of England,
The Abbot there did hold.

The High Justice, and many mo,
Had taken into their hand
Wholly all the Knight's debt,
To put that Knight to wrong.

They deemed the Knight wonder sore
The Abbot and his meiny,
But he come this ilk day
Disherited shall he be.

" He will not come yet," said the Justice,
" I dare well undertake ! "
But in sorrow time for them all,
The Knight came to the gate.

Then bespake that gentle Knight
Until his meiny,
" Now, put on your simple weeds
That ye brought from the sea ! "
[They put on their simple weeds,]

They came to the gates anon,
The Porter was ready himself,

And welcomed them everych one.
"Welcome, Sir Knight!" said the Porter;
"My Lord, to meat is he;
And so is many a gentleman
For the love of thee!"
The Porter swore a full great oath
"By God that made me!
Here be the best coresed horse
That ever yet saw I me!
Lead them into the stable!" he said,
"That easèd might they be!"
"They shall not come therein!" said the Knight,
"By God that died on a tree!"
Lords were to meat yset
In that Abbot's hall:
The Knight went forth, and kneeled down,
And salued them, great and small.
"Do gladly, Sir Abbot!" said the Knight,
"I am come to hold my day!"
The first word the Abbot spake,
"Hast thou brought my pay?"
"Not one penny!" said the Knight,
"By God that makèd me!"
"Thou art a shrewd debtor!" said the Abbot;
"Sir Justice, drink to me!
What doest thou here," said the Abbot,
"But thou hadst brought thy pay?"
"For God!" then said the Knight,
"To pray of a longer day!"
"Thy day is broke!" said the Justice;
"Land gettest thou none!"
"Now, good Sir Justice! be my friend!
And fend me of my fone!"
"I am hold with the Abbot!" said the Justice,
"Both with cloth and fee!"
"Now, good Sir Sheriff! be my friend!"
"Nay, for God!" said he.
"Now, good Sir Abbot! be my friend!
For thy courtesy;
And hold my lands in thy hand
Till I have made thee gree:

And I will be thy true servant
And truly serve thee
Till ye have four hundred pounds
Of money good and free."
  The Abbot sware a full great oath,
" By God that died on a tree !
Get thee land where thou mayest ;
For thou gettest none of me !"
  " By dear worthy God," then said the Knight,
" That all this world wrought !
But I have my land again,
Full dear it shall be bought !
God that was of Maiden born,
Leave us well to speed !
For it is good to assay a friend
Or that a man have need !"
  The Abbot loathly on him 'gan call :
And villainously him 'gan look :
" Out," he said, " thou false Knight !
Speed thee out of my hall !"
  " Thou liest !" then said the gentle Knight,
" Abbot in thy hall !
False Knight was I never,
By God that made us all !"
Up then stood that gentle Knight :
To the Abbot, said he,
" To suffer a Knight to kneel so long,
Thou canst no courtesy !
In jousts and in tournament
Full far then have I be ;
And put myself as far in press
As any that ever I see."
  " What will ye give more," said the Justice,
" And the Knight shall make a release ?
And else I dare safely swear
Ye hold never your land in peace !"
  " An hundred pounds !" said the Abbot.
  The Justice said, " Give him two !"
  " Nay, by God !" said the Knight,
" Yet get ye it not so !
Though ye would give a thousand more,

Yet wert thou never the near!
Shalt there never be mine heir,
Abbot! Justice! ne Friar!"
He started him to a board anon,
Till a table round,
And there he shook out of a bag
Even four hundred pound.
"Have here thy gold, Sir Abbot!" said the Knight,
"Which that thou lentest me!
Hadst thou been courteous at my coming,
Rewarded shouldst thou have be!"
    The Abbot sat still, and eat no more,
For all his royal fare :
He cast his head on his shoulder,
And fast began to stare.
    "Take me my gold again!" said the Abbot,
"Sir Justice, that I took thee!"
    "Not a penny!" said the Justice,
"By God that died on the tree!"
    "Sir Abbot, and ye Men of Law!
Now have I held my day!
Now shall I have my land again
For ought that you can say!"

    The Knight started out of the door,
Away was all his care!
And on he put his good clothing,
The other he left there.
He went him forth full merry singing
As men have told in tale,
His Lady met him at the gate
At home in Verysdale.
    "Welcome, my Lord!" said his Lady,
"Sir, lost is all your good?"
    "Be merry, Dame!" said the Knight,
"And pray for Robin Hood!
That ever his soul be in bliss ;
He helped me out of my teen.
Ne had not been his kindness,
Beggars had we been!
The Abbot and I accorded be ;

He is served of his pay !
The good yeoman lent it me,
As I came by the way."

This Knight then dwelled fair at home,
The sooth for to say,
Till he had got four hundred pounds
All ready for to pay.
He purveyed him an hundred bows,
The strings well dight ;
An hundred sheafs of arrows good,
The heads burnished full bright :
And every arrow an ell long
With peacock well ydight ;
Ynocked all with white silver,
It was a seemly sight.
He purveyed him an hundred men,
Well harnessed in that stead,
And himself in that same set
And clothed in white and red.
He bare a lancegay in his hand,
And a man led his mail,
And riden with a light song
Unto Bernysdale.
But at Wentbridge there was a wrestling,
And there tarried was he :
And there was all the best yoemen
Of all the West country.
A full fair game there was up set;
A white bull up i-pight;
A great courser, with saddle and bridle
With gold burnished full bright;
A pair of gloves, a red gold ring,
A pipe of wine, in fay :
What man beareth him best, I wis
The prize shall bear away.
There was a yoeman in that place,
And best worthy was he.
And for he was far and fremd bestead
Yslain he should have be.

The Knight had ruth of his yeoman
In place where that he stood :
He said, " The yeoman should have no harm,
For love of ROBIN HOOD ! "
  The Knight pressed into the place,
An hundred followed him free,
With bows bent and arrows sharp
For to shend that company.
They shouldered all and made him room
To wit what he would say ;
He took the yeoman by the hand
And gave him all the play ;
He gave him five marks for his wine,
There it laid on the mould :
And bade it should be set abroach,
Drink who so would !
Thus long tarried this gentle Knight
Till that play was done :
So long abode ROBIN fasting,
Three hours after the noon.

The third fytte.

ITHE and listen, Gentlemen !
All that now be here,
Of Little JOHN, that was the Knight's man,
Good mirth ye shall hear.
  It was upon a merry day
That young men would go shoot,
Little JOHN fetched his bow anon
And said he " would them meet."
  Three times, Little JOHN shot about,
And always he sleste [*slit*] the wand :
The proud Sheriff of NOTTINGHAM
By the Marks 'gan stand.
  The Sheriff swore a full great oath,
" By Him that died on the tree !
This man is the best archer
That yet saw I me !

Say me now, wight young man !
What is now thy name ?
In what country wert thou born ?
And where is thy woning wane ? "
  " In Holderness, I was born,
I-wis, all of my dame :
Men call me REYNOLD GREENLEAF,
When I am at home."
  " Say me, REYNOLD GREENLEAF !
Wilt thou dwell with me ?
And every year, I will thee give
Twenty marks to thy fee ! "
  " I have a Master," said Little JOHN,
" A courteous Knight is he ;
May ye get leave of him, the better may it be
  The Sheriff got Little JOHN
Twelve months of the Knight ;
Therefore he gave him right anon
A good horse and a wight.
Now is Little JOHN a Sheriff's man,
God give us well to speed !
But always thought Little JOHN
To quite him well his meed.
  " Now, so God me help ! " said Little JOHN,
" And be my true lewte !
I shall be the worst servant to him
That ever yet had he ! "
  It befel upon a Wednesday,
The Sheriff on hunting was gone,
And Little JOHN lay in his bed, and was forgot at home,
Therefore he was fasting till it was past the noon.
  " Good Sir Steward, I pray thee,
Give me to dine ! " said Little JOHN.
" It is long for GREENLEAF, fasting so long to be.
Therefore I pray thee, Steward, my dinner give thou me ! '
  " Shalt thou never eat nor drink," said the Steward,
" Till my lord be come to town ! "
  " I make my avow to God," said Little JOHN
" I had lever to crack thy crown ! "
  The Butler was full uncourteous,
There he stood on floor ;

He started to the buttery, and shut fast the door.
Little JOHN gave the Butler such a rap
His back went nigh in two
Though he lived an hundred winters, the worse he should go.
He spurned the door with his foot, it went up well and fine!
And there he made a large 'livery
Both of ale and wine.
   " Sir, if ye will not dine," said Little JOHN,
" I shall give you to drink!
And though ye live an hundred winters,
On Little JOHN ye shall think! "
Little JOHN eat and little JOHN drank, the while he would.
   The Sheriff had in his kitchen a Cook,
A stout man and a bold,
" I make mine avow to God!" said the Cook,
" Thou art a shrewd hind,
In any household to dwell! for to ask thus to dine!"
And there he lent Little JOHN
Good strokes three.
   " I make mine avow," said Little JOHN,
" These strokes liketh well.
Thou art a bold man and a hardy,
And so thinketh me!
And ere I pass from this place
Assayed better shalt thou be!"
   Little JOHN drew a good sword,
The Cook took another in hand;
They thought nothing for to flee,
But stiffly for to stand.
There they fought sore together,
Two mile way and more;
Might neither other harm do
The maintenance of an hour.
   " I make mine avow to God," said Little JOHN,
" And by my true lewte!
Thou art one of the best swordsmen
That ever yet saw I me,
Couldst thou shoot as well in a bow,
To green wood, thou shouldst with me!
And two times in the year, thy clothing
Ychanged should be!

And every year of ROBIN HOOD,
Twenty marks to thy fee!"
    " Put up thy sword," said the Cook,
" And fellows will we be!"
    Then he fetch to Little JOHN,
The nombles of a doe,
Good bread, and full good wine.
They eat and drank thereto.
And when they had drunken well,
Their troths together they plight,
That they would be with ROBIN
That ilk same night.
They did them to the treasure house
As fast as they might go;
The locks that were good steel,
They brake them everych one.
They took away the silver vessels,
And all that they might get;
Piece, mazers, ne spoons,
Would they none forget.
Also they took the good pence,
Three hundred pounds and more:
And did them strait to ROBIN HOOD
Under the green-wood hoar.
    " God thee save, my dear master!
And CHRIST thee save and see!"
    And then said ROBIN to Little JOHN,
" Welcome might thou be!
And also that fair yeoman,
Thou bringest there with thee!
What tidings from Nottingham,
Little JOHN? tell thou me!"
    " Well thee greeteth the proud Sheriff!
And send thee here by me,
His Cook and his silver vessels,
And three hundred pounds and three!"
    " I make mine avow to God!" said ROBIN,
" And to the Trinity!
It was never by his good-will
This good is come to me!"
    Little JOHN him there bethought

On a shrewd wile.   Five miles in the forest he ran.
Him happed at his will!
Then he met the proud Sheriff
Hunting with hounds and horn.
Little JOHN could his courtesy,
And kneeled him beforne.
  " God thee save, my dear Master!
And CHRIST thee save and see!"
    " REYNOLD GREENLEAF!" said the Sheriff,
" Where hast thou now be?"
    " I have been in this forest;
A fair sight can I see;
It was one of the fairest sights
That ever yet saw I me!
Yonder I see a right fair hart,
His colour is of green!
Seven score of deer upon a herd,
Be with him all bedeen,
His tynde are so sharp, Master,
Of sixty and well mo,
That I durst not shoot for dread,
Lest they would me slo!"
    " I make mine avow to God!" said the Sheriff,
" That sight would I fain see!"
    " Busk you thitherward, my dear Master
Anon, and wend with me!"
    The Sheriff rode, and Little JOHN,
Of foot he was full smart;
And when they came afore ROBIN,
" Lo, here is the master Hart!"
    Still stood the proud Sheriff:
A sorry man was he!
" Woe the worth, REYNOLD GREENLEAF,
Thou hast betrayed me!"
    " I make mine avow to God," said Little JOHN,
" Master, ye be to blame!
I was mis-served of my dinner,
When I was with you at home!"
    Soon he was to supper set,
And served with silver white:
And when the Sheriff saw his vessel,

For sorrow, he might not eat !
    " Make good cheer," said ROBIN HOOD,
" Sheriff ! for charity !
And for the love of Little JOHN
Thy life is granted to thee ! "
    When they had supped well,
The day was all agone,
ROBIN commanded Little JOHN
To draw off his hosen and his shoon,
His kirtle and his courtepy,
That was furred well fine ;
And took him a green mantle,
To lap his body therein.
ROBIN commanded his wight young men,
Under the green-wood tree,
They shall lay in that same suit,
That the Sheriff might them see.
    All night lay that proud Sheriff,
In his breech and in his shirt :
No wonder it was in green wood
Though his sides do smart.
    " Make glad cheer," said ROBIN HOOD,
" Sheriff, for charity !
For this is our order, I-wis,
Under the green-wood tree ! "
    " This is harder order," said the Sheriff,
" Than any Anchor or Frere !
For all the gold in merry England,
I would not long dwell here ! "
    " All these twelve months," said ROBIN,
" Thou shalt dwell with me !
I shall thee teach, proud Sheriff,
An outlaw for to be ! "
    " Ere I here another night lie," said the Sheriff,
" ROBIN, now I pray thee !
Smite off my head, rather to-morn,
And I forgive it thee !
Let me go then," said the Sheriff,
" For saint charity !
And I will be thy best friend,
That yet had ye ! "

" Thou shalt swear me an oath ! " said ROBIN,
" On my bright brand,
Thou shalt never await me scathe !
By water ne by land !
And if thou find any of my men,
By night, or by day,
Upon thine oath, thou shalt swear
To help them that thou may ! "
    Now has the Sheriff ysworn this oath,
And home he began to gone ;
He was as full of green wood,
As ever was heap of stone.

❡ The fourth fytte.

HE Sheriff dwelled in Nottingham,
    He was fain that he was gone,
    And ROBIN and his merry men
    Went to wood anon.
    " Go we to dinner ? " said Little JOHN.
ROBIN HOOD said, " Nay !
For I dread our Lady be wroth with me ;
For she [has] sent me not my pay ! "
    " Have no doubt, Master ! " said Little JOHN.
"Yet is not the sun not at rest :
For I dare say and safely swear
The Knight is true and trust ! "
    " Take thy bow in thy hand ! " said ROBIN.
" Let MUCH wend with thee !
And so shall WILLIAM SCATHELOCK ;
And no man abide with me !
And walk up under the Sayles,
And to Watling Street ;
And wait after such unketh guest,
Upchance ye may them meet.
Whether he be messenger,
Or a man that mirths can ;
Of my good, he shall have some
If he be a poor man ! "
    Forth then started Little JOHN,

Half in tray or teen,
And girded him with a full good sword
Under a mantle of green.
They went up to the Sayles,
These yeomen all three,
They looked East, they looked West,
They might no man see.
But as they looked in Bernysdale,
By the highway
Then were they 'ware of two black monks,
Each on a good palfrey.
  Then bespake Little JOHN,
To MUCH he 'gan say :
" I dare lay my life to wed
These monks have brought our pay ! "
  " Make glad cheer," said Little JOHN,
" And frese our bows of yew !
And look your hearts be sicker and sad,
Your strings trusty and true ! "
  The monk had fifty and two [men]
And seven somers full strong,
There rideth no Bishop in this land
So royally I understand.
  " Brethren," said Little JOHN,
" Here are no more but we three ;
But we bring them to dinner,
Our Master, dare we not see ! "
  " Bend your bows ! " said Little JOHN,
" Make all yon press to stand !
The foremost monk, his life and his death,
Are closed in my hand.
Abide, churl Monk ! " said Little JOHN,
" No further that thou go,
If thou dost, by dear-worthy God !
Thy death is in my hand !
And evil thrift on thy head ! " said Little JOHN,
" Right under thy hat's band :
For thou hast made our Master wroth,
He is fasting so long ! "
  " Who is your Master ? " said the Monk.
Little JOHN said, " ROBIN HOOD ! "

" He is a strong thief ! " said the Monk ;
" Of him heard I never good ! "
   " Thou liest then ! " said Little JOHN,
" And that shall rue thee !
He is a yeoman of the forest ;
To dine, he hath bidden thee!"
   MUCH was ready with a bolt,
Readily and anon,
He set the Monk tofore the breast
To the ground that he can gone.
Of fifty-two wight young yeomen
There abode not one ;
Save a little page and a groom
To lead the somers with Little JOHN.
   They brought the Monk to the lodge door,
Whether he were loth or lief,
For to speak with ROBIN HOOD,
Maugre in their teeth.
   ROBIN did adown his hood,
The Monk when that he see,
The Monk who was not so courteous
His hood then let he be.
   " He is a churl, Master ! by dear-worthy God ! "
Then said Little JOHN.
   " Thereof no force ! " said ROBIN,
" For courtesy can he none !
How many men," said ROBIN,
" Had this Monk, JOHN ? "
   " Fifty and two when that we met ;
But many of them be gone."
   " Let blow a horn ! " said ROBIN,
" That fellowship may us know ! "
   Seven score of wight yeomen
Came pricking on a row,
And everych of them a good mantle
Of scarlet and of ray,
All they came to good ROBIN
To wit what he would say.
They made the Monk to wash and wipe,
And sit at his dinner,
ROBIN HOOD and Little JOHN

They served him both in-fere.
"Do gladly, Monk!" said ROBIN.
"Grammercy, Sir!" said he.
"Where is your Abbey, when ye are at home;
And who is your avow?"
"St. Mary's Abbey," said the Monk,
"Though I be simple here."
"In what office?" said ROBIN.
"Sir! the High Cellarer."
"Ye be the more welcome," said ROBIN.
"So ever might I thee."
"Fill of the best wine!" said ROBIN,
"This Monk shall drink to me!
But I have great marvel," said ROBIN,
"Of all this long day,
I dread our Lady be wroth with me,
She sent me not my pay!"
"Have no doubt, Master!" said Little JOHN,
"Ye have no need, I say:
This Monk, it hath brought, I dare well swear!
For he is of her Abbey."
"And She was a borrow," said ROBIN,
"Between a Knight and me,
Of a little money that I him lent
Under the green-wood tree;
And if thou hast that silver ybrought,
I pray thee let me see,
And I shall help thee eftsoons
If thou have need to me!"
The Monk swore a full great oath,
With a sorry cheer,
"Of the borrowhood thou speakest to me
Heard I never ere!"
"I make mine avow to God!" said ROBIN,
"Monk, thou art to blame!
For God is held a righteous man,
And so is his dame.
Thou toldest with thine own tongue
Thou mayst not say 'Nay!'
How thou art her servant,
And servest her every day:

And thou art made her messenger,
My money for to pay.
Therefore I can the more thanks,
Thou art come to thy day!
What is in your coffers?" said ROBIN;
"True, then, tell thou me?"
   "Sir!" he said, "twenty marks!
Also might I thee!"
   "If there be no more," said ROBIN,
"I will not one penny.
If thou hast myster of any more,
Sir, more I shall lend to thee!
And if I find more," said ROBIN,
"Iwis, thou shalt it forgo;
For of thy spending silver, Monk!
Thereof will I right none."
   "Go now forth, Little JOHN,
And the truth, tell thou me!
If there be no more but twenty marks
No penny [of] that I see!"
   Little JOHN spread his mantle down,
As he had done before,
And he told out of the Monk's mail
Eight hundred pound and more.
   Little JOHN let it lie full still,
And went to his Master in haste;
   "Sir!" he said, "the Monk is true enough;
Our Lady hath doubled your cast!"
   "I make mine avow to God!" said ROBIN,
"Monk, what told I thee!
Our Lady is the truest woman
That ever yet found I me!
By dear worthy God!" said ROBIN,
"To seek all England through;
Yet found I never to my pay,
A much better borrow.
Fill of the best wine, and do him drink!" said ROBIN:
" And greet well thy Lady hend;
And if she have need to ROBIN HOOD,
A friend she shall him find:
And if she needeth any more silver,

Come thou again to me!
And, by this token she hath me sent,
She shall have such three! "
     The Monk was going to London ward,
There to hold great Mote,
The Knight that rode so high on horse
To bring him under foot.
     " Whither be ye away? " said ROBIN.
     " Sir, to manors in this land,
To reckon with our Reeves
That have done much wrong."
     " Come now forth, Little JOHN!
And hearken to my tale!
A better yeoman, I know none
To seek a Monk's mail.
How much is in yonder other corser? " said ROBIN,
" The sooth must we see! "
     " By our Lady! " then said the Monk,
" That were no courtesy;
To bid a man to dinner,
And sith him beat and bind! "
     " It is our old manner! " said ROBIN,
" To leave but little behind."
     The Monk took the horse with spur,
No longer would he abide!
     " Ask to drink! " then said ROBIN,
" Or that ye further ride? "
     " Nay, for God! " said the Monk,
" Me rueth I came so near!
For better cheap, I might have dined
In Blyth or in Doncaster! "
     " Greet well, your Abbot! " said ROBIN,
" And your Prior, I you pray!
And bid him send me such a Monk
To dinner every day! "

     Now let we that Monk be still;
And speak we of the Knight!
Yet he came to hold his day
While that it was light.
He did him strait to Bernysdale,

Under the green-wood tree.
And he found there ROBIN HOOD
And all his merry meiny.
The Knight light down off his good palfrey.
ROBIN when he 'gan see ;
So courteously he did adown his hood
And set him on his knee.
  "God thee save, ROBIN HOOD,
And all this company ! "
  "Welcome, be thou, gentle Knight ὶ
And right welcome to me ! "
Then bespake him ROBIN HOOD,
To that Knight so free,
" What need driveth thee to green wood ?
I pray thee, Sir Knight, tell me !
And welcome be, thou gentle Knight !
Why hast thou been so long ? "
  " For the Abbot and high Justice
Would have had my land ? "
  " Hast thou thy land again ? " said ROBIN,
" Truth then tell thou me ! "
  " Yea, for God ! " said the Knight,
" And that I thank God and thee !
But take not a grief," said the Knight,
" That I have been so long,
I came by a wrestling,
And there I helped a poor yeoman,
Who with wrong was put behind."
  " Nay, for God ! " said ROBIN,
" Sir Knight, that thank I thee !
What man that helpeth a good yeoman,
His friend then will I be."
  " Have here four hundred pounds ! " then said the Knight
" The which ye lent me,
And here is also twenty marks for your courtesy ! "
  " Nay, for God ! " then said ROBIN,
" Thou brook it well for aye ;
For our Lady, by her Cellarer,
Hath sent to me my pay !
And if I took it twice,
A shame it were to me !

But truly, gentle Knight,
Welcome art thou to me ! "
  When ROBIN had told his tale,
He laughed and had good cheer,
  " By my troth ! " then said the Knight,
" Your money is ready here ! "
  " Brook it well ! " said ROBIN,
" Thou gentle Knight so free !
And welcome be thou, gentle Knight,
Under my trystel tree !
But what shall these bows do ? " said ROBIN,
" And these arrows yfeathered free ? "
  " By God ! " then said the Knight,
" A poor present to thee ! "
  "Come now forth, Little JOHN,
And go to my treasure,
And bring me there four hundred pounds
The Monk overtold it me.
Have here four hundred pounds,
Thou gentle Knight and true !
And buy horse and harness good,
And gilt thy spurs all new !
And if thou fail any spending,
Come to ROBIN HOOD !
And, by my troth, thou shalt none fail
The whiles I have any good ;
And brook well thy four hundred pounds
Which I lent to thee !
And make thyself no more so bare ;
By the counsel of me."

Thus then helped him, good ROBIN,
The Knight all of his care :
God that sits in heaven high
Grant us well to fare !

The fifth fytte.

Ow hath the Knight his leave ytake,
And went him on his way.
ROBIN HOOD and his merry men
Dwelled still full many a day.
Lithe and listen, Gentlemen !
And hearken what I shall say,
How the proud Sheriff of NOTTINGHAM
Did cry a full fair Play,
That all the best archers of the North
Should come upon a day ;
And he that shooteth alder best,
The game shall bear away !
He that shooteth alder best
Furthest, fair, and low,
At a pair of finely butts,
Under the green-wood shaw,
A right good arrow he shall have,
The shaft of silver white,
The head and feathers of rich red gold,
In England is none like.
    This then heard good ROBIN,
Under his trystel tree.
" Make you ready, ye wight young men,
That shooting will I see !
Busk you, my merry young men,
Ye shall go with me !
And I will wit the Sheriff's faith ;
True and if be he ! "
    When they had their bows ybent,
Their tackles feathered free,
Seven score of wight young men
Stood by ROBIN's knee.
    When they came to Nottingham,
The butts were fair and long,
Many were the bold archers
That shooted with bowès strong.
" There shall but six shoot with me,

The others shall keep my head,
And stand with good bows bent
That I be not deceived."
    The fourth outlaw, his bow 'gan bend,
And that was ROBIN HOOD:
And that beheld the proud Sheriff,
All by the butt he stood.
Thrice ROBIN shot about,
And always sliced the wand;
And so did good " GILBERT
With the white hand."
Little JOHN and good SCATHELOCK
Were archers good and free:
Little MUCH and good REYNOLD
The worst would they not be!
    When they had shot about,
These archers fair and good:
Ever more was the best,
Forsooth, ROBIN HOOD.
Him was delivered the good arrow,
For best worthy was he:
He took the gift so courteously;
To green wood would he!
They cried out on ROBIN HOOD,
And great horns 'gan they blow!
    "Woe worth the treason!" said ROBIN;
"Full evil thou art to know!
And woe be thou, thou proud Sheriff!
Thus gladding thy guest,
Otherwise thou behote me
In yonder wild forest,
But had I thee in green wood,
Under my trystel tree,
Thou shouldst leave me a better wed,
Than thy true lewte."
    Full many a bow there was bent,
And arrows let they glide!
Many a kirtle there was rent,
And hurt many a side!
The outlaws' shot was so strong
That no man might them drive.

And the proud Sheriff's men
They fled away full blyve.
ROBIN saw the [am]bushment to broke,
In green wood he would have been;
Many an arrow there was shot
Among that company.
Little JOHN was hurt full sore,
With an arrow in his knee,
That he might neither go nor ride:
It was full great pity!
  "Master!" then said Little JOHN,
"If ever thou lovest me;
And for that ilk Lord's love
That died upon a tree!
And for the meeds of my service,
That I have servèd thee:
Let never the proud Sheriff
Alive now find me!
But take out thy brown sword
And smite all off my head!
And give me wounds dead and wide,
No life on me be left!"
  "I would not that," said ROBIN,
"JOHN! that thou be slo,
For all the gold in merry England,
Though it lay now on a row!"
  "God forbid!" said Little MUCH,
"That dièd on a tree!
That thou shouldst, Little JOHN!
'Part our company!"
  Up he took him on his back,
And bare him well nigh a mile:
Many a time, he laid him down,
And shot another while.
  Then was there a fair Castle
A little within the wood;
Double ditched it was about,
And wallèd, by the rood:
And there dwelt that gentle Knight,
Sir RICHARD AT THE LEE,
That ROBIN had lent his good

E

Under the green-wood tree.
　In he took good ROBIN
And all his company.
　"Welcome be thou, ROBIN HOOD!
Welcome art thou, to me!
And much thank thee of thy comfort
And of thy courtesy,
And of thy great kindness
Under the green-wood tree!
I love no man, in all this world
So much as I do thee!
For all the proud Sheriff of NOTTINGHAM;
Right here shalt thou be!
Shut the gates, and draw the bridge;
And let no man come in!
And arm you well, and make you ready!
And to the wall ye win!
For one thing, ROBIN! I thee behote
I swear by St. Quintin!
These twelve days thou wonest with me,
To sup, eat, and dine!"
　Boards were laid and cloths spread
Readily and anon:
ROBIN HOOD and his merry men
To meat 'gan they gone.

❧ The sixth fytte.

ITHE and listen, Gentlemen!
　And hearken unto your song!
How the proud Sheriff of NOTTINGHAM
　And men of armès strong
Full fast came to the High Sheriff
　The country up to rout,
And they beset the Knight's Castle,
　The walls all about.
　　The proud Sheriff loud 'gan cry
And said, "Thou traitor Knight!
Thou keepest here the King's enemy!
Against the laws and right!"

" Sir, I will avow that I have done
The deeds that here be dight,
Upon all the lands that I have,
As I am a true Knight,
Wend forth, Sirs, on your way ;
And do no more to me,
Till ye wit our King's will
What he will say to thee ! "
    The Sheriff thus, had his answer
Without any leasing.
Forth he yode to London town,
All for to tell the King.
There he told them of that Knight,
And eke of ROBIN HOOD ;
And also of the bold archers,
That noble were and good.
He would avow that he had done
To maintain the outlaws strong ;
He would be Lord, and set you at nought
In all the North land.
    " I will be at Nottingham," said the King,
" Within this fortnight !
And take I will, ROBIN HOOD ;
And so I will that Knight !
Go now home, Sheriff," said the King,
" And do as I thee bid.
And ordain good archers ynow
Of all the wide country ! "
    The Sheriff had his leave ytake ;
And went him on his way.
And ROBIN HOOD to green wood,
Upon a certain day,
And Little JOHN was whole of the arrow
That shot was in his knee ;
And did him straight to ROBIN HOOD
Under the green-wood tree.
    ROBIN HOOD walked in the forest
Under the leavès green,
The proud Sheriff of NOTTINGHAM,
Thereof he had great teen.
The Sheriff there failed of ROBIN HOOD

He might not have his prey.
Then he awaited this gentle Knight,
Both by night and by day.
Ever he awaited that gentle Knight,
Sir RICHARD AT THE LEE,
As he went on hawking by the river side
And let his hawks flee;
Took he there, this gentle Knight,
With men of armès strong,
And led him home to Nottingham ward
Ybound both foot and hand.
The Sheriff swore a full great oath,
By Him that died on rood,
He had lever than a hundred pound
That he had ROBIN HOOD.
    This heard the Knight's wife
A fair Lady and free,
She set her on a good palfrey;
To green wood anon rode she.
When she came to the forest,
Under the green-wood tree,
Found she there ROBIN HOOD
And all his fair meiny.
" God [save] thee, good ROBIN!
And all thy company,
For our dear Lady's love
A boon, grant thou me!
Let thou never my wedded Lord
Shamely yslain be!
He is fast ybound to Nottingham ward,
For the love of thee!"
    Anon then said good ROBIN,
To that Lady free :
" What man hath your Lord ytake?
    " For sooth, as I thee say,
He is not yet three miles
Passèd on your way."
    Up then started good ROBIN,
As a man that had been wood;
" Busk you, my merry young men,
For Him that died on a rood!

And he that this sorrow forsaketh,
By Him that died on a tree!
Shall he never in green wood be,
Nor longer dwell with me!"
   Soon there were good bows ybent,
Mo than seven score;
Hedge ne ditch spare they none
That were them before.
   " I make mine avow to God," said ROBIN,
" The Knight would I fain see;
And if I may him take,
Yquit then shall it be!"
   And when they came to Nottingham
They walkèd in the street,
And with the proud Sheriff ywis
Soon gan they meet.
   " Abide, thou proud Sheriff!" he said,
" Abide, and speak with me!
Of some tidings of our King
I would fain hear of thee!
This seven year, by dear-worthy God!
Ne yede I so fast on foot;
I make mine avow to God, thou proud Sheriff!
That it is not for thy good."
   ROBIN bent a good bow,
An arrow he drew at his will;
He hit so the proud Sheriff,
Upon the ground he lay full still:
And or he might up arise,
On his feet to stand;
He smote off the Sheriff's head,
With his bright brand.
   " Lie thou there, thou proud Sheriff!
Evil might thou thrive!
There might no man to thee trust
The whiles thou wert alive!"
   His men drew out their bright swords,
That were so sharp and keen,
And laid on the Sheriff's men
And drived them down bydene.
   ROBIN started to that Knight,

And cut a two his bond;
And took him in his hand a bow,
And bade him by him stand.
  " Leave thy horse thee behind,
And learn for to run !
Thou shalt with me to green wood
Through mire, moss, and fen !
Thou shalt with me to green wood
Without any leasing,
Till that I have got us grace
Of EDWARD, our comely King."

The seventh fytte.

HE King came to Nottingham
With Knights in great array
For to take that gentle Knight
And ROBIN HOOD, if he may.
  He asked men of that country
After ROBIN HOOD,
And after that gentle Knight
That was so bold and stout.
When they had told him the case,
Our King understood their tale
And seizèd in his hand
The Knight's land all.
All the pass of Lancashire
He went both far and near ;
Till he came to Plom[p]ton Park
He failed many of his deer.
There our King was wont to see
Herdès many a one,
He could unneath find one deer
That bare any good horn.
  The King was wondrous wroth withal,
And swore, " By the Trinity !
I would I had ROBIN HOOD !
With eyen I might him see !

And he that would smite off the Knight's head,
And bring it to me ;
He shall have the Knight's lands
Sir RICHARD AT THE LEE.
I give it him with my charter,
And seal it [with] my hand,
To have and hold for evermore
In all merry England."
  Then bespake a fair old Knight,
That was true in his fay,
" O my liege Lord the King,
One word I shall you say !
There is no man in this country
May have the Knight's lands
While ROBIN HOOD may ride or gone
And bear a bow in his hands,
That he ne shall lose his head,
That is the best ball in his hood :
Give it to no man, my Lord the King !
That ye will any good ! "
  Half a year dwelled our comely King
In Nottingham, and well more,
Could he not hear of ROBIN HOOD,
In what country that he were :
But always went good ROBIN
By halke and eke by hill,
And always slew the King's deer
And welt them at his will.
  Then bespake a proud for'ster
That stood by our King's knee,
" If ye will see good ROBIN
Ye must do after me !
Take five of the best Knights
That be in your lead,
And walk down by yon Abbey
And get you monks' weed !
And I will be your leadsman
And lead you the way !
And or ye come to Nottingham,
Mine head then dare I lay !
That ye shall meet with good ROBIN.

In life if that he be :
Or ye come to Nottingham
With eyen ye shall him see ! "
   Full hastily our King was dight,
So were his Knightès five,
Everych of them in monks' weed,
And hasted them thither blithe.
Our King was great above his cowl,
A broad hat on his crown.
Right as he were Abbot like,
They rode up into the town.
Stiff boots our King had on,
For sooth as I you say,
He rode singing to green wood,
The convent was clothed in grey.
His mail horse and his great somers
Followed our King behind,
Till they came to green wood
A mile under the lynde.
   There they met with good Robin
Standing on the way,
And so did many a bold archer,
For sooth as I you say.
   Robin took the King's horse,
Hastily in that stead :
And said, " Sir Abbot ! by your leave ;
A while ye must abide !
We be yeoman of this forest,
Under the green-wood tree,
We live by our King's deer,
Under the green-wood tree ;
And ye have churches and rents both,
And gold full great plenty :
Give us some of your spending,
For saint charity ! "
   Then bespake our comely King,
Anon then said he,
" I brought no more to green wood,
But forty pounds with me.
I have lain at Nottingham,
This fortnight with our King ;

And spent I have full much good
On many a great Lording :
And I have but forty pounds,
No more than have I me.
But if I had a hundred pounds,
I would give it to thee !"
  ROBIN took the forty pounds,
And departed it in two parts :
Halfendell he gave his merry men,
And bade them merry to be.
Full courteously ROBIN 'gan say,
  " Sir, have this for your spending !
We shall meet another day."
  "Grammercy ! " then said our King.
"But well thee greeteth EDWARD our King,
And sent to thee his seal ;
And biddeth thee come to Nottingham,
Both to meat and meal ! "
  He took out the broad targe
And soon he let him see.
ROBIN could his courtesy,
And set him on his knee.
  " I love no man in all the world
So well as I do my King !
Welcome is my Lord's seal !
And monk for thy tiding,
Sir Abbot, for thy tidings,
To-day, thou shalt dine with me !
For the love of my King,
Under my trystel tree."
  Forth he led our comely King
Full fair by the hand ;
Many a deer there was slain,
And full fast dightand.
ROBIN took a full great horn,
And loud he 'gan blow,
Seven score of wight young men
Came ready on a row.
All they kneeled on their knee
Full fair before ROBIN.
  The King said, himself until,

And swore, " By Saint Austin!
Here is a wondrous seemly sight!
Methinketh, by God's pine!
His men are more at his bidding
Than my men be at mine."
  Full hastily was their dinner ydight,
And thereto 'gan they gone;
They served our King with all their might,
Both Robin and Little John.
Anon before our King was set
The fat venison,
The good white bread, the good red wine,
And thereto the fine ale brown.
  " Make good cheer!" said Robin,
" Abbot, for charity!
And for this ilk tiding
Blessèd might thou be!
Now shalt thou see what life we lead,
Or thou hence wend,
That thou may inform our King
When ye together lend."
  Up they start all in haste,
Their bows were smartly bent:
Our King was never so sore aghast;
He wended to have been shent!
Two yards there were up set
Thereto 'gan they gang.
  " By fifty paces," our King said,
" The marks were too long!"
  On every side a rose garland,
They shot under the line.
  " Whoso faileth of the rose garland," saith Robin
" His tackle he shall tine,
And yield it to his Master,
Be it never so fine!
(For no man will I spare,
So drink I ale or wine!)
And bear a buffet on his head
Iwis right all bare."
And all that fell in Robin's lot,
He smote them wondrous sore.

Twice ROBIN shot about,
And ever he cleaved the wand;
And so did good " GILBERT,
With the good white hand."
Little JOHN and good SCATHELOCK,
For nothing would they spare.
When they failed of the garland
ROBIN smote them full sore.

At the last shot, that ROBIN shot
For all his friends' fare;
Yet he failed of the garland
Three fingers and more.
Then bespake good GILBERT,
And thus he 'gan say,
" Master," he said, " your tackle is lost,
Stand forth and take your pay!"
" If it be so," said ROBIN,
" That may no better be;
Sir Abbot, I deliver thee mine arrow!
I pray thee, Sir, serve thou me!"
" It falleth not for mine order," said our King,
" ROBIN, by thy leave,
For to smite no good yeoman,
For doubt I should him grieve."
" Smite on boldly," said ROBIN,
" I give thee large leave!"
Anon our King, with that word,
He folded up his sleeve,
And such a buffet he gave ROBIN,
To ground he yede full near.
" I make mine avow to God," said ROBIN,
" Thou art a stalwart frere!
There is pith in thine arm," said ROBIN,
" I trow thou canst well shoot."

Thus our King and ROBIN HOOD,
Together then they met.
ROBIN beheld our comely King,
Wistly in the face:
So did Sir RICHARD AT THE LEE,
And kneeled down in that place.

And so did all the wild outlaws,
When they see them kneel.
" My Lord, the King of England,
Now I know you well."
" Mercy, then, ROBIN," said our King,
" Under your trystel tree,
Of thy goodness and thy grace,
For my men and me ! "
" Yes, for God ! " said ROBIN,
" and also God me save !
I ask mercy, my Lord the King,
And for my men I crave ! "
" Yes, for God ! " then said our King,
" And thereto 'sent I me ;
With that thou leave the green wood,
And all thy company ;
And come home, Sir, to my Court,
And there dwell with me."
" I make mine avow to God ! " said ROBIN,
" And right so shall it be,
I will come to your Court,
Your service for to see !
And bring with me, of my men,
Seven score and three.
But me like well your service,
I come again full soon ;
And shoot at the dun deer
As I wont to done."

❡ The eighth fytte.

Ast thou any green cloth," said our King,
" That thou wilt sell now to me ? "
" Yea, for God ! " said ROBIN,
" Thirty yards and three."
" ROBIN," said our King,
" Now pray I thee !
Sell me some of that cloth
To me and my meiny."

"Yes, for God!" then said ROBIN,
" Or else I were a fool!
Another day ye will me clothe,
I trow against the yule."
    The King cast off his cowl then,
A green garment he did on,
And every knight also, i-wis,
Another had full soon.
When they were clothed in Lincoln green,
They cast away their gray.
"Now we shall to Nottingham!
All thus," our King 'gan say.
    Their bows bent, and forth they went,
Shooting all in-fere
Toward the town of Nottingham,
Outlaws as they were.
    Our King and ROBIN rode together,
For sooth as I you say,
And they shot Pluck-buffet,
As they went by the way.
And many a buffet our King won
Of ROBIN HOOD that day ;
And nothing spared good ROBIN
Our King in his pay.
    "So God me help!" said our King,
" Thy game is nought to lere ;
I should not get a shot of thee,
Though I shoot all this year!"

    All the people of Nottingham,
They stood and beheld,
They saw nothing but mantles of green
That covered all the field :
Then every man to other 'gan say,
" I dread our King be slone ;
Come ROBIN HOOD to the town, ywis
In life he left never one!"
    Full hastily they began to flee,
Both yeomen and knaves,
And old wives that might evil go
They hippèd on their staves.

The King laughed full fast,
And commanded them again:
When they see our comely King
I-wis they were full fain.
They eat and drank and made them glad,
And sang with notès high.
Then bespake our comely King
To Sir RICHARD AT THE LEE:
He gave him there his land again;
A good man he bade him be.
ROBIN thanked our comely King
And set him on his knee.

Had ROBIN dwelled in the King's Court
But twelve months and three;
That he had spent an hundred pound,
And all his men's fee.
In every place where ROBIN came,
Evermore he laid down,
Both for Knights and for Squires
To get him great renown.
By then the year was all agone
He had no man but twain,
Little JOHN and good SCATHELOCK
With him all for to gone.
ROBIN saw young men shoot
Full far upon a day.
"Alas," then said good ROBIN,
"My wealth is went away!
Sometime I was an archer good,
A stiff, and eke a strong,
I was counted the best archèr
That was in merry England.
Alas," then said good ROBIN,
"Alas, and well a wo!
If I dwell longer with the King,
Sorrow will me slo!"
Forth then went ROBIN HOOD,
Till he came to our King:
"My Lord the King of England,
Grant me mine asking!

I made a chapel in Bernysdale,
That seemly is to see:
It is of MARY MAGDALENE;
And thereto would I be!
I might never in this seven night
No time to sleep ne wink;
Neither all these seven days
Neither eat ne drink:
Me longeth sore to Bernysdale.
I may not be therefro,
Barefoot and woolward I have hight
Thither for to go."
"If it be so," then said our King,
"It may no better be!
Seven nights I give thee leave,
No longer, to dwell from me."
"Grammercy, Lord!" then said ROBIN,
And set him on his knee.
He took his leave full courteously
To green wood then went he.

When he came to green wood
In a merry morning,
There he heard the notès small
Of birds, merry singing.
"It is far gone," said ROBIN,
"That I was last here.
Me list a little for to shoot
At the dun deer."
ROBIN slew a full great hart,
His horn then 'gan he blow,
That all the outlaws of that forest,
That horn could they know.
And gathered them together
In a little throw,
Seven score of wight young men
Came ready on a row,
And fair did off their hoods
And set them on their knee.
"Welcome!" they said, "our Master!
Under this green-wood tree!"

Robin dwelled in green wood
Twenty years and two ;
For all dread of Edward our King
Again would he not go.
Yet was he beguiled i-wis
Through a wicked woman,
The Prioress of Kirkesley.
That nigh was of his kin,
For the love of a Knight,
Sir Roger of Donkesley.
That was her own special
(Full evil might they thee!)
They took together their counsel
Robin Hood for to slee,
And how they might best do that deed
His banes for to be.

Then bespake good Robin,
In place where as he stood,
" To-morrow, I must to Kirkesley
Craftily to be let blood ! "
Sir Roger of Doncaster,
By the Prioress he lay :
And there they betrayed good Robin Hood
Through their false play.

Christ have mercy on his soul!
(That died on the rood)
For he was a good outlaw,
And did poor men much good.

⁋ Explicit. King Edward and Robin Hood and Little John. Imprinted at London in Fleet street at the sign of the Sun. By Wynken de Worde.

English Carols.

[From a Manuscript at Balliol College, Oxford.]

English Carols.

From a Manuscript at Balliol College, Oxford.

Mater, ora filium,
ut post hoc exilium
nobis donet gaudium
beatorum omnium !

AIR maiden, who is this bairn
That thou bearest in thine arm?
Sir it is a Kinges Son,
That in Heaven above doth wone.
Mater, ora, etc.

Man to father he hath none,
But Himself God alone!
Of a maiden He would be born,
To save mankind that was forlorn !
Mater, ora, etc.

The Kings brought him presents,
Gold, myrrh, and frankincense
To my Son full of might,
King of Kings and Lord of right!
Mater, ora, etc.

Fair maiden pray for us
Unto thy Son, sweet Jesus,
That He will send us of His grace
In heaven on high to have a place!
Mater, ora, etc.

Ave Maria, now say we so,
Maid and mother were never no mo !

AUDE MARIA! Christes mother,
   Mary mild of thee I mean ;
Thou bare my Lord, thou bare my brother,
   Thou bare a lovely child and clean!
Thou stoodest full still without blin
When in thy ear that errand was done so,
Tho gracious God thee light within.
     Gabrielis nuncio !

Gaude Maria! [preva]lent with grace
   When Jesus thy Son on thee was bore,
Full nigh thy breast thou gan Him brace,
   He sucked, He sighed, He wept full sore.
Thou fed'st the flower that never shall fade
With maiden's milk, and sung thereto
Lullay, my sweet! I bare thee, babe!
     Cum pudoris lilio.

Gaude Maria! thy mirth was away,
   When Christ on cross, thy Son, gan die,
Full dolefully on Good Friday,
   That many a mother's son it sy.
His blood us brought from care and strife
His watery wound us washed from woe,
The third day from death to life
     Fulget resurrectio.

Gaude Maria! thou bird so bright,
   Brighter than blossom that bloweth on hill!
Joyfull thou were to see that sight,
   When the Apostles, so sweet of will,
All and some did shriek full shrill
When the fairest of shape went you fro,
From earth to heaven he styed full still,
     Motu quod fertur proprio.

Gaude Maria! thou rose of Ryse!
Maiden and mother both gentle and free,
Precious princess, peerless of price,
Thy bower is next the Trinity!
Thy Son as law asketh a right,
In body and soul thee took Him to,
Thou reignes with Him right as we find.
In coeli palatio.

Now, blessed bird, we pray thee a boon,
Before thy Son for us thou fall,
And pray Him, as He was on the rood done
And for us drank eisell and gall,
That we may wone within that wall
Wherever is well without woe,
And grant that grace unto us all.
In perenni gaudio.

Of a rose, a lovely rose
And of a rose I sing a song!

EARKEN to me both old and young,
How a rose began to spring,
A fairer rose to my liking
Sprung there never in Kinges land.

Six branches are on that rose beme,
They be both bright and sheen.
The rose is called Mary, heaven queen,
Of her bosom a blossom sprung.

The first branch was of great might,
That sprung on Christmas night!
The star shone over Bethlehem bright,
That men might see both broad and long.

The second branch was of great honour,
It was sent from heaven tower!
Blessed be that fair flower,
    Break it shall the fiendes bonds!

The third branch wide spread,
There Mary lay in her bed,
The bright stream three Kings led
    To Bethlem there that branch they found.

The fourth branch sprung into hell,
The fiendes boast for to fell,
There might no soul therein dwell,
    Blessed be that time that branch gan spring!

The fifth branch was fair in foot,
That sprung to heaven, top and root,
There to dwell and be our bote,
    And yet is seen in priestes hands.

The sixth branch by and by,
It is the five joys of mild Mary!
Now Christ save all this company,
    And send us good life and long!

Make me merry both more and less,
For now is the time of Christymas!

ET no man come into this hall,
Groom, page, nor yet marshall,
But that some sport he bring withal!
    For now is the time of Christmas!

If that he say, he can not sing,
Some other sport then let him bring!
That it may please at this feasting!
    For now is the time of Christmas!

If he say he can naught do,
Then for my love ask him no mo!
But to the stocks then let him go!
For now is the time of Christmas!

Can I not sing but Hoy!
The jolly shepherd made so much joy!

HE shepherd upon a hill he sat,
He had on him his tabard and his hat,
His tar-box, his pipe, and his flagat,
His name was called Jolly, Jolly Wat!
    For he was a good herds-boy,
      Ut hoy!
    For in his pipe he made so much joy.
      Can I not sing but hoy.

The shepherd upon a hill was laid,
His dog to his girdle was tayd,
He had not slept but a little braid
But "gloria in excelsis" was to him said
      Ut hoy!
    For in his pipe he made so much joy!
      Can I not sing, etc.

The shepherd on a hill he stood,
Round about him his sheep they yode,
He put his hand under his hood,
He saw a star as red as blood.
      Ut hoy!
    For in his pipe he made so much joy.
      Can I not sing, etc.

Now farewell Mall, and also Will,
For my love go ye all still,
Unto I come again you till,
And ever more will ring well thy bell.
      Ut hoy!
    For in his pipe he made so much joy!
      Can I not sing, etc.

Now must I go there Christ was born,
Farewell! I come again to-morn,
Dog, keep well my sheep fro the corn!
And warn well Warroke when I blow my horn!
Ut hoy!
For in his pipe he made so much joy!
Can I not sing, etc.

When Wat to Bethlehem come was,
He sweat, he had gone faster than a pace,
He found Jesus in a simple place,
Between an ox and an ass.
Ut hoy!
For in [his] pipe he made so much joy!
Can I not sing, etc.

The shepherd said anon right:
I will go see yon farly sight,
Where as the angel singeth on height,
And the star that shineth so bright!
Ut hoy!
For in [his] pipe he made so much joy!
Can I not sing, etc.

Jesus, I offer to thee here my pipe,
My skirt, my tarbox and my scrip,
Home to my fellows now will I skip,
And also look unto my sheep!
Ut hoy!
For in his pipe he made so much joy!
Can I not sing, etc.

Now farewell, mine own herds-man Wat!
Yea, fore God, Lady, even so I hat!
Lull well Jesus in thy lap,
And farewell Joseph, with thy round cap!
Ut hoy!
For in his pipe he made so much joy!
Can I not sing, etc.

Now may I well both hope and sing,
For I have been at Christ's bearing,
Home to my fellows now will I fling,
Christ of heaven to His bliss us bring!
Ut hoy!
For in his pipe he made so much joy!
Can I not sing, etc.

Now have good day, now have good day!
I am Christmas, and now I go my way!

ERE have I dwelt with more and less,
From Hallow-tide till Candlemas!
And now must I from you hence pass,
Now have good day!

I take my leave of King and Knight,
And Earl, Baron, and lady bright!
To wilderness I must me dight!
Now have good day!

And at the good lord of this hall,
I take my leave, and of guestes all!
Methinks I hear Lent doth call,
Now have good day!

And at every worthy officer,
Marshall, panter, and butler,
I take my leave as for this year,
Now have good day!

Another year I trust I shall
Make merry in this hall!
If rest and peace in England may fall!
Now have good day!

But often times I have heard say,
That he is loth to part away,
That often biddeth "have good day!"
　　Now have good day!

Now fare ye well all in-fere!
Now fare ye well for all this year,
Yet for my sake make ye good cheer!
　　Now have good day!

　　Now sing we with angels
　　Gloria in excelsis!

A BABE is born to bliss us bring;
I heard a maid lullay and sing;
She said "dear Son, leave thy weeping,
Thy Father is the King of bliss."
　　Now sing we, etc.

"Lullay," she said and sang also,
"Mine own dear Son, why art thou woe?
Have I not done as I should do?
Thy grievance tell me what it is."
　　Now sing we, etc.

"Nay, dear mother, for thee weep I nought,
But for the woe that shall be wrought
To me, or I mankind have bought,
Was never sorrow like it, i-wis."
　　Now sing we, etc.

"Peace, dear Son, tell me not so!
Thou art my child, I have no mo!
Should I see men mine own Son slo?
Alas, my dear Son, what means this?"
　　Now sing we, etc.

"My hands, mother, that ye may see,
Shall be nailed unto a tree!
My feet also fast shall be ;
Men shall weep that shall see this!"
    Now sing we, etc.

"Ah, dear Son, hard is my hap!
See my child that sucked my pap,
His hands, his feet that I did wrap
Be so nailed, that never did amiss!"
    Now sing we, etc.

"Ah, dear mother, yet shall a spear
My heart in sunder all to-tear ;
No wonder if I carefull were,
And weep full sore to think on this!"
    Now sing we, etc.

"Ah, dear Son, shall I see this ?
Thou art my child and I thy mother, i-wis !
When Gabriel called me, full of grace,
He told me nothing of this!"
    Now sing we, etc.

"Ah, dear mother, through my hair
To thrust in thorns they will not spare!
Alas, mother, I am full of care
That ye shall see this heaviness!"
    Now sing we, etc.

"Ah dear Son, leave thy weeping!
Thou bringst my heart in great mourning ;
A careful song now may I sing,
This tidings hard to me it is!"
    Now sing we, etc.

"Ah, peace, dear mother, I thee pray!
And comfort me all that ye may,
And sing 'by by, lullay lullay,'
To put away all heaviness."
    Now sing we, etc.

Caput apri refero
Resonens laudes domino.

HE boar's head in hands I bring,
With garlands gay and birds singing!
I pray you all help me to sing,
    Qui estis in convivio!

The boar's head I understand,
Is chief service in all this land,
Wheresoever it may be found,
    Servitur cum sinapio!

The boar's head I dare well say,
Anon after the twelfth day,
He taketh his leave and goeth away!
    Exivit tunc de patria!

I pray you be merry and sing with me,
In worship of Christ's Nativity!

NTO this world this day did come
Jesus Christ, both God and man,
Lord and servant in one person,
Born of the blessed Virgin Mary!
    I pray, etc.

He that was rich without any need
Appeared in this world in right poor weed,
To make us, that were poor indeed,
Rich without any need truly!
    I pray, etc.

A stable was his chamber, a crach was his bed,
He had not a pillow to lay under His head,
With maiden's milk that babe was fed,
In poor clothes was lapped the Lord Almighty!
    I pray, etc.

A noble lesson here is us taught,
To set all worldly riches at nought!
But pray we that we may be thither brought
Where riches is everlastingly!
> *I pray, etc.*

EXPLICIT.

> *Noël, noël, noël, noël!*
> *This is the salutation of Gabriel!*

 IDINGS true
There be come new,
Sent from the Trinity,
By Gabriel from Nazareth
A city of Galilee!
A clean maiden,
A pure virgin,
By her humility
Hath born the Person
Second in divinity!
> *Noël!*

When that He presented was
Before her fair visage,
In most demure and goodly wise
He did to her homage!
"I am sent, Lady,
From heaven so high,
That Lord's heritage,
For He of thee
Now born will be,
I am sent on the message!"
> *Noël!*

"Hail, Virgin celestial!
The meekest that ever was
Hail, temple of the Deity
Hail, Virgin pure!
I thee ensure,

Within a little space
Thou shalt conceive,
And Him receive
That shall bring great solace."
  Noël!

Then bespake the Virgin again,
And answered womanly,
"Whatsoever my Lord commandeth me
I will obey truly!
Ecce, sum humillima
Ancilla domini,
Secundum verbum tuum
fiat mihi!
  Noël!

Man, move thy mind and joy this feast,
Veritas de terra orta est!

AS I came by the way
I saw a sight seemly to see,
Three shepherds ranging in a kay,
Upon the field keeping their fee.
A star, they said, they did espy,
Casting the beams out of the east,
And angels making melody
  Veritas de terra orta est!

Upon that sight they were aghast,
Saying these words, as I say thee:
"To Bethlehem shortly let us haste,
And there we shall the truthe see!"
The angel said unto them all three,
To their comfort or ever be ceased,
"*Consolamini and merry be,*
  Veritas de terra orta est!"

From heaven, out of the highest see,
Righteousness hath taken the way,
With mercy meddled plenteously,
And so conceived in a may,
Miranda res this is in fay!
So saith the prophet in his gest;
Now is He born, scripture doth say:
    Veritas de terra orta est!

Then passed the shepherds from that place,
And followed by the starres beam,
That was so bright afore their face,
It brought them straight unto Bethlem.
So bright it shone, on all the realm
Till they came there they would not rest,
To Jewry and Jerusalem!
    Veritas de terra orta est!

    All this time this song is best:
    Verbum caro factum est!

HIS night there is a child born
That sprang out of Jesse's thorn;
We must sing and say therefore
    Verbum caro factum est!

Jesus is the child's name,
And Mary mild is his dame;
All our sorrow shall turn to game,
    Verbum caro factum est!

It fell upon high midnight,
The stars shone both fair and bright,
The angels sang with all their might
    Verbum caro factum est!

Now kneel we down on our knee,
And pray we to the Trinity,
Our help, our succour for to be!
    Verbum caro factum est!

Now sing we, sing we,
Gloria tibi domine!

HRIST keep us all, as he well can,
A solis ortus cardine!
For He is both God and man,
Qui natus est de virgine!
Sing we, etc.

As He is Lord both day and night,
Venter puellae baiulat,
So is Mary mother of might,
Secreta quae non noverat.
Sing we, etc.

The holy breast of chastity,
verbo concepit filium,
So brought before the Trinity,
Ut castitatis lilium!
Sing we, etc.

Between an ox and an ass
enixa est puerpera;
In poor clothing clothed He was
[Qui] regnat super aethera!
Sing we, etc.

EXPLICIT.

The Examination

of Master William Thorpe, priest,
of heresy, before Thomas Arundell,
Archbishop of Canterbury,
the year of our Lord,
M.CCCC. and
seven.

❡ The Examination

of the honourable Knight, Sir John
Oldcastle, Lord Cobham, burnt
by the said Archbishop,* in
the first year of King
Henry the Fifth.

❡ Be no more ashamed to hear it, than ye were
and be, to do it.

[* This is incorrect, Archbishop ARUNDELL condemned Sir JOHN OLD-
CASTLE on September 25th, 1413, who was then sent to the Tower, see
pp. 125, 132 : from which he escaped ; and being recaptured in Wales in
1417, was burnt on the 14th December of that year.   But in the meantime, Archbishop ARUNDELL had died on the 14th February, 1414 ; and
HENRY CHICHELEY had become Archbishop.]

❡ Unto the Christian Reader.

RACE and peace in our Lord JESUS CHRIST. Read here with judgement, good Reader! the Examination of the blessed Man of GOD, and there thou shalt easily perceive wherefore our Holy Church (as the most unholy sort of all the people will be called) make all their examinations in darkness; all the lay people clean excluded from their counsels.

For if their lies had been openly confuted, and also that the Accused of Heresy might as well have been admitted to reason their Articles with Counsel, whether they were heresy or no[t], as the Accused of Treason against the King is admitted to his Council to confute his cause and Articles, whether they be treason or not, they should never have murdered nor prisoned so many good Christian men as they have done.

For their cloaked lies could never have continued so long in the light, as they have done in corners. They, good men! when they come in the pulpit, and preach against the Truth, cry, " If their learning [i.e., of the Protestants] were good and true, they would never go in corners; but speak it openly ! "

Whereunto I answer, that besides that CHRIST and his Apostles were compelled (for because of the furiousness of their fathers, the Bishops and Priests, which only, that time also, would be called Holy Church) oftentimes for to walk secretly, and absent themselves, and give place to their malice. Yet we have daily examples, of more than one or two, that have not spared nor feared for to speak, and also [to] preach openly the Truth; which have been taken of them, prisoned, and brent: besides others that for fear of death, have abjured and carried faggots. Of whose Articles and Examination there is no layman that can shew a word.

Who can tell wherefore, not many years past, there were Seven burnt in Coventry on one day? Who can tell wherefore that good priest and holy martyr, Sir [the reverend] THOMAS HITTON *was brent, now this year, at Maidstone in Kent? I am sure, no man! For this is their cast* [contrivance] *ever when they have put to death or punished any man: after their secret Examinations, to slander him of such things as he never thought; as they may do well enough, seeing there is no man to contrary them.*

Wherefore I exhort thee, good brother! whosoever thou be that readest this treatise, mark it well, and consider it seriously! and there thou shalt find, not only what the Church is, their doctrine of the Sacrament, the Worshipping of Images, Pilgrimage, Confession, Swearing, and Paying of Tithes: but also thou mayest see what strong and substantial arguments of Scripture and Doctors, and what clerkly reasons my Lord the head and Primate of the Holy Church in England (as he will be taken) bringeth against this poor, foolish, simple, and mad losell, knave, and heretic, as he calleth him. And also the very cause wherefore all their Examinations are made in darkness.

And the Lord of all Light shall lighten thee with the candle of His grace, for to see the Truth! Amen.

❡ This I have corrected and put forth in the English that now is used in England, for our Southern men; nothing thereto adding, ne yet therefrom minishing. And I intend hereafter, with the help of GOD to put it forth in his own old English, which shall well serve, I doubt not, both for the Northern men and the faithful brethren of Scot- land.

[William of Thorpe's Preface.]

THE LORD GOD that knoweth all things, wotteth well that I am right sorrowful for to write or make known this Sentence beneath written, where that of mine even Christian, set in high state and dignity, so great blindness and malice may be known; that they, that presume of themselves to destroy vices and to plant in men virtues, neither dread to offend GOD, nor lust [*desire*] to please Him: as their works shew. For, certes, the bidding of GOD and His Law (which, in the praising of His most Holy Name, He commandeth to be known and kept of all men and women, young and old; after the cunning and power that He hath given to them), the Prelates of this land and their ministers, with the comente [*community*] of priests chiefly consenting to them, enforce them most busily to withstand and destroy the holy Ordinance of GOD. And therethrough, GOD is greatly wroth and moved to take hard vengeance, not only on them that do the evil, but also on them all that consent to the Antichrist's limbs; which know or might know their malice and their falsehood, and [ad]dress them not to withstand their malice and great pride.

Nevertheless, four things moveth me to write this Sentence beneath.

The first thing, that moveth me hereto is this, that whereas it was known to certain friends that I came from the prison of Shrewsbury, and (as it befell in deed), that I should to the prison of Canterbury; then divers friends, in divers places, spake to me full heartfully and full tenderly, and commanded me then, if it so were that I should be examined before the Archbishop of CANTER-BURY, that, if I might in any wise, I should write mine Apposing and mine Answering. And I promised to my special friends, that if I might, I would gladly do their biddings, as I might.

The second thing that moveth me to write this Sentence is this. Divers friends which have heard that I have been examined before the Archbishop, have come to me in prison and counselled me busily, and coveted greatly that I should do the same thing. And other brethren have sent to me, and required me, on GOD's behalf! that I should write out and make known both mine Apposing and mine Answering "for the profit that," as they say, "over my [ac]knowledging may come thereof." But this, they bade me, that I should be busy in all my wits to go as near the Sentence and the words as I could; both that were spoken to me, and that I spake: up[on] adventure this Writing came another time, before the Archbishop and his Council. And of this counselling I was right glad! for in my conscience, I was moved to do this thing; and to ask hereto the special help of GOD.

And so then, I considering the great desire of divers friends of sundry places, according all in one; I occupied all my mind and my wits so busily, that through GOD's grace, I perceived by their meaning and their charitable desire some profit might come therethrough.

For Soothfastness and Truth hath these conditions. Wherever it is impugned, it hath a sweet smell, and thereof comes a sweet savour. And the more violent the enemies [ad]dress themselves to oppress and to with-stand the Truth, the greater and the sweeter smell cometh thereof. And therefore this heavenly smell of GOD's Word will not, as a smoke, pass away with the wind; but it will descend and rest in some clean soul that thirsteth thereafter.

And thus, some deal, by this Writing, may be perceived, through GOD's grace, how that the enemies of the Truth, standing boldly in their malice, enforce them to withstand the freedom of CHRIST's Gospel; for which freedom, CHRIST became man, and shed his heart's blood. And therefore it is great pity and sorrow that many men and women do their own wayward will; nor busy them not to know nor to do the pleasant will of GOD.

Ye men and women that hear the Truth and Soothfastness, and hear or know of this, perceiving what is now in the Church, ought therethrough to be the more moved in all their wits to able them to grace, and set lesser price by themselves: that they, without tarrying, forsake wilfully [*voluntarily*] and bodily all the wretchedness of this life; since they know not how soon, nor when, nor where, nor by whom GOD will teach them, and assay their patience. For, no doubt, who that ever will live piteously, that is charitably, in CHRIST JESU shall suffer now, here in this life, persecution in one wise or another, that is, if we shall be saved.

It behoveth us to imagine full busily, the vilite and foulness of sin, and how the LORD GOD is displeased therefore: and of this vilite of hideousness of sin, it behoveth us to busy us in all our wits for to abhor and hold in our mind a great shame of sin, ever! and so then we owe [*ought*] to sorrow [heartily therefore, and ever flying all occasion thereof. And then [it] behoveth us to take upon us sharp penance, continuing therein, for to obtain of the LORD, forgiveness of our foredone sins, and grace to abstain us hereafter from sin! And but if [*except*] we enforce us to do this wilfully and in convenient time, the LORD (if He will not utterly destroy and cast us away!) will, in divers manners, move tyrants against us, for to constrain us violently for to do penance, which we would not do wilfully. And, trust! that this doing is a special grace of the LORD, and a great token of life and mercy!

And, no doubt, whoever will not apply himself, as is said before, to punish himself wilfully, neither will suffer patiently, meekly, and gladly the rod of the LORD, howsoever that He will punish him: their wayward wills and their impatience are unto them earnest of everlasting damnation.

But because there are but few in number that do able them thus faithfully to grace, for to live here simply and purely, and without gall of malice and of grudging, herefore the lovers of this world hate and pursue them that they know patient, meek, chaste, and wilfully poor, hating and fleeing all worldly vanities and fleshly lusts. For, surely, their virtuous conditions are even contrary to the manners of this world.

The third thing that moveth me to write this Sentence is this. I thought I shall busy me in myself to do faithfully, that all men and women occupying all their business in knowing and in keeping of GOD's commandments, able them so to grace, that they might understand truly the Truth, and have and use virtue and prudence; and so to serve to be lightened from above with heavenly wisdom: so that all their words and their works may be hereby made pleasant sacrifices unto the LORD GOD; and not only for help for their own souls, but also for edification of all Holy Church.

For I doubt not but all they that will apply them to have this foresaid business shall profit full mickle both to friends and to foes. For some enemies of the Truth, through the grace of GOD, shall, through charitable folks, be made astonied in their conscience, and peradventure converted from vices to virtues; and also they that labour to know and to keep faithfully the biddings of GOD, and to suffer patiently all adversities, shall hereby comfort many friends.

And the fourth thing that moveth me to write this Sentence is this. I know my sudden and unwarned Apposing and Answering that all they that will of good heart without feigning able themselves wilfully and gladly, after their cunning and their power, to follow CHRIST patiently, travailing busily, privily and apertly, in work and in word, to withdraw whomsoever that they may from vices, planting in them (if they may) virtues, comforting them and furthering them that standeth in grace; so that therewith they be not borne up into vainglory through presumption of their wisdom, nor enflamed with any worldly prosperity: but ever meek and patient, purposing to abide steadfastly in the Will of GOD, suffering wilfully and gladly, without any grudging whatsoever, the rod the LORD will chastise them with.

Then this good LORD will not forget to comfort all such men and women in all their tribulations, and at every point of temptation that any enemy purposeth for to do against them ([to] such faithful lovers specially, and patient followers of CHRIST), the LORD sendeth His wisdom from above to them! which the adversaries of the Truth may not know nor understand; but through their old and new unshamefast sins, those tyrants and enemies of Soothfastness shall be so blinded and obstinate in evil, that they shall ween themselves to do pleasant sacrifices unto the LORD GOD in their malicious and wrongful pursuing and destroying of innocent men's and women's bodies; which men and women for their very virtuous living and for their true knowledging of the Truth and their patient, wilful, and glad suffering of persecution for righteousness, deserve through the grace of GOD to be heirs of the endless bliss of heaven.

And for [*on account of*] the fervent desire and the great

love that those men have, as to stand in Soothfastness and witness of it, though they be, suddenly and unwarned, brought forth to be Apposed of their adversaries : the HOLY GHOST yet, that moveth and ruleth them, through His charity, will, in the hour of their Answering, speak in them, and shew His wisdom, that all their enemies shall not again say [*gainsay*] and against stand lawfully [*by right*].

And therefore all they that are stedfast in the faith of GOD, yea, which (through diligent keeping of His commandments, and for their patient suffering of whatsoever adversity that cometh to them) hope surely in His mercy, purposing to stand continually in perfect charity : for those men and women dread not so the adversities of this life, that they will fear (after their cunning and their power) to [ac]knowledge prudently the truth of GOD's Word! when, where, and to whom that they think their [ac]knowledging may profit. Yea, and though therefore, persecution come to them, in one wise or another, certes, they patiently take it! knowing their conversation to be in heaven.

It is a high reward and a special grace of GOD for to have and enjoy as the everlasting inheritance of heaven, for the suffering of one persecution in so short a time as is the term of this life. For, lo, this heavenly heritage and endless reward is the LORD GOD Himself! which is the best thing that may be. This Sentence witnesseth the LORD GOD Himself, whereas He said to ABRAHAM, *I am thy mede!* And as the LORD said He was, and is the mede of ABRAHAM; so He is of all His other saints.

This most blessed and best mede He grant to us all! for His holy name, that made us of nought, and sent His only most dear worthy Son, our Lord JESU CHRIST, for to redeem us with His most precious
heart's blood.
Amen.

[The Examination of sir William of Thorpe.]

NOWN be it to all men that read or hear this Writing beneath, that on the Sunday next [*August 7th*] after the Feast of St. Peter that we call Lammas [*August 1st*], in the year of our Lord a thousand four hundred seventh year, I, WILLIAM of Thorpe, being in prison in the castle of Saltwood [*near Hythe, in Kent*], was brought before THOMAS ARUNDELL, Archbishop of CANTERBURY, and [Lord] Chancellor then of England.

And when that I came to him, he stood in a great chamber, and much people [were] about him; and when that he saw me, he went fast into a closet [*private room*], bidding all secular men [*laymen*] that followed him, to go forth from him soon; so that no man was left then in that closet, but the Archbishop himself, a physician that was called MALVEREN [*i.e., JOHN MALVERNE, S.T.P.*], Parson of St. Dunstan's [Church, in Tower Street] in London, and two other persons unknown to me, which were Ministers of the Law [*i.e., the Canon Law : later on, they are called Clerks, i.e., Chaplains*].

Archbishop. And I standing before them, by and by, the Archbishop said to me, " WILLIAM ! I know well, that thou hast, this twenty winter and more [*i.e., from before 1387*], travelled about busily, in the North country and in other divers countries [*counties*] of England, sowing about false doctrine : having great business, if thou might, with thine untrue teaching and shrewd will, for to infect and poison all this land. But, through the grace of GOD ! thou art now withstanded, and brought into my ward ! so that I shall now sequester thee from thine evil purpose, and let [*hinder*] thee to envenom the sheep of my Province. Nevertheless, St. PAUL saith, *If it may be, as far as in us is, we owe* [ought] *to have peace with all men.* Therefore, WILLIAM ! if thou wilt now, meekly, and of good heart, without any feigning, kneel down and lay thy hand upon a book, and kiss it; promising faithfully as I shall here charge thee, that 'thou wilt submit thee to my correction and stand to mine ordinance, and fulfil it duly by all thy cunning and power,' thou shalt yet find me gracious unto thee!"

William. Then said I, to the Archbishop, "Sir, since ye deem me an heretic out of belief, will ye give me here audience to tell my *Belief.*"

Archbishop. And he said, "Yea, tell on!"

William. And I said, "*I believe that there is not but one GOD Almighty, and in this Godhead and of this Godhead are three Persons; that is the Father, the Son, and the soothfast HOLY GHOST. And I believe that all these three Persons are even in power, in cunning, and in might, full of grace and of all goodness: for whatever that the Father doth or can or will, that thing also the Son doth can and will; and in all their power cunning and will, the HOLY GHOST is equal to the Father and to the Son.*

Over this, I believe that, through counsel of this most blessed Trinity (in most convenient time, before ordained), for the salvation of mankind, the second Person of this Trinity was ordained to take the form of Man, that is the Kind of man. And I believe that this second Person, our Lord JESU CHRIST was conceived, through the HOLY GHOST, into the womb of the most blessed Virgin MARY without any man's seed. And I believe that after nine months, CHRIST was born of this most blessed Virgin without any pain or breaking of the closter of her womb, and without filth of her virginity.

And I believe that CHRIST our Saviour was circumcised in the eighth day after his birth, in fulfilment of the Law; and his name was called JESUS, which was called of the angel before he was conceived in the womb of MARY his mother.

And I believe that CHRIST, as he was about thirty years old, was baptized in the flood of Jordan of JOHN [the] Baptist, and in likeness of a dove the HOLY GHOST descended there upon him; and a voice was heard from heaven, saying, Thou art my well beloved Son! In Thee, I am full pleased!

And I believe that CHRIST was moved then by the HOLY GHOST for to go into [the] desert, and there he fasted forty

*days and forty nights without bodily meat and drink.   And
I believe that by and by, after his fasting, when the manhood
of* CHRIST *hungered, the Fiend came to him and tempted him
in gluttony, in vainglory, and in covetise : but in all those
temptations* CHRIST *concluded* [confounded] *the Fiend and
withstood him.*

And then, without tarrying, JESU *began to preach, and to say
unto the people,* Do ye penance ! for the Realm of Heaven
is now at hand !

And I believe that CHRIST, *in all his time here, lived most holily;
and taught the Will of his Father most truly : and I believe
that he suffered therefore most wrongfully, greatest reproofs
and despisings.*

And after this, when CHRIST *would make an end here, of his
temporal life, I believe that, in the day next before that he
would suffer passion on the morn, in form of bread and wine,
he ordained the Sacrament of his flesh and blood, that is his
own precious body, and gave it to his Apostles for to eat,
commanding them, and by them all their after-comers, that
they should do it, in this form that he shewed to them, use
themselves and teach and common forth to other men and
women this most worshipful holiest Sacrament ; in mindful-
ness of his holiest Living and of his most true Teaching, and
of his wilful and patient Suffering of the most painful Passion.*

And I believe that thus, CHRIST *our Saviour, after that he had
ordained this most worthy Sacrament of his own precious
body, he went forth wilfully against his enemies, and he suffered
them most patiently to lay their hands most violently upon
him, and to bind him, and to lead him forth as a thief,
and to scorn and buffet him, and all to blow or* [de]*file him
with their spittings.*

Over this, I believe that CHRIST *suffered, most meekly and
patiently, his enemies for to ding* [beat] *out with sharp
scourges, the blood that was between his skin and his flesh :
yea, without grudging,* CHRIST *suffered wicked Jews to
crown him with most sharp thorns, and to strike him with
a reed.   And, after,* CHRIST *suffered wicked Jews to draw*
[lay] *him out upon the Cross, and for to nail him
there, upon foot and hand; and so, through this pitiful
nailing,* CHRIST *shed out wilfully, for man's life, the
blood that was in his veins : and then,* CHRIST *gave*

wilfully his spirit into the hands or power of his Father. And so, as he would, and when he would, CHRIST died wilfully, for man's sake, upon the Cross. And notwithstanding that CHRIST was wilfully, painfully, and most shamefully put to death as to the world, there was left blood and water in his heart, as he before ordained that he would shed out this blood and this water for man's salvation. And therefore he suffered the Jews to make a blind [ignorant] Knight to thrust him into the heart with a spear; and this the blood and water that was in his heart, CHRIST would shed out for man's love.

And, after this, I believe that CHRIST was taken down from the Cross, and buried.

And I believe that on the third day, by the power of his godhead, CHRIST rose again from death to life. And forty days thereafter, I believe that CHRIST ascended up into heaven; and that he there sitteth on the right hand of GOD the Father Almighty. And the tenth day after his up going, he sent to his Apostles the HOLY GHOST, that he had promised them before.

And I believe that CHRIST shall come and judge all mankind, some to everlasting peace, and some to everlasting pains.

And as I believe in the Father, and in the Son, that they are one GOD Almighty; so I believe in the HOLY GHOST that is also, with them, the same GOD Almighty.

And I believe [in] an Holy Church, that is, all they that have been, and that now are, and always to the end of the world shall be, a people the which shall endeavour them to know, and keep the commandments of GOD; dreading over all things to offend GOD, and loving and seeking most to please Him. And I believe that all they that have had, and yet have, and all they that yet shall have the foresaid virtues, surely standing in the Belief of GOD, hoping steadfastly in His merciful doings, continuing to their end in perfect charity, wilfully patiently and gladly suffering persecutions by the example of CHRIST chiefly and His Apostles; and these have their names written in the Book of Life. Therefore I believe that the gathering together of this people living now in this life, is the Holy Church of GOD, fighting here on earth against the Fiend, the prosperity of the world, and their fleshly lusts. Wherefore, seeing that all the gathering together of this Church beforesaid, and every part thereof, neither coveteth, nor willeth, nor loveth, nor seeketh anything, but to eschew the offence of GOD, and to do His pleasing will : meekly, gladly, and wilfully, of all mine heart, I submit myself unto this Holy Church of CHRIST ; to be ever buxom and obedient to the ordinance of it, and of every member thereof, after my knowledge and power, by the help of GOD.

Therefore I [ac]knowledge now, and evermore shall (if GOD will !) that, of all my heart, and of all my might, I will submit me only to the rule and governance of them whom, after my knowledge, I may perceive, by the having and using of the beforesaid virtues, to be members of the Holy Church.

Wherefore these Articles of Belief and all others, both of the Old Law and of the New, which, after the commandment of GOD, any man ought to believe, I believe verily in my soul, as a sinful deadly wretch of my cunning and power ought to believe ; praying the LORD GOD, for His holy name, for to increase my belief, and help my unbelief.

And for because, to the praising of GOD's name, I desire above all things to be a faithful member of Holy Church, I make this Protestation before you all four that are now here present, coveting that all men and women that [are] now absent knew the same ; that what thing soever before this time I have said or done, or what thing here I shall do or say at any time hereafter, I believe that all the Old Law and the New Law given and ordained by the counsel of these three Persons in the Trinity, were given and written to [for] the salvation of mankind. And I believe these Laws are sufficient for the man's salvation. And I believe every Article of these Laws to the intent that these Articles were ordained and commanded, of these three Persons of the most blessed Trinity, to be believed. And therefore to the rule and the ordinance of these, GOD's Laws, meekly, gladly, and wilfully, I submit me with all mine heart : that whoever can or will, by authority of GOD's Law, or by open reason, tell me that I have erred, or now err, or any time hereafter shall err in any Article of Belief (from which inconvenience, GOD keep me, for his goodness !) I submit me to be reconciled, and to be buxom and obedient unto these Laws of GOD, and to every Article of them. For by authority specially of these Laws, I will, through the grace of GOD, be unied [united] charitably unto these Laws.

Yea, Sir, and over this, I believe and admit all the Sentences,

*authorities, and reasons of the Saints and Doctors, according
unto Holy Scripture, and declaring it truly. I submit me
wilfully and meekly to be ever obedient, after my cunning and
power, to all these Saints and Doctors as they are obedient in
work and in word to GOD and his Law: and further, not
to my knowledge; nor for any earthly power, dignity, or state,
through the help of GOD.*

"But, Sir, I pray you tell me, if after your bidding, I
shall lay my hand upon the book, to the intent to swear
thereby?"

Archbishop. And the Archbishop said unto me, "Yea!
wherefore else?"

William. And I said to him, " Sir, a book is nothing else
but a thing coupled together of diverse creatures [*created
things*] ; and to swear by any creature, both GOD's Law and
man's law is against. But, Sir, this thing I say here to you,
before these your Clerks, with my foresaid *Protestation*, that
how, where, when, and to whom, men are bounden to swear
or to obey, in any wise, after GOD's Laws, and Saints and
good Doctors according with GOD's Law ; I will, through
GOD's grace, be ever ready thereto, with all my cunning and
power!

"But I pray you, Sir, for the charity of GOD! that ye
will, before that I swear as I have rehearsed to you, tell me
how or whereto that I shall submit me ; and shew me
whereof that ye will correct me, and what is the ordinance
that ye will thus oblige me to fulfil?"

Archbishop. And the Archbishop said unto me, "I will,
shortly, that now thou swear here to me, that thou shalt forsake all the opinions which the Sect of Lollards hold, and is
slandered [*charged*] with ; so that, after this time, neither
privily nor apertly, thou hold any opinion which I shall, after
that thou hast sworn, rehearse to thee here. Nor thou shalt
favour no man nor woman, young nor old, that holdeth any
of these foresaid opinions ; but, after thy knowledge and
power, thou shalt enforce thee to withstand all such dis-
troublers of Holy Church in every diocese that thou comest
in ; and them that will not leave their false and damnable
opinions, thou shalt put them up, publishing them and their
names ; and make them known to the Bishop of the diocese

that they are in, or to the Bishop's Ministers. And, over
this, I will that thou preach no more, unto the time that
I know, by good witness and true, that thy conversation
be such that thy heart and thy mouth accord truly in one
contrarying [of] all the lewd learning that thou hast taught
herebefore."

And I, hearing these words, thought in my heart that this
was an unlawful asking; and I deemed myself cursed of
GOD, if I consented hereto: and I thought how SUSANNA
said, *Anguish is to me on every side!*

Archbishop. And in that I stood still, and spake not;
the Archbishop said to me, "Answer one wise or another!"

William. And I said, "Sir, if I consented to you thus, as
ye have here rehearsed to me; I should become an Appealer, or
every Bishop's Spy! Summoner of all England! For an [*if*] I
should thus put up and publish the names of men and women,
I should herein deceive full many persons: yea, Sir, as it is
likely, by the doom of my conscience, I should herein be
cause of the death, both of men and women; yea, both
bodily and ghostly. For many men and women that stand
now in the Truth, and are in the way of salvation, if I should
for the learning and reading of their *Belief* publish them
or put them therefore up to Bishops or to their unpiteous
Ministers, I know some deal by experience, that they
should be so distroubled and dis-eased with persecution or
otherwise, that many of them, I think, would rather choose
to forsake the Way of Truth than to be travailed, scorned,
and slandered or punished as Bishops and their Ministers
now use [*are accustomed*] for to constrain men and women to
consent to them.

"But I find in no place in Holy Scripture, that this
office that ye would now enfeoff me with, accordeth to any
priest of CHRIST's sect, nor to any other Christian man.
And therefore to do thus, were to me a full noyous bond to be
bounden with, and over grievous charge. For I suppose that
if I thus did, many men and women in the world, yea, Sir,
might justly, unto my confusion say to me that 'I were a
traitor to GOD and to them!' since, as I think in mine
heart, many men and women trust so mickle in me in this
case, that I would not, for the saving of my life, do thus to
them. For if I thus should do, full many men and women

would, as they might full truly, say that ' I had falsely and cowardly forsaken the Truth, and slandered shamefully the Word of GOD ! ' For if I consented to you, to do hereafter your will, for bonchief and mischief that may befall to me in this life, I deem in my conscience that I were worthy here-fore to be cursed of GOD, as also of all His Saints ! From which inconvenience keep me and all Christian people, Almighty GOD ! now and ever, for His holy name ! "

Archbishop. And then the Archbishop said unto me, " O thine heart is full hard, endured [*hardened*] as was the heart of PHARAOH ; and the Devil hath overcome thee, and perverted thee ! and he hath so blinded thee in all thy wits, that thou hast no grace to know the truth, nor the measure of mercy that I have proffered to thee ! Therefore, as I per-ceive now by thy foolish answer, thou hast no will to leave thine old errors. But I say to thee, lewd losell ! [*base lost one ! or base son of perdition !*] either thou quickly consent to mine ordinance, and submit thee to stand to my decrees, or, by Saint Thomas ! thou shalt be disgraded [*degraded*], and follow thy fellow in Smithfield ! "

And at this saying, I stood still and spake not ; but I thought in mine heart that GOD did to me a great grace, if He would, of His great mercy, bring me to such an end. And in mine heart, I was nothing [a]fraid with this menacing of the Archbishop.

And I considered, there, two things in him. One, that he was not yet sorrowful, for that he had made WILLIAM SAUTRE wrongfully to be burnt [*on Feb.* 12, 1401, *at Smithfield*]. And as I considered that the Archbishop thirsted yet after more shedding out of innocent blood. And fast therefore I was moved in all my wits, for to hold the Archbishop neither for Prelate, nor for priest of GOD ; and for that mine inward man was thus altogether departed from the Arch-bishop, methought I should not have any dread of him. But I was right heavy and sorrowful for that there was none audience of secular [*lay*] men by : but in mine heart, I prayed the LORD GOD to comfort me and strengthen me against them that there were against the Soothfastness. And I pur-posed to speak no more to the Archbishop and his Clerks [*Chaplains*] than me need behoved.

And all thus I prayed GOD, for His goodness, to give me

then and always grace to speak with a meek and an easy
spirit; and whatsoever thing that I should speak, that I
might thereto have true authorities of Scriptures and open
reason.

A Clerk. And for that I stood still, and nothing spake,
one of the Archbishop's Clerks said unto me, " What thing
musest thou? Do thou, as my Lord hath now commanded
to thee here! "

And yet I stood still, and answered him not.

Archbishop. And then, soon after, the Archbishop said
to me, " Art thou not yet bethought, whether thou wilt do as
I have here said to thee? "

William. And I said then to him, " Sir, my father and
mother (on whose souls GOD have mercy! if it be His will)
spent mickle money in divers places about my learning; for
the intent to have made me a priest to GOD. But when
I came to years of discretion, I had no will to be priest;
and therefore my friends were right heavy to me. And then
methought their grudging against me was so painful to
me, that I purposed therefore to have left their company.
And when they perceived this in me, they spake some time
full fair and pleasant words to me : but for that they might
not make me to consent, of good heart, to be a priest, they
spake to me full ofttimes very grievous words, and menaced
me in divers manners, shewing to me full heavy cheer.
And thus, one while in fair manner, another while in
grievous, they were long time, as methought, full busy
about me, ere I consented to them to be a priest.

"But, at the last, when, in this matter, they would no
longer suffer mine excusations; but either I should consent
to them, or I should ever bear their indignation; yea, 'their
curse,' as they said. Then I seeing this, prayed them that
they would give me license for to go to them that were
named wise priests and of virtuous conversation, to have
their counsel, and to know of them the office and the charge
of priesthood.

"And hereto my father and my mother consented full
gladly, and gave me their blessing and good leave to go, and
also money to spend in this journey.

"And so then I went to those priests whom I heard to be of
best name and of most holy living, and best learned and

most wise of heavenly wisdom : and so I communed with them unto the time that I perceived, by their virtuous and continual occupations, that their honest and charitable works [sur]passed their fame, which I heard before of them. Wherefore, sir, by the example of the doctrine of them, and specially for the godly and innocent works which I perceived of them and in them ; after my cunning and power I have exercised me then, and in this time, to know perfectly GOD's Law : having a will and desire to live thereafter, willing that all men and women exercised themselves faithfully thereabout.

" If then, Sir, either for pleasure or displeasure of them that are neither so wise, nor of so virtuous conversation (to my knowledge, nor by common fame of other men's knowledge in this land) as these men were, of whom I took my counsel and information ; I should now forsake, thus suddenly and shortly, and unwarned, all the learning that I have exercised myself in, this thirty winter [*i.e.*, *from* 1377] and more, my conscience should ever be herewith out of measure unquieted. And as, Sir, I know well that many men and women should be therethrough greatly troubled and slandered ; and (as I said, Sir, to you before) for mine untruth and false cowardness many a one should be put into full great reprefe [*reproof*]. Yea, Sir, I dread that many a one, as they might then justly, would curse me full bitterly : and, Sir, I fear not but the curse of GOD (which I should deserve herein) would bring me to a full evil end, if I continued thus.

"And if through remorse of conscience, I repented me at any time, returning into the Way which you do your diligence to constrain me now to forsake ; yea, Sir, all the Bishops of this land, with full many other priests, would defame me, and pursue me as a Relapse : and they that now have (though I be unworthy) some confidence in me, hereafter would never trust to me, though I could teach and live never so virtuously more that I can or may.

" For if, after your counsel, I left utterly all my Learning : I should hereby, first wound and defile mine own soul ; and also I should herethrough give occasion to many men and women of full sore hurting. Yea, Sir, it is likely to me, if I consented to your will, I should herein by mine evil example in it, as far as in me were, slay many folk ghostly, that I should never deserve for to have grace of GOD to the edifying of His Church, neither of myself, nor of none other man's life, and [be] undone both before GOD and man.

"But, Sir, by example chiefly of some, whose names I will not now rehearse, [NICHOLAS DE] H[EREFORD], of J[OHN] P[URVEY], and B[OWLAND]; and also by the present doing of PHILIP of REPINGTON that [*after being a Lollard*] is now become Bishop of LINCOLN [*consecrated on March* 28, 1405; *and about a year following this Examination was made, on September* 19, 1408, *a Cardinal*] : I am now learned, as many more hereafter through GOD's grace shall be learned, to hate and to flee all such slander that these foresaid men chiefly hath defiled principally themselves with. And in it that in them is, they have envenomed all the Church of GOD; for the slanderous revoking at the Cross of Paul's, of H[EREFORD], P[URVEY], and of B[OWLAND], and how now PHILIP REPINGTON pursueth CHRIST's people. And the feigning that these men dissemble by worldly prudence, keeping them cowardly in their preaching and communing, within the bonds and terms, which, without blame, may be spoken and shewed out to the most worldly livers, will not be unpunished of GOD. For to the point of truth that these men shewed out some time, they not will now stretch forth their lives: but by example, each one of them, as their words and works shew, they busy them, through their feigning, for to slander and to pursue CHRIST in his members, rather than they will be pursued."

Archbishop. And the Archbishop said to me, "These men the which thou speakest of now, were fools and heretics, when they were counted wise men of thee and other such losells : but now they are wise men, though thou and such others deem them unwise. Nevertheless, I wist never none, that right said; that any while were envenomed with your contagiousness, that is contaminated and spotted doctrine."

William. And I said to the Archbishop, "Sir, I think well that these men and such others are now wise as to this world, but as their words sounded sometime and their works shewed outwardly, it was likely to move me that they had earnest of the wisdom of GOD, and that they should have deserved mickle grace of GOD to have saved their own souls and many other men's, if they had continued faithful in wilful poverty and in other simple virtuous living; and specially if they had with these foresaid virtues, continued in their busy fruitful sowing of GOD's Word, as, to many men's knowledge, they occupied them a season in all their wits full busily to know the pleasant Will of GOD, travailing all their members full busily for to do thereafter purely, and chiefly to the praising of the most holy name of GOD and for grace of edification and salvation of Christian people. But woe worth false covetise! and evil counsel! and tyranny! by which they and many men and women are led blindly into an evil end."

Archbishop. Then the Archbishop said to me, "Thou and such other losells of thy sect would shave your beards full near, for to have a benefice! For, by Jesu! I know none more covetous shrews than ye are, when that ye have a benefice. For, lo, I gave to JOHN PURVEY a benefice but a mile out of this Castle [*i.e., the vicarage of West Hythe, near Saltwood Castle in Kent, which PURVEY held from August* 11, 1401, *till he resigned it on October* 8, 1403], and I heard more complaints about his covetousness for tithes and other misdoings, than I did of all men that were advanced within my diocese."

William. And I said to the Archbishop, "Sir, PURVEY is neither with you now for the benefice that ye gave him, nor holdeth he faithfully with the learning that he taught and writ before time; and thus he sheweth himself neither to be hot nor cold: and therefore he and his fellows may sore[ly] dread that if they turn not hastily to the Way that they have forsaken, peradventure they be put out of the number of CHRIST's chosen people."

Archbishop. And the Archbishop said, "Though PURVEY be now a false harlot [*debased man. This term was at this time applied also to men*], I quite me [*absolve myself in respect*] to him: but come he more for such cause before me, ere we depart, I shall know with whom he holdeth! But I say to thee, Which are these holy men and wise of whom thou hast taken thine information?"

William. And I said, "Sir, Master JOHN WYCLIFFE was holden of full many men, the greatest Clerk [*Divine*] that they

knew then living; and therewith he was named a passing
ruely man and an innocent in his living : and herefore great
many commoned [*communed*] oft with him, and they loved so
much his learning that they writ it, and busily enforced
them to rule themselves thereafter. Therefore, Sir, this foresaid learning of Master JOHN WYCLIFFE is yet holden of full
many men and women, the most agreeable learning unto the
living and teaching of CHRIST and his Apostles, and most
openly shewing and declaring how the Church of CHRIST
hath been, and yet should be, ruled and governed. Therefore so many men and women covet this learning, and purpose, through GOD's grace, to conform their living like to
this learning of WYCLIFFE.

"Master JOHN AISTON taught and writ accordingly, and full
busily, where, and when, and to whom that he might : and
he used it himself right perfectly, unto his life's end.

"And also PHILIP of REPINGTON, while he was a Canon of
Leicester [*He was Chancellor of Oxford in* 1397, *and again
in* 1400]; NICHOLAS HER[E]FORD; DAVID GOTRAY of
Pakring, Monk of Bylande and a Master of Divinity; and
JOHN PURVEY, and many others, which were holden right
wise men and prudent, taught and writ busily this foresaid
learning, and conformed them thereto. And with all these
men I was oft right homely [*quite at home*], and communed
with them long time and oft : and so, before all other men,
I choose wilfully to be informed of them and by them, and
especially of WYCLIFFE himself; as of the most virtuous and
godly wise men that I heard of or knew. And therefore of
him specially, and of these men I took my learning, that I
have taught; and purpose to live thereafter, if GOD will ! to
my life's end.

"For though some of these men be contrary to the learning
that they taught before, I wot well that their learning was
true which they taught ; and therefore, with the help of GOD,
I purpose to hold and to use the learning which I heard of
them while they sat on MOSES' chair, and specially while they
sat on the chair of CHRIST. But after the works that they
now do, I will not do ! with GOD's help. For they feign and
hide and contrary the Truth which before they taught out
plainly and truly. For as I know well, when some of these
men hath been blamed for their slanderous doing, they grant

not that they have taught amiss, or erred before time ; but that they were constrained by pain[s] to leave to tell out the Sooth : and thus they choose now rather to blaspheme GOD than to suffer awhile here bodily persecution for Soothfastness that CHRIST shed out his heart-blood for."

Archbishop. And the Archbishop said, "That learning that thou callest Truth and Soothfastness is open slander to Holy Church, as it is proved of Holy Church. For albeit that WYCLIFFE your author [*founder*] was a great Clerk, and though that many men held him a perfect liver : yet his doctrine is not approved of Holy Church, but many Sentences of his learning are damned [*condemned*] as they are well worthy.

" But as touching PHILIP of REPINGTON that was first Canon, and after Abbot of Leicester, which is now Bishop of LINCOLN; I tell thee that the Day is now comen for which he fasted the Even ! For neither he holdeth now, now will hold the learning that he thought when he was Canon of Leicester ; for no Bishop of this land pursueth now more sharply them that hold thy Way than he doth."

William. And I said, "Sir, full many men and women wondereth upon him, and speaketh him mickle shame, and holdeth him for a cursed enemy of the Truth."

Archbishop. And the Archbishop said to me, " Wherefore tarriest thou me thus here, with such fables ? Wilt thou shortly, as I said to thee, submit thee to me or no ? "

William. And I said, " Sir, I tell you at one word. I dare not, for the dread of GOD, submit me to you after the tenour and Sentence that ye have above rehearsed to me."

Archbishop. And then, as if he had been wroth, he said to one of his Clerks, " Fetch hither quickly the *Certification* that came to me from Shrewsbury, under the Bailiff's seal, witnessing the errors and heresies which this losell hath venemously witnessed there ! "

Then hastily the Clerk took out and laid forth on a cupboard divers rolls and writings ; among which there was a little one, which the Clerk delivered to the Archbishop.

And by and by the Archbishop read this roll containing this sentence.

❡ *The third Sunday* [April 17th] *after Easter* [March 27th],
the year of our Lord 1407, WILLIAM THORPE *came unto the
town of Shrewsbury, and, through leave granted to him to preach,
he said openly in St. Chad's Church, in his sermon,*
> *That the Sacrament of the Altar after the consecration was
> material bread.*
> *And that images should in no wise be worshipped.*
> *And that men should not go on any pilgrimages.*
> *And that priests have no title to tithes.*
> *And that it is not lawful to swear in any wise.*

Archbishop. And when the Archbishop had read thus
this roll, he rolled it up again, and said to me, " Is this
wholesome learning to be among the people ? "

William. And I said to him, " Sir, I am both ashamed on
their behalf, and right sorrowful for them that have certified
you these things thus untruly : for I never preached nor taught
thus, privily nor apertly."

Archbishop. And the Archbishop said to me, " I will give
credence to these worshipful men which have written to me
and witnessed under their seals there among them.   Though
thou now deniest this, weenest thou that I will credence to
thee !   Thou, losell ! hast troubled the worshipful comminalty of Shrewsbury, so that the Bailiffs and comminal-
alty of that town have written to me, praying me, that am
Archbishop of CANTERBURY, Primate, and Chancellor of
England, *that I will vouchsafe to grant them, that if thou shalt
be made, as thou art worthy I to suffer open jouresse* [? penance or
pillory] *for thine heresies, that thou may have thy jouresse openly
there among them ; so that all they whom thou and such like losells
have there perverted, may, through fear of thy deed* [*i.e.*, martyr-
dom] *be reconciled again to the unity of Holy Church ; and also
they that stand in true faith of Holy Church may through thy
deed be more stablished therein.*"   And as if this asking had
pleased the Archbishop, he said, " By my thrift ! this hearty
prayer and fervent request shall be thought on ! "

But certainly neither the prayer of the men of Shrewsbury,
nor the menacing of the Archbishop made me anything afraid :
but, in the rehearsing of this malice, and in the hearing of it,
my heart greatly rejoiced, and yet doth. I thank GOD, for the
grace that I then thought, and yet think, shall come to all

the Church of GOD herethrough, by the special merciful doing of the LORD.

William. And as having no dread of the malice of tyrants, by trusting stedfastly in the help of the LORD, with full purpose for to [ac]knowledge the Soothfastness, and to stand thereby after my cunning and power, I said to the Archbishop, " Sir, if the truth of GOD's Word might now be accepted as it should be, I doubt not to prove by likely evidence, that they that are famed to be out of the faith of Holy Church in Shrewsbury and in other places also, are in the true faith of Holy Church. For as their words sound and their works shew to man's judgement, dreading and loving faithfully GOD ; their will, their desire, their love, and their business, are most set to dread to offend GOD and to love for to please Him in true and faithful keeping of His commandments.

" And again, they that are said to be in the faith of Holy Church at Shrewsbury and in other places, by open evidence of their proud, envious, malicious, covetous, lecherous, and other foul words and works, neither know nor have will to know nor to occupy their wits truly and effectuously in the right faith of Holy Church. Wherefore [none of] all these, nor none that follow their manners, shall any time come verily in the faith of Holy Church, except they enforce them more truly to come in the way which now they despise. For these men and women that are now called Faithful and holden Just, neither know, nor will exercise themselves to know, of faithfulness, one commandment of GOD. And thus full many men and women now, and specially men that are named to be " principal limbs of Holy Church," stir GOD to great wrath ; and deserve His curse for that they call or hold them "just men" which are full unjust, as their vicious words, their great customable swearing, and their slanderous and shameful works shew openly and witness. And herefore such vicious men and unjust in their own confusion call them " unjust men and women," which after their power and cunning, busy themselves to live justly after the commandment of GOD.

" And where, Sir, ye say, that I have distroubled the cominalty of Shrewsbury and many other men and women with my teaching ; if it thus be, it is not to be wondered [at] of

wise men, since all the comminalty of the city of Jerusalem
was distroubled of CHRIST's own person, that was Very GOD
and Man, and [the] most prudent preacher that ever was or
shall be.   And also all the Synagogue of Nazareth was
moved against CHRIST, and so full-filled with ire towards him
for his preaching, that the men of the Synagogue rose up and
cast CHRIST out of their city, and led him up to the top of a
mountain for to cast him down there headlong.   Also according hereto, the LORD witnesseth by MOSES, that He shall
put dissension betwixt His people, and the people that contrarieth and pursueth His people.   Who, Sir, is he that shall
preach the truth of GOD's Word to that unfaithful people,
and shall let [hinder] the Soothfastness of the gospel, and the
prophecy of GOD Almighty to be fulfilled ? "

Archbishop.   And the Archbishop said to me, "It followeth
of these thy words, that thou, and such other, thinkest that
ye do right well for to preach and teach as ye do, without
authority of any Bishop.   For ye presume that the LORD
hath chosen you only, for to preach as faithful disciples and
special followers of CHRIST ! "

William.   And I said, " Sir, by authority of GOD's law,
and also of Saints and Doctors, I am learned to deem that it
is every priest's office and duty for to preach busily, freely,
and truly the Word of GOD.

" For, no doubt, every priest should purpose first in his soul
and covet to take the order of priesthood chiefly for to make
known to the people the Word of GOD, after his cunning and
power, approving his words ever to be true by his virtuous
works ; and for this intent we suppose that Bishops and
other prelates of Holy Church should chiefly take and use
their prelacy.   And for the same cause, Bishops should give
to priests their orders.   For Bishops should accept no man to
priesthood, except that he had good will and full purpose,
and were well disposed and well learned to preach.   Wherefore, Sir, by the bidding of CHRIST, and by example of His
most holy living, and also by the witnessing of His holy
apostles and prophets, we are bound under full great pain to
exercise us after our cunning and power (as every priest is
likewise charged of GOD), to fulfil duly the office of priesthood.   We presume not hereof, ourselves, for to be esteemed, neither in our own reputation nor in none other

man's, faithful disciples and special followers of CHRIST: but, Sir, as I said to you before, we deem this, by authority chiefly of GOD's Word, that it is the chief duty of every priest to busy him faithfully to make the law of GOD known to His people; and so to comune [*communicate*] the commandment of GOD charitably, how that we best, where, when, and to whom that ever we may, is our very duty. And for the will and business that we owe of due debt to do justly our office, through the stirring and special help, as we trust, of GOD, hoping stedfastly in His mercy, we desire to be the faithful disciples of CHRIST: and we pray this gracious LORD, for His holy name! that He make us able for to please Him with devout prayers and charitable priestly works, that we may obtain of Him to follow Him thankfully."

Archbishop. And the Archbishop said to me, "Lewd losell! whereto makest thou such vain reasons to me? Asketh not Saint PAUL, *How should priests preach, except they be sent?* But I sent thee never to preach! For thy venomous doctrine is so known throughout England, that no Bishop will admit thee for to preach, by witnessing of their Letters! Why then, lewd idiot! willst thou presume to preach, since thou art not sent nor licensed of thy Sovereign to preach? Saith not Saint PAUL that *Subjects owe* [ought] *to obey their Sovereigns; and not only good and virtuous, but also tyrants that are vicious!*"

William. And I said to the Archbishop, "Sir, as touching your Letter of License or other Bishops', which, ye say, we should have to witness that we were able to be sent for to preach; we know well that neither you, Sir, nor any other Bishop of this land will grant to us any such Letters of License but [*except*] we should oblige [*bind*] us to you and to other Bishops by unlawful oaths for to pass not the bounds and terms which ye, Sir, or other Bishops will limit to us. And since in this matter, your terms be some too large, and some too strait; we dare not oblige us thus to be bound to you for to keep the terms which you will limit to us, as ye do to Friars and such other preachers: and therefore, though we have not your Letter, Sir, nor Letters of other Bishops written with ink upon parchment; we dare not herefore leave the office of preaching; to which preaching, all priests, after their cunning and power are bound, by divers testimonies of GOD's Law and of great Doctors, without any mention making of Bishops' Letters.

"For as mickle as we have taken upon us the office of
priesthood, though we are unworthy thereto, we come and
purpose to fulfil it, with the help of GOD, by authority of
His own law, and by witness of great Doctors and Saints
according hereto, trusting stedfastly in the mercy of GOD.
For that [*because*] He commandeth us to do the office of
priesthood, He will be our sufficient Letters and witness, if
we, by the example of his living and teaching specially
occupy us faithfully to do our office justly: yea, that people
to whom we preach, be they faithful or unfaithful, shall be
our Letters, that is, our witness bearers; for that Truth where
it is sown may not be unwitnessed. For all that are converted and saved by learning of GOD's Word and by working
thereafter are witness bearers, that the Truth and Soothfastness which they heard and did after, is cause of their
salvation. And again, all unfaithful men and women which
heard the Truth told out to them and would not do thereafter,
also all they that might have heard the Truth and would
not hear it, because that they would not do thereafter, all
these shall bear witness against themselves, and the Truth
(which they would not hear, or else heard it and despised to
do thereafter through their unfaithfulness) is and shall be
cause of their damnation.

"Therefore, Sir, since this foresaid witnessing of GOD, and
of divers Saints and Doctors, and of all the people good and
evil sufficeth to all true preachers: we think that we do not
the office of the priesthood, if that we leave our preaching
because that we have not or may not have duly Bishops'
Letters to witness that we are sent of them to preach. This
Sentence approveth Saint PAUL where he speaketh of himself and of faithful Apostles and disciples, saying thus, *We
need no letters of commendation as some other preachers do; which
preach for covetousness of temporal goods, and for men's praising.*

"And where ye say, Sir, Saint PAUL biddeth *subjects obey
their Sovereigns*; this is Sooth, and may not be denied. But
there are two manner of Sovereigns; virtuous sovereigns
and vicious tyrants. Therefore to these last Sovereigns,
neither men nor women that be subject owe [*ought*] to obey.
In two manners. To virtuous Sovereigns and charitable,
subjects owe to obey wilfully and gladly in hearing of their
good counsel, in consenting to their charitable biddings, and

in working after their fruitful works. This Sentence, PAUL
approveth where he saith thus to subjects, *Be ye mindful of
your Sovereigns that speak to you the Word of GOD ; and follow
you the faith of them, whose conversation you know to be virtuous.*

" For as PAUL saith after, These Sovereigns to whom subjects owe to obey in following of their manners, work busily
in holy studying how they may withstand and destroy vices,
first in themselves and after in all their subjects, and
and how they may best plant in them virtues. Also these
Sovereigns make devout and fervent prayers for to purchase
[*obtain*] grace of GOD, that they and their subjects may,
over all things, dread to offend Him, and to love for to
please Him. Also these Sovereigns to whom PAUL biddeth us obey, as it is said before, live so virtuously that
all they that will live well may take of them good example
to know and to keep the commandments of GOD.

" But, in this foresaid wise, subjects owe [*ought*] not to obey
nor to be obedient to tyrants, while they are vicious tyrants ;
since their will, their counsel, their biddings, and their works
are so vicious that they owe [*ought*] to be hated and left.
And though such tyrants be masterful and cruel in boasting
and menacing, in oppressions and divers punishings ; Saint
PETER biddeth the servants of such tyrants to obey meekly
to such tyrants, suffering patiently their malicious cruelness.
But PETER counselleth not any servant or subject to obey to
any Lord, or Prince, or Sovereign, in anything that is not
pleasing to GOD."

Archbishop. And the Archbishop said unto me, " If the
Sovereign bid his subject do that thing that is vicious, this
Sovereign herein is to blame : but the subject, for his
obedience, deserveth meed of GOD. For obedience pleaseth
more to GOD than any sacrifice."

William. And I said, " SAMUEL the Prophet said to
SAUL the wicked King, that *GOD was more pleased with
the obedience of His commandment, than with any sacrifice of
beasts* : but DAVID saith, and Saint PAUL and Saint GRE-
GORY accordingly together, that not only they that do evil
are worthy of death and damnation ; but also all they that
consent to evil doers. And, Sir, the law of Holy Church
teacheth, in the *Decrees*, that no servant to his Lord, nor
child to the father or mother, nor wife to her husband,

nor monk to his abbot, ought to obey, except in lefull [*loyal*] things and lawful."

Archbishop. And the Archbishop said to me, "All these allegings that thou bringest forth are nought else but proud presumptuousness. For hereby thou enforcest [*endeavourest*] thee to prove, that thou and such others are so just, that ye owe [*ought*] not to obey to Prelates: and thus against the learning of Saint PAUL that telleth you *not to preach, but if ye were sent*, of your own authority, ye will go forth and preach, and do what ye list!"

William. And I said, "Sir, [re]presenteth not every priest the office of the Apostles or the office of the disciples of CHRIST?"

Archbishop. And the Archbishop said, "Yea!"

William. And I said, "Sir, as the 10th Chapter of Matthew and the last Chapter of Mark witnesseth, CHRIST sent his Apostles for to preach. And the 10th Chapter of Luke witnesseth CHRIST sent his two and seventy disciples for to preach in every place that CHRIST was to come to. And Saint GREGORY in the *Common Law* saith, that every man that goeth to priesthood taketh upon him the office of preaching: for as he saith, *that priest stirreth GOD to great wrath, of whose mouth is not heard the voice of preaching.* And as other more glosses upon EZEKIEL witness, that the priest that preacheth not busily to the people shall be partaker of their damnation, that perish through his default: and though the people be saved by other special grace of GOD than by the priest's preaching; yet the priests (in that they are ordained to preach, and preach not) as before GOD, they are man-slayers. For as far as in them is, such priests as preach not busily and truly, slayeth all the people ghostly, in that they withhold from them the Word of GOD, that is [the] life and sustenance of men's souls. And Saint ISIDORE saith, *Priests shall be damned for* [the] *wickedness of the people, if they teach not them that are ignorant, and condemn them that are sinners.* For all the work and witness of priests standeth in preaching and teaching; that they edify all men, as well by cunning of faith, as by discipline of works, that is virtuous teaching. And, as the gospel witnesseth, CHRIST said in his teaching, *I am born and come into this world to bear witness to the Truth, and he that is of the Truth heareth my voice.*

" ¶ Then, Sir, since by the word of Christ specially, that is his voice, priests are commanded to preach; whatsoever priest that it be, that hath not goodwill and full purpose to do thus, and ableth not himself after his cunning and power to do his office, by the example of Christ and his Apostles : whatsoever other thing that he doeth, displeaseth GOD. For, lo, Saint GREGORY saith, *That thing left, that a man is bound chiefly to do ; whatsoever other thing that a man doeth, it is unthankful to the HOLY GHOST.* And therefore saith [ROBERT GROSSETÊTE, Bishop of] LINCOLN, *That priest that preacheth not the Word of GOD, though he be seen to have none other default, he is Antichrist and Sathanas, a night-thief and a day-thief, a slayer of souls, and an angel of light turned into darkness.*

"Wherefore, Sir, these authorities and others well considered, I deem myself damnable, if I, either for pleasure or displeasure of any creature, apply me not diligently to preach the Word of GOD : and in the same damnation, I deem all those priests which, of good purpose and will, enforce them not busily to do thus, and also all them that have purpose or will to let [*hinder*] any priest of this business."

Archbishop. And the Archbishop said to those three Clerks that stood before him, " Lo, Sirs, this is the manner and business of this losell and such others, to pick out such sharp sentences of Holy Scripture and of Doctors to maintain their sect and lore [*teaching*] against the ordinance of Holy Church. And therefore, losell ! is it, that thou covetest to have again the *Psalter* that I made to be taken from thee at Canterbury, to record sharp verses against us ! But thou shalt never have that *Psalter*, nor none other book, till that I know that thy heart and thy mouth accord fully to be governed by Holy Church."

William. And I said, " Sir, all my will and power is, and ever shall be, I trust to GOD ! to be governed by Holy Church."

Archbishop. And the Archbishop asked me, " What was Holy Church ? "

William. And I said, "Sir, I told you before, what was Holy Church : but since ye ask me this demand, I call CHRIST and his saints, Holy Church."

Archbishop. And the Archbishop said unto me, " I wot

well that CHRIST and his saints are Holy Church in heaven; but what is Holy Church in earth?"

William. And I said, "Sir, though Holy Church be every one in charity; yet it hath two parts. The first and principal part hath overcomen perfectly all the wretchedness of this life, and reigneth joyfully in heaven with CHRIST. And the other part is here yet in earth, busily and continually fighting, day and night, against temptations of the Fiend, forsaking and hating the prosperity of this world, despising and withstanding their fleshly lusts; which only are the pilgrims of CHRIST, wandering towards heaven by steadfast faith, and grounded hope, and by perfect charity. For these heavenly pilgrims may not, nor will not, be letted [*hindered*] of their good purpose by reason of any Doctors discording from Holy Scripture, nor by the floods of any tribulation temporal, nor by the wind of any pride of boast, or of menacing of any creature; for they are all fast grounded upon the sure stone CHRIST, hearing his word and loving it, exercising them faithfully and continually in all their wits to do thereafter."

Archbishop. And the Archbishop said to his Clerks, "See ye not how his heart is endured [*hardened*], and how he is travailled with the Devil, occupying him thus busily to allege such Sentences to maintain his errors and heresies! Certain, thus, he would occupy us here all day, if we would suffer him!"

NE of the **Clerks** answered, "Sir, he said, right now, that this *Certification* that came to you from Shrewsbury is untruly forged against him. Therefore, Sir, appose you him now here, in all the points which are certified against him; and so we shall hear of his own mouth his answers, and witness them."

Archbishop. And the Archbishop took the *Certification* in his hand, and looked thereon awhile; and then he said to me, "Lo, herein is certified against thee, by worthy men and faithful of Shrewsbury, that thou preachedst there *openly in Saint Chad's Church, that the Sacrament of the Altar was material bread after the consecration.* What sayest thou? Was this truly preached?"

William. And I said, "Sir, I tell you truly that I touched nothing there of the Sacrament of the Altar, but in this wise, as I will, with GOD's grace, tell you here.

I   12

'As I stood there in the pulpit, busying me to teach the commandment of GOD, there knelled a sacring-bell; and therefore mickle people turned away hastily, and with great noise ran from towards me. And I seeing this, say to them thus, ' Good men! ye were better to stand here full still and to hear GOD's Word. For, certes, the virtue and the mede of the most holy Sacrament of the Altar standeth much more in the Belief thereof that ye ought to have in your soul, than it doth in the outward Sight thereof. And therefore ye were better to stand quietly to hear GOD's Word, because that through the hearing thereof, men come to very true belief.' And otherwise, Sir, I am certain I spake not there, of the worthy Sacrament of the Altar."

Archbishop. And the Archbishop said to me, " I believe thee not! whatsoever thou sayest, since so worshipful men have witnessed against thee. But since thou deniest that thou saidest thus there, what sayest thou now? Resteth there, after the consecration, in the [h]ost, material bread or no?"

William. And I said, " Sir, I know of no place in Holy Scripture, where this term, *material bread*, is written: and therefore, Sir, when I speak of this matter, I use not [*am not accustomed*] to speak of material bread."

Archbishop. Then the Archbishop said to me, " How teachest thou men to believe in this Sacrament?"

William. And I said, " Sir, as I believe myself, so I teach other men."

Archbishop. He said, "Tell out plainly thy belief hereof!"

William. And I said, with my Protestation, " Sir, *I believe that the night before that CHRIST JESU would suffer wilfully Passion for mankind on the morn after, he took bread in his holy and most worshipful hands, lifting up his eyes, and giving thanks to GOD his Father, blessed this bread and brake it, and gave it to his disciples, saying to them,* Take, and eat of this, all of you! This is my body!

"And that this is, and ought to be all men's belief, MATTHEW, MARK, LUKE, and PAUL witnesseth.

"Other belief, Sir, have I none, nor will have, nor teach: for I believe that this sufficeth in this matter. For in this belief, with GOD's grace, I purpose to live and die: [ac]-knowledging as I believe and teach other men to believe, that *the worshipful Sacrament of the Altar is the Sacrament of CHRIST's flesh and his blood, in form of bread and wine."*

Archbishop. And the Archbishop said to me, " It is sooth, that this Sacrament is very CHRIST's body in form of bread : but thou and thy sect teachest it to be the substance of bread ! Think you this true teaching ? "

William. And I said, " Neither I nor any other of the sect that ye damn [*condemn*], teach any otherwise than I have told you, nor believe otherwise, to my knowing.

" Nevertheless, Sir, I ask of you, for charity ! that will ye tell me plainly, how ye shall understand this text of Saint PAUL, where he saith thus, *This thing feel you in yourselves, that is, in CHRIST JESU, while he was in the form of GOD.* Sir, calleth not PAUL here, *the form of GOD*, the substance or kind of GOD ? Also, Sir, saith not the Church, in the *Hours* of the most blessed Virgin, accordingly hereto, where it is written thus, *Thou Author of Health ! remember that some time thou took, of the undefiled Virgin, the form of our body !* Tell me, for charity ! therefore, Whether *the form of our body* be called here, *the kind of our body*, or no ? "

Archbishop. And the Archbishop said to me, " Wouldst thou make me declare this text after thy purpose, since the Church hath now determined that 'there abideth no substance of bread after the consecration in the Sacrament of the Altar !' Believest thou not, on this Ordinance of the Church?"

William. And I said, " Sir, whatsoever Prelates have or-dained in the Church, our Belief standeth ever whole. I have not heard that the ordinance of men under Belief, should be put into Belief."

Archbishop. And the Archbishop said to me, " If thou hast not learned this before, learn now, to know that thou art out of belief, if, in this matter, and others, thou believest not as Holy Church believeth ! What say Doctors treating of this Sacrament ? "

William. And I said, " Sir, Saint PAUL, that was a great Doctor of Holy Church, speaking to the people and teaching the right belief of this most holy Sacrament, calleth it *bread that we break.*   And also in the Canon of the *Masse*, after the consecration, this most worthy Sacrament is called *holy bread.* And every priest in this land, after he hath received this Sacrament, saith to this wise, *That thing which we have taken with* *our mouth, we pray GOD, that we may take it with a pure and clean mind* : that is, as I understand, 'We pray GOD, that we may receive, through very belief, this holy Sacrament worthily.' And, Sir, Saint AUGUSTINE saith, *That thing that is sense is bread, but that men's faith asketh to be informed of, is very CHRIST's body.* And also FULGENTIUS, an ententif Doctor, saith, *As it were an error to say that CHRIST was but a substance, that is Very Man and not Very GOD, or to say that CHRIST was Very GOD and not Very Man ; so is it,* this Doctor saith, *an error to say that the Sacrament of the Altar is but a substance.* And also, Sir, accordingly hereto, in the *Secret* of the mid-*Mass* of Christmas day, it is written thus, *Idem refulsit DEUS, sic terrena substantia nobis conferat quod divinum est ;* which sentence, with the *Secret* of the fourth ferye *quatuor temporum Septembris,* I pray you, Sir, declare here openly in English ! "

Archbishop. And the Archbishop said to me, " I perceive well enough whereabout thou art ! and how the Devil blindeth thee, that thou maist not understand the ordinance of Holy Church, nor consent thereto ! But I command thee now, answer me shortly, ' Believest thou that, after the consecration of this foresaid Sacrament, there abideth substance of bread or not ? ' "

William. And I said, " Sir, as I understand, it is all one to grant or to believe that there dwelleth substance of bread, and to grant or to believe that this most worthy Sacrament of CHRIST's own body is one Accident without Subject. But, Sir, for as mickle as your asking passeth mine understanding, I dare neither deny it nor grant it, for it is a School matter [*a subject for debate in the University Schools*], about which I busied me never for to know it : and therefore I commit this term *accidens sine subjecto,* to those Clerks which delight them so in curious and subtle sophistry, because they determine oft so difficult and strange matters, and wade and wander so in them, from argument to argument, with *pro* and *contra,* till they wot not where they are ! nor understand not themselves ! But the shame that these proud sophisters have to yield them to men and before men, maketh them oft fools, and to be concluded shamefully before GOD."

Archbishop. And the Archbishop said to me, " I purpose not to oblige thee to the subtle arguments of Clerks, since

thou art unable thereto! but I purpose to make thee obey to
the determination of Holy Church."

William. And I said, " Sir, by open evidence and great
witness, a thousand years after the Incarnation of CHRIST,
that determination which I have, here before you, rehearsed
was accepted of Holy Church, as sufficient to the salvation
of all them that would believe it faithfully, and work thereafter charitably. But, Sir, the determination of this matter,
which was brought in since the Fiend was loosed by Friar
THOMAS [ACQUINAS, *d.* 1274] again, specially calling the most
worshipful Sacrament of CHRIST's own body, an *Accident without Subject* ; which term, since I know not that GOD's law
approveth it in this matter, I dare not grant : but utterly I
deny to make this friar's sentence [*enunciation*] or any such
other my belief ; do with me, GOD ! what Thou wilt ! "

Archbishop. And the Archbishop said to me, " Well,
well ! thou shalt say otherwise ere that I leave thee ! "

" **B**UT what sayest thou to this second point that is re-
corded against thee, by worthy men of Shrewsbury,
saying that thou preachedst openly there that *the
images ought not to be worshipped in any wise* ? "

William. And I said, " Sir, I preached never thus, nor,
through GOD's grace, I will not, any time, consent to think
nor to say thus ; neither privily, nor apertly. For, lo, the
LORD witnesseth by MOSES, that the things which He made
were *right good,* and so then they were, and yet arc, and shall
be good and worshipful in their kind. And thereto, to the
end that GOD made them to, they are all preisable [*valuable*]
and worshipful ; and specially man that was made after the
image and likeness of GOD is full worshipful in his kind :
yea, this holy image, that is man, GOD worshippeth [*respecteth*].
And herefore every man should worship others in kind, and
also for heavenly virtues that men use charitably. Also I
say, wood, tin, gold, silver, or any other matter that images
are made of; all these creatures [*created things*] are worshipful
in their kind, and to the end that GOD made them for.

" But the carving, casting, nor painting of any imagery
made with man's hands (albeit that this doing be accepted of
men of highest state and dignity, and ordained of them to be
a calendar [*horn book*] to lewd men that neither can nor will

be learned to know GOD in His Word, neither by His creatures, nor by His wonderful and divers workings); yet this
imagery ought not to be worshipped in the form, nor in the
likeness of man's craft : nevertheless that every matter that
painters paint with, since it is GOD's creature ought to be
worshipped in the kind and to the end that GOD made and
ordained it to serve man."

Archbishop. Then the Archbishop said to me, " I grant
well that nobody oweth [*ought*] to do worship to any such
images for themselves; but a crucifix ought to be worshipped
for the Passion of CHRIST that is painted therein, and so
brought therethrough to man's mind : and thus the images
of the blessed Trinity and of [the] Virgin MARY, CHRIST's
mother, and other images of the saints ought to be worshipped.
For, lo, earthly kings and lords, which use to send their
letters ensealed with their arms or with their privy signet, to
men that are with them, are worshipped of these men. For
when these men receive their lord's letters, in which they see
and know the wills and biddings of their lords, in worship of their
lords, they do off their caps to these letters : why not, then,
since in images made with man's hands, we may read and
know many divers things of GOD and of His saints, shall we
not worship their images ? "

William. And I said, with my foresaid Protestation, " I
say that these worldly usages of temporal lords that ye speak
now of, may be done in case without sin : but this is no simi-
litude to worship images made by man's hand, since that
MOSES, DAVID, SOLOMON, BARUCH, and other saints in the
Bible, forbid so plainly the worshipping of all such images."

Archbishop. Then the Archbishop said to me, " Lewd
losell! In the Old Law, before that CHRIST took mankind
[*human nature*], was no likeness of any person of the Trinity
neither shewed to man nor known of man ; but now since
CHRIST became man, it is lawful to have images to shew His
manhood. Yea, though many men which are right great
Clerks, and others also, hold it an error to paint the Trinity;
I say, it is well done to make and to paint the Trinity
in images. For it is a great moving of devotion to men, to
have and to behold the Trinity and other images of Saints
carved, cast, and painted. For beyond the sea, are the best
painters that ever I saw. And, sirs! I tell you, this is their

manner; and it is a good manner! When that an image-maker shall carve, cast in mould, or paint any images; he shall go to a priest, and shrive him as clean as if he should die, and take penance, and make some certain vow of fasting, or of praying, or of pilgrimages doing: praying the priest specially to pray for him, that he may have grace to make a fair and a devout image."

William. And I said, "Sir, I doubt not, if these painters that ye speak of, or any other painters understood truly the text of MOSES, of DAVID, of the Wise Man [*i.e.*, SOLOMON], of BARUCH, and of other Saints and Doctors, these painters should be moved to shrive them to GOD, with full inward sorrow of heart; taking upon them to do right sharp penance for the sinful and vain craft of painting, carving, or casting that they had used; promising GOD faithfully never to do so after, [ac]knowledging openly before all men, their reprovable earning. And also, sir, these priests, that shrive, as ye do say, painters, and enjoin them to do penance, and pray for their speed, promising to them help of their prayers for to be curious [*cunning*] in their sinful crafts, sin herein more grievously than the painters. For these priests do comfort and give them counsel to do that thing, which of great pain (yea, under the pain of GOD's curse!) they should utterly forbid them. For, certes, Sir, if the wonderful working of GOD, and the holy living and teaching of CHRIST and of his Apostles and Prophets were made known to the people by holy living and true and busy teaching of priests; these things, Sir, were sufficient books and kalendars to know GOD by, and His Saints: without any images made with man's hand: but, certes, the vicious living of priests and their covetousness are [the] chief cause of this error and all other viciousness that reigneth among the people."

Archbishop. Then the Archbishop said to me, "I hold thee a vicious priest, and a curst! and all them that are of thy sect! for all priests of Holy Church and all images that move men to devotion; thou and such others go about to destroy! Losell! were it a fair thing to come into a church, and see therein none image?"

William. And I said, "Sir, they that come to the church, for to pray devoutly to the LORD GOD, may in their inward wits be the more fervent [when] that all their outward wits be closed from all outward seeing and hearing and from all distroublance and lettings [*hindrances*]. And since CHRIST blessed them that saw him not bodily, and have believed faithfully in him: it sufficeth then, to all men, through hearing and knowing of GOD's Word, and to do thereafter, for to believe in GOD, though they see never images made with man's hands, after any Person of the Trinity, or of any other Saint."

Archbishop. And the Archbishop said to me with a fervent spirit, " I say to thee, losell! that it is right well done to make and to have an image of the Trinity! Yea, what sayest thou ? Is it not a stirring thing to behold such an image ? "

William. And I said, " Sir, ye said, right now, that in the Old Law, ere Christ took mankind, no likeness of any Person of the Trinity was shewed to men ; wherefore, Sir, ye said it was not then lawful to have images : but now ye say, since CHRIST is become man, it is lawful to make and to have an image of the Trinity, and also of other saints. But, sir, this thing would I learn of you ! Since the Father of heaven, yea, and every Person of the Trinity was, without beginning, GOD Almighty, and many holy prophets, that were dedely [*deathly, i.e., liable to death*] men, were martyrized violently in the Old Law, and also many men and women then died holy Confessors : why was it not *then*, as lawful and necessary as now, to have made an image of the Father of heaven, and to have made and had other images of martyrs, prophets, and holy confessors to have been kalendars to advise men and move them to devotion, as ye say that images now do ? "

Archbishop. And the Archbishop said, " The Synagogue of Jews had not authority to approve these things, as the Church of Christ hath now."

William. And I said, " Sir, Saint GREGORY was a great man in the New Law, and of great dignity ; and as the Common [? *Canon*] Law witnesseth, he commended greatly a Bishop, in that he forbade utterly the images made with man's hand, should be worshipped."

Archbishop. And the Archbishop said, " Ungracious losell! thou favourest no more the truth, than a hound ! Since at the Rood[s] at the North Door [*of Saint Paul's Church*] at London, at our Lady at Walsingham, and many other divers places in England, are many great and preisable

[*precious*] miracles done: should not the images of such holy
saints and places, at [*on account of*] the reverence of GOD,
and our Lady, and other saints, be more worshipped, than
other places and images where no such miracles are done ? "

William. And I said, " Sir, there is no such virtue in any
imagery, that any images should herefore be worshipped ;
wherefore I am certain that there is no miracle done of GOD
in any place in earth, because that any images made with
man's hand, should be worshipped. And herefore, Sir, as
I preached openly at Shrewsbury and other places, I say now
here before you : that nobody should trust that there were
any virtue in imagery made with man's hand, and herefore
nobody should vow to them, nor seek them, nor kneel to
them, nor bow to them, nor pray to them, nor offer anything to them, nor kiss them, nor incense them. For,
lo, the most worthy of such images, the Brazen Serpent, by
MOSES made, at GOD's bidding ! the good King HEZEKIAH
destroyed worthily and thankfully ; for because it was
incensed. Therefore, Sir, if men take good heed to the
writing and to the learning of Saint AUGUSTINE, of Saint
GREGORY, and of Saint JOHN CHRYSOSTOM, and of other
Saints and Doctors, how they speak and write of miracles
that shall be done now in the last end of the world ; it is to
dread that, for the unfaithfulness of men and women, the
Fiend hath great power for to work many of the miracles that
now are done in such places. For both men and women
delight now, more for to hear and know miracles, than they do
to know GOD's Word or to hear it effectuously. Wherefore,
to the great confusion of all them that thus do, Christ saith,
The generation of adulterers requireth tokens, miracles, and wonders.
Nevertheless, as divers Saints say, now, when the faith of
GOD is published in Christendom, the Word of God sufficeth
to man's salvation, without such miracles ; and thus also the
Word of GOD sufficeth to all faithful men and women, without any such images.

"But, good Sir, since the Father of heaven, that is GOD in
His Godhead, is the most unknown thing that may be, and the
most wonderful Spirit, having in it no shape or likeness of
any members of any dedely [*deadly, i.e., liable to death*] creature : in what likeness, or what image, may GOD the Father
be shewed or painted ? "

Archbishop. And the Archbishop said, "As Holy Church hath suffered, and yet suffereth the images of all the Trinity, and other images to be painted and shewed, sufficeth to them that are members of Holy Church. But since thou art a rotten member cut away from Holy Church, thou favourest not the ordinance thereof! But since the day passeth, leave we this matter!"

Rchbishop. And then he said to me, "What sayest thou, to the third point that is certified against thee, preaching openly in Shrewsbury that *Pilgrimage is not lawful*? And, over this, thou saidest that *those men and women that go on pilgrimages to Canterbury, to Beverley, to Carlington, to Walsingham, and to any such other places, are accursed; and made foolish, spending their goods in waste.*"

William. And I said, "Sir, by this *Certification*, I am accused to you, that I should teach that *no pilgrimage is lawful*. But I never said thus. For I know that there be true pilgrimages, and lawful and full pleasant to GOD; and therefore, Sir, howsoever mine enemies have certified you of me, I told at Shrewsbury of two manner of pilgrimages."

Archbishop. And the Archbishop said to me, "Whom callest thou true pilgrims?"

William. And I said, "Sir, with my Protestation, I call them true pilgrims travelling towards the bliss of heaven, which (in the state, degree, or order that GOD calleth them) do busy them faithfully for to occupy all their wits bodily and ghostly, to know truly and keep faithfully the biddings of GOD, hating and fleeing all the seven deadly sins and every branch of them, ruling them virtuously, as it is said before, with all their wits, doing discreetly wilfully and gladly all the works of mercy, bodily and ghostly, after their cunning and power abling them to the gifts of the HOLY GHOST, disposing them to receive in their souls, and to hold therein the right blessings of CHRIST; busying them to know and to keep the seven principal virtues: and so then they shall obtain herethrough grace for to use thankfully to GOD all the conditions of charity; and then they shall be moved with the good Spirit of GOD for to examine oft and diligently their conscience, that neither wilfully nor wittingly they err in any Article of Belief, having continually (as frailty will

suffer) all their business to dread and to flee the offence of
GOD, and to love over all things and to seek ever to do His
pleasant will.

"Of these pilgrims, I said, 'Whatsoever good thought that
they any time think, what virtuous word that they speak, and
what fruitful work that they work; every such thought, word,
and work is a step numbered of GOD towards Him into heaven.
These foresaid pilgrims of GOD delight sore, when they hear
of saints or of virtuous men and women, how they forsook
wilfully the prosperity of this life, how they withstood the
suggestion of the Fiend, how they restrained their fleshly
lusts, how discreet they were in their penance doing, how
patient they were in all their adversities, how prudent they
were in counselling of men and women, moving them to
hate all sin and to flee them and to shame ever greatly
thereof, and to love all virtues and to draw to them, imagin-
ing how CHRIST and his followers (by example of him) suffered
scorns and slanders, and how patiently they abode and took
the wrongful menacing of tyrants, how homely they were and
serviceable to poor men to relieve and comfort them bodily
and ghostly after their power and cunning, and how devout
they were in prayers, how fervent they were in heavenly
desires, and how they absented them from spectacles of vain
seeings and hearings, and how stable they were to let [hinder]
and to destroy all vices, and how laborious and joyful they
were to sow and plant virtues. These heavenly conditions
and such others, have the pilgrims, or endeavour them for to
have, whose pilgrimage GOD accepteth.'

"And again I said, 'As their works shew, the most part of
men or women that go now on pilgrimages have not these
foresaid conditions; nor loveth to busy them faithfully for to
have. For (as I well know, since I have full oft assayed)
examine, whosoever will, twenty of these pilgrims! and he
shall not find three men or women that know surely a Commandment of GOD [i.e., one of the Ten Commandments], nor
can say their Pater noster and Ave MARIA! nor their Credo,
readily in any manner of language. And as I have learned,
and also know somewhat by experience of these same pilgrims,
telling the cause why that many men and women go hither
and thither now on pilgrimages, it is more for the health of
their bodies, than of their souls! more for to have richesse and

prosperity of this world, than for to be enriched with virtues in their souls! more to have here worldly and fleshly friendship, than for to have friendship of GOD and of His saints in heaven. For whatsoever thing a man or woman doth, the friendship of GOD, nor of any other Saint, cannot be had without keeping of GOD's commandments.'

"For with my Protestation, I say now, as I said at Shrewsbury, 'though they that have fleshly wills, travel for their bodies, and spend mickle money to seek and to visit the bones or images, as they say they do, of this saint and of that : such pilgrimage-going is neither praisable nor thankful to GOD, nor to any Saint of GOD ; since, in effect, all such pilgrims despise GOD and all His commandments and Saints. For the commandments of GOD they will neither know nor keep, nor conform them to live virtuously by example of CHRIST and of his Saints.'

"Wherefore, Sir, I have preached and taught openly, and so I purpose all my lifetime to do, with GOD's help, saying that 'such fond people waste blamefully GOD's goods in their vain pilgrimages, spending their goods upon vicious hostelars [*innkeepers*], which are oft unclean women of their bodies; and at the least, those goods with the which, they should do works of mercy, after GOD's bidding, to poor needy men and women.'

" ❡ These poor men's goods and their livelihood, these runners about offer to rich priests! which have mickle more livelihood than they need : and thus those goods, they waste wilfully, and spend them unjustly, against GOD's bidding, upon strangers; with which they should help and relieve, after GOD's will, their poor needy neighbours at home. Yea, and over this folly, ofttimes divers men and women of these runners thus madly hither and thither into pilgrimage, borrow hereto other men's goods (yea, and sometimes they steal men's goods hereto), and they pay them never again.

"Also, Sir, I know well, that when divers men and women will go thus after their own wills, and finding out one pilgrimage, they will ordain with them before[hand] to have with them both men and women that can well sing wanton songs; and some other pilgrims will have with them bagpipes: so that every town that they come through, what with the noise of their singing, and with the sound of their piping, and with the jangling of their Canterbury bells, and with the

barking out of dogs after them, they make more noise than
if the King came there away, with all his clarions and many
other minstrels.   And if these men and women be a month
out in their pilgrimage, many of them shall be, a half year
after, great janglers, tale-tellers, and liars."

Archbishop. And the Archbishop said to me, "Lewd
losell! thou seest not far enough in this matter! for thou
considerest not the great travail of pilgrims ; therefore thou
blamest that thing that is praisable! I say to thee, that it
is right well done ; that pilgrims have with them both singers
and also pipers : that when one of them that goeth barefoot
striketh his toe upon a stone and hurteth him sore and
maketh him to bleed ; it is well done, that he or his fellow,
begin then a song or else take out of his bosom a bagpipe for to
drive away with such mirth, the hurt of his fellow.   For with
such solace, the travail and weariness of pilgrims is lightly
and merrily brought forth."

William. And I said, " Sir, Saint PAUL teacheth men, *to
weep with them that weep.*"

Archbishop. And the Archbishop said, " What janglest
thou against men's devotion ?   Whatsoever thou or such
other say, I say, that the pilgrimage that now is used, is to
them that do it, a praisable and a good mean[s] to come the
rather to grace.   But I hold thee unable to know this grace !
for thou enforcest thee to let [*hinder*] the devotion of the
people, since by authority of Holy Scripture, men may lawfully have and use such solace as thou reprovest!   For
DAVID in his last *Psalm,* teacheth me to have divers instruments of music for to praise therewith GOD."

William. And I said, "Sir, by the sentence [*opinions*] of
divers Doctors expounding the *Psalms* of DAVID, the music
and minstrelsy that DAVID and other Saints of the Old Law
spake of, owe [*ought*], now, neither to be taken nor used by
the letter ; but these instruments with their music ought to
be interpreted ghostly [*spiritually*] : for all those figures are
called Virtues and Grace, with which virtues men should
please GOD and praise His name.   For Saint PAUL saith,
All such things befell to them in figure.   Therefore, Sir, I
understand that the letter of this *Psalm* of DAVID and of such
other *Psalms* and sentences, doth slay them that taken them
now literally.   This sentence, I understand, Sir, CHRIST ap-

proveth himself, putting out the minstrels, ere that he would quicken the dead damsel."

Archbishop. And the Archbishop said to me, "Lewd losell! is it not lawful for us to have organs in the church, for to worship therewithal GOD?"

William. And I said, "Yea, Sir, by man's ordinance; but, by the ordinance of GOD, a good sermon to the people's understanding, were mickle more pleasant to GOD!"

Archbishop. And the Archbishop said that "organs and good delectable songs quickened and sharpened more men's wits, than should any sermon!"

William. But I said, "Sir, lusty men and worldly lovers delight and covet and travail to have all their wits quickened and sharpened with divers sensible solace: but all the faithful lovers and followers of CHRIST have all their delight to hear GOD's Word, and to understand it truly, and to work thereafter faithfully and continually. For, no doubt, to dread to offend GOD, and to love to please Him in all things, quickeneth and sharpeneth all the wits of CHRIST's chosen people, and ableth them so to grace, that they joy greatly to withdraw their ears, and all their wits and members from all worldly delight, and from all fleshly solace. For Saint JEROME, as I think, saith, *Nobody may joy with this world, and reign with CHRIST.*"

Archbishop. And the Archbishop, as if he had been displeased with mine answer, said to his Clerks, "What guess ye this idiot will speak there, where he hath none dread; since he spaketh thus now, here in my presence? Well, well, by God! thou shalt be ordained for!"

AND then he spake to me, all angerly, "What sayest thou to this fourth point that is certified against thee, preaching openly and boldly in Shrewsbury, *That priests have no title to tithes?*"

William. And I said, "Sir, I named there no word of tithes in my preaching. But, more than a month after [? *June*, 1407] that I was arrested, there in prison [*at Shrewsbury*], a man came to me into the prison, asking me 'What I said of tithes?'

"And I said to him, 'Sir, in this town, are many Clerks and Priests; of which some of them are called Religious Men, though many of them be Seculars. Therefore, ask ye of them this question!'

" And this man said to me, ' Sir, our prelates say that we are also obliged to pay our tithes of all things that renew to us; and that they are accursed that withdraw any part wittingly from them of their tithes.'

"And I said, Sir, to that man, as with my Protestation, I say now here before you, that ' I had wonder[ed] that any priest dare say *men to be accursed*, without ground of GOD's Word.'

" And the man said, 'Sir, our priests say that they curse men thus, by authority of GOD's Law.'

" And I said, ' Sir, I know not where this sentence of cursing is authorized now in the *Bible*. And therefore, Sir, I pray you that ye will ask the most cunning Clerk of this town, that ye may know where this sentence, " cursing them that tythe not now," is written in GOD's Law: for if it were written there, I would right gladly be learned [*informed*] where.'

" But, shortly, this man would not go from me, to ask this question of another body ; but required me, there, as I would answer before GOD ! if, in this case, the cursing of priests were lawful and approved of GOD ?

" And, shortly, therewith came to my mind the learning of Saint PETER, teaching priests especially, *to hallow the LORD CHRIST in their hearts, being evermore ready, as far as in them is, to answer through faith and hope, to them that ask of them a reason.* And this lesson PETER teacheth me to use, with a meek spirit, and with dread of the LORD.

"Wherefore, Sir, I said to this man, in this wise, ' In the Old Law, which ended not fully till the time that CHRIST rose up again from death to life, GOD commanded tithes to be given to the Levites for the great business and daily travail that pertained to their office: but Priests, because their travail was mickle more easy and light than was the office of the Levites, GOD ordained that Priests should take for their lifelode [*livelihood*] to do their office, the tenth part of those tithes that were given to the Levites.

" ' But now,' I said, ' in the New Law, neither CHRIST nor any of his Apostles took tithes of the people, nor commanded the people to pay tithes, neither to Priests nor to Deacons. But CHRIST taught the people to do almesse [*alms*], that is, works of mercy to poor needy men, of surplus that is superfluouse [*superfluity*] of their temporal goods which they had more than them needed reasonably to their necessary livelihood. And thus,' I said, ' not of tithes, but of pure alms of the people CHRIST lived and his Apostles, when they were so busy in teaching of the Word of GOD to the people, that they might not travail otherwise for to get their livelihood. But after CHRIST's Ascension, and when the Apostles had received the HOLY GHOST, they travailed with their hands for to get their livelihood when that they might thus do for [*on account of*] busy preaching. Therefore, by example of himself, St. PAUL teacheth all the priests of CHRIST for to travail with their hands, when for busy teaching of the people, they might thus do. And thus all these priests (whose priesthood GOD accepteth now, or will accept ; or did [accept] in the Apostles' time, and after their decease) will do, to the world's end.

"' But as *Cisterciensis* telleth, in the thousand year of our Lord JESUS CHRIST, two hundred and eleventh year, one Pope, the tenth GREGORY, ordained new tithes first to be given to priests now in the New Law. But Saint PAUL in his time (whose trace or example, all priests of GOD enforce them to follow), seeing the covetousness that was among the people (desiring to destroy this foul sin, through the grace of GOD, and true virtuous living and example of himself) wrote and taught all priests for *to follow him, as he followed* CHRIST, patiently, willingly, and gladly in high poverty. Wherefore PAUL saith this, *The LORD hath ordained, that they that preach the Gospel shall live by the Gospel. But we,* saith PAUL, *that covet and busy us to be faithful followers of* CHRIST, *use not this power.* For, lo, as PAUL witnessed afterward, when he was full poor and needy, preaching among the people, he was not chargeous [*chargeable*] unto them, but with his hands he travailed, not only to get his own living, but also the living of other poor and needy creatures. And since the people were never so covetous nor so avarous [*avaricious*], I guess, as they are now ; it were good counsel that all priests took good heed to this heavenly learning of PAUL : following him here, in wilful poverty, nothing charging the people for their bodily livelihood.

"' But because that many priests do contrary PAUL in this foresaid doctrine, PAUL biddeth the people take heed to those priests, that follow him, as he had given them example : as if

Paul would say thus to the people, "Accept ye none other priests, than they that live after the form that I have taught you!" For, certain, in whatsoever dignity or order that any priest is in, if he conform him not to follow Christ and his Apostles in wilful poverty and in other heavenly virtues, and specially in true preaching of God's Word; though such a one be named a Priest, yet he is no more but a Priest in name: for the work of a very Priest such a one wanteth! This sentence [*opinion*] approveth Augustine, Gregory, Chrysostom, and [Grossetête, *Bishop of*] Lincoln plainly.'"

Archbishop. And the Archbishop said to me, " Thinkest thou this wholesome learning for to sow openly, or yet privily among the people! Certain, this doctrine contrarieth plainly the ordinance of Holy Fathers : which have ordained, granted, and licensed priests to be in divers degrees; and to live by tithes and offerings of the people, and by other duties."

William. And I said, " Sir, if priests were now in measurable measure and number; and lived virtuously, and taught busily and truly the Word by the example of Christ and of his Apostles, without tithes offerings and other duties that priests now challenge and take : the people would give them freely sufficient livelihood."

A Clerk. And a Clerk said to me, " How wilt thou make this good, that the people will give freely to priests their livelihood; since that now, by the law, every priest can scarcely constrain the people to give them their livelihood?"

William. And I said, " Sir, it is now no wonder, though the people grudge to give the priests the livelihood that they ask! for mickle people know, now, how that priests should live; and how that they live contrary to Christ and His Apostles. And therefore the people are full heavy to pay, as they do, their temporal goods to Parsons and to other Vicars and Priests; which should be faithful dispensators of the parish's goods, taking to themselves no more but a scarce living of tithes nor of offerings by the Ordinance of the Common Law. For whatsoever priests take of the people, be it tithes or offering, or any other duty or service, the priests ought not to have thereof no more but a bare living : and to depart [*give away*] the residue to the poor men and women, specially of the parish of whom they take this temporal living.

K   12

But the most deal [*greater portion*] of priests now waste their parish's goods, and spendeth them at their own will, after the world in their vain lusts : so that in few places poor men have duly, as they should have, their own sustenance, neither of tithes nor of offerings, nor of other large wages and foundations that priests take of the people in divers manners, above that they need for needful sustenance of meat and clothing. But the poor needy people are forsaken and left of priests, to be sustained of the paroshenis [*parishioners*]; as if the priests took nothing of the parishioners, for to help the poor people with. And thus, Sir, into over great charges of the parishioners, they pay their temporal goods twice ; where once might suffice, if priests were true dispensators.

"Also, Sir, the parishioners that pay their temporal goods, be they tithes or offerings, to priests that do not their office among them justly, are partners of every sin of those priests : because that they sustain those priests' folly in their sin, with their temporal goods. If these things be well considered, what wonder is it then, Sir, if the parishioners grudge against these dispensators ? "

Archbishop. Then the Archbishop said to me, " Thou that shouldest be judged and ruled by Holy Church, presumptuously, thou deemest Holy Church to have erred in the ordinance of tithes and other duties to be paid to priests ! It shall be long ere thou thrive, losell ! that thou despisest thy ghostly Mother ! How darest thou speak this, losell ! among the people ? Are not tithes given to priests for to live by ? "

William. And I said, " Sir, Saint PAUL saith that tithes were given in the Old Law to Levites and to Priests, that came of the lineage of LEVI. But *our priest, he* saith, *came not of the lineage of LEVI, but of the lineage of JUDAH ; to which JUDAH, no tithes were promised to be given.* And therefore PAUL saith, *Since the priesthood is changed from the generation of LEVI to the generation of JUDAH, it is necessary that changing also be made of the Law.* So that priests live now without tithes and other duties that they now claim ; following CHRIST and his Apostles in wilful poverty, as they have given them example. For since CHRIST lived all the time of His preaching by pure [*the simple*] alms of the people, and (by example of him) his Apostles lived in the same wise, or else by the travail of their hands, as it is said above; every priest, whose

priesthood CHRIST approveth, knoweth well, and confesseth
in word and in work that *a disciple oweth* [ought] *not to be above
his Master, but it sufficeth to a disciple to be as his Master,* simple
and pure, meek and patient : and by example specially of his
Master CHRIST, every priest should rule him in all his living;
and so, after his cunning and power, a priest should busy
him to inform and to rule whomsoever he might charitably."

Archbishop. And the Archbishop said to me, with a great
spirit, " GOD's curse have thou and thine for this teaching !
for thou wouldest hereby make the Old Law more free and
perfect than the New Law !   For thou sayest it is lawful for
Levites and to Priests to take tithes in the Old Law, and so
to enjoy their privileges; but to us priests in the New Law,
thou sayest it is not lawful to take tithes !   And thus, thou
givest the Levites of the Old Law more freedom, than to
priests of the New Law ! "

William. And I said, " Sir, I marvel, that ye understand
this plain text of PAUL thus !   Ye wot well, that the Levites
and Priests in the Old Law, that took tithes, were not so free
nor so perfect as CHRIST and his Apostles that took no tithes !
And, Sir, there is a Doctor, I think that it is Saint JEROME,
that saith thus, *The priests that challenge now in the New Law,
tithes, say, in effect that CHRIST is not become Man, nor that he
hath yet suffered death for man's love.*   Whereupon, this Doctor
saith this sentence, *Since tithes were the hires and wages limited
to Levites and to Priests of the Old Law, for bearing about of
the Tabernacle, and for slaying and flaying of beasts, and for
burning of sacrifice, and for keeping of the Temple, and for trumping
of battle before the host of Israel, and other divers observances that
pertained to their office; those priests, that will challenge or take
tithes, deny that CHRIST is comen in flesh, and do the Priest's office
of the Old Law, for whom tithes were granted : for else,* as the
Doctor saith, *priests take now tithes wrongfully."*

Archbishop. And the Archbishop said to his Clerks,
" Heard ye ever losell speak thus !   Certain, this is the
learning of them all, that wheresoever they come, and they
may be suffered, they enforce them to expugn the freedom of
Holy Church ! "

William. And I said, " Sir, why call you the taking of
tithes and of such other duties that priests challenge now
wrongfully ' the freedom of Holy Church'; since neither

CHRIST nor his Apostles challenged nor took such duties? Herefore these takings of priests now, are not called justly 'the freedom of Holy Church' : but all such giving and taking ought to be called and holden 'the slanderous covetousness of men of the Holy Church.'"

Archbishop. And the Archbishop said to me, "Why, losell! wilt not thou and others that are confedered [*confederated*] with thee, seek out of Holy Scripture and of the sentence of Doctors, all sharp authorities against Lords and Knights and Squires, and against other secular men, as thou dost against priests?"

William. And I said, "Sir, whatsoever men or women, Lords or Ladies, or any others that are present in our preaching specially, or in our communing, after our cunning, we to tell to them their office and their charges: but, Sir, since CHRYSOSTOM saith *the priests are the stomach of the people*, it is needful in preaching and also in communing, to be most busy about this priesthood, since by the viciousness of priests, both Lords and Commons are most sinfully infected and led into the worst. And because that the covetousness of priests, and pride and the boast that they have and make, of their dignity and power, destroyeth not only the virtues of priesthood in priests themselves : but also, over this, it stirreth GOD to take great vengeance both upon Lords and Commons, which suffer these priests charitably."

Archbishop. And the Archbishop said to me, "Thou judgest every priest proud that will not go arrayed as thou dost! By God! I deem him to be more meek that goeth every day in a scarlet gown, than thou, in that threadbare blue gown! Whereby knowest thou a proud man?"

William. And I said, "Sir, a proud priest may be known when he denieth to follow CHRIST and his Apostles in wilful poverty and other virtues; and coveteth worldly worship, and taketh it gladly, and gathereth together with pleting [? *pleading*] menacing or with flattering, or with simony, any worldly goods : and most if a priest busy him not chiefly in himself, and after in all other men and women, after his cunning and power, to withstand sin."

Archbishop. And the Archbishop said to me, "Though thou knewest a priest to have all these vices, and though thou sawest a priest, lovely, lie now by a woman, knowing

her fleshly; wouldest thou herefore deem this priest damnable? I say to thee, that in the turning about of thy hand,
such a sinner may be verily repented!"

William. And I said, "Sir, I will not damn any man for
any sin that I know done or may be done; so that the sinner
leaveth his sin! But, by authority of Holy Scripture, he
that sinneth thus openly, as ye shew here, is damnable for
doing of such a sin; and most specially a priest that should
be [an] example to all others for to hate and fly sin: and in
how short time that ever ye say, that such a sinner may be
repented, he oweth [*ought*] not, of him that knoweth his
sinning, to be judged verily repentant, without open evidence
of great shame and hearty sorrow for his sin. For whosoever,
and specially a priest, that useth pride, envy, covetousness,
lechery, simony, or any other vices; and sheweth not, as open
evidence of repentance, as he hath given evil example and
occasion of sinning: if he continue in any such sin as long as
he may, it is likely that sin leaveth him and he not sin; and,
as I understand, such a one sinneth unto death, for whom
nobody oweth [*ought*] to pay, as Saint JOHN saith."

A Clerk. And a Clerk said to the Archbishop, " Sir, the
longer that ye appose him, the worse he is! and the more
that ye busy you to amend him, the waywarder he is! for he
is of so shrewd a kind, that he shameth not only to be himself
a foul nest; but, without shame, he busieth him to make his
nest fouler!"

Archbishop. And the Archbishop said to his Clerk,
"Suffer a while, for I am at an end with him! for there is
one other point certified against him; and I will hear what
he saith thereto."

AND so then, he said to me, "Lo, it is here certified
against thee, that thou preachedst openly at Shrewsbury *that it is not lawful to swear in any case.*"

William. And I said, " Sir, I preached never so
openly, nor I have not taught in this wise, in any place. But,
Sir, as I preached in Shrewsbury, with my Protestation I say
to you now here, That by the authority of the Gospel and of
Saint JAMES, and by witness of divers Saints and Doctors, I
have preached openly, in one place or other, that it is not lawful in any case to swear by any creature. And, over this, Sir,

have also preached and taught, by the foresaid authorities, that nobody should swear in any case, if that without oath, in any wise, he that is charged to swear, might excuse him to them that have power to compel him to swear in leful things and lawful: but if a man may not excuse him without oath to them that have power to compel him to swear, then he ought to swear only by GOD, taking Him only, that is Soothfastness, for to witness the soothfastness."

A Clerk. And then a Clerk asked me, " If it were not leful [*lawful*] to a subject, at the bidding of his Prelate, for to kneel down and touch the Holy Gospel book, and kiss it saying, *So help me, GOD ! and this holy doom !* for he should, after his cunning and power, do all things, that his Prelate commandeth him ? "

William. And I said to them, " Sirs, ye speak here full generally and largely ! What, if a Prelate commanded his subject to do an unlawful thing, should he obey thereto ? "

Archbishop. And the Archbishop said to me, " A subject ought not to suppose that his Prelate will bid him do an unlawful thing. For a subject ought to think that his Prelate will bid him do nothing but that he will answer for before GOD, that it is lefull [*lawful*]: and then, though the bidding of the Prelate be unlawful, the subject hath no peril to fulfil it; since that he thinketh and judgeth that whatsoever thing his Prelate biddeth him do, that is leful to him for to do it."

William. And I said, " Sir, I trust not hereto ! But to our first purpose ! Sir, I tell you that I was once in a gentleman's house, and there were then two Clerks there, a Master of Divinity and a Man of Law; which Man of Law was also communing in divinity. And among other things, these men spake of oaths. And the Man of Law said, 'At the bidding of his Sovereign which had power to charge him to swear, he would lay his hand upon a book, and hear his charge; and if his charge, to his understanding were unlawful, he would hastily withdraw his hand from the book; and if he perceived his charge to be leful he would hold still his hand upon the book, taking there only GOD to witness that he would fulfil that leful charge after his power.' And the Master of Divinity said then to him thus, ' Certain, he that layeth his hand upon a book in this wise, and maketh there a promise to do that thing that he is commanded, is obliged there, by book oath, then, to fulfil his charge. For, no doubt, he that chargeth him to lay his hand thus upon a book, touching the book and swearing by it, and kissing it, promising in this form, to do this thing or that, will say and witness, that he that toucheth thus a book and kisseth it, hath sworn upon that book; and all other men that see that men thus do, and also all those that hear thereof in the same wise, will say and witness that *this man hath sworn upon a book!* Wherefore,' the Master of Divinity said, ' it was not leful, neither to give nor to take any such charge upon a book! for every book is nothing else but divers creatures [*created things*], of which it is made of: therefore to swear upon a book, is to swear by creatures! and this swearing is ever unleful.'

" This sentence witnesseth CHRYSOSTOM, plainly blaming them greatly, that bring forth a book for to swear upon, charging Clerks that in nowise they constrain anybody to swear, whether they think a man to swear true or false."

And the Archbishop and his Clerks scorned me, and blamed me greatly for this saying. And the Archbishop menaced me with great punishment and sharp, except I left this opinion of swearing.

William. And I said, " Sir, this is not mine opinion; but it is the opinion of CHRIST our Saviour! and of Saint JAMES! and of CHRYSOSTOM! and of other divers Saints and Doctors ! "

Then the Archbishop bad a Clerk read this *Homily* of CHRYSOSTOM, which *Homily* this Clerk held in his hand written in a roll; which roll the Archbishop caused to be taken from my fellow at Canterbury: and so then this Clerk read this roll, till he came to a clause where CHRYSOSTOM saith that *it is sin, to swear well.*

A Clerk (? Malveren). And then a Clerk, MALVEREN as I guess, said to the Archbishop, " Sir, I pray you wit of him, how that he understandeth CHRYSOSTOM here, saying it to be *sin, to swear well.*"

Archbishop. And so the Archbishop asked me, " How I understood here CHRYSOSTOM ?

William. And, certain, I was somewhat afraid to answer hereto; for I had not busied me to study about the sense hereof: but lifting up my mind to GOD, I prayed Him, of grace. And, as fast, as I thought how CHRIST said to his apostles, *When, for my name, ye shall be brought before judges, I will give into your mouth, wisdom, that your adversaries shall not against say* [gainsay]; and trusting faithfully in the Word of GOD, I said, "Sir, I know well, that many men and women have now swearing so in custom, that they know not, nor will not know that they do evil for to swear as they do: but they think and say, that they do well for to swear as they do; though they know well that they swear untruly. For they say, 'They may by their swearing, though it be false, [a]void blame or temporal harm; which they should have, if they swore not thus.'

"And, Sir, many men and women maintain strongly that they swear well, when that thing is sooth that they swear for.

"Also full many men and women say now that 'It is well done to swear by creatures, when they may not (as they say) otherwise be believed.'

"And also full many men and women now say that 'It is well done to swear by GOD and by our Lady, and by other Saints; for to have them in mind!'

"But since all these sayings are but excusations [*excuses*] and sin, methinketh, Sir, that this sentence of CHRYSOSTOM may be alleged well against all such swearers: witnessing that these sin grievously; though they think themselves for to swear in this foresaid wise, well. For it is evil done and great sin for to swear truth, when, in any manner, a man may excuse him without oath."

Archbishop. And the Archbishop said that "CHRYSOSTOM might be thus understood."

A Clerk. And then a Clerk said to me, "Wilt thou tarry my Lord no longer! but submit thee here meekly to the ordinance of Holy Church; and lay thine hand upon a book, touching the Holy Gospel of GOD, promising, not only with thy mouth but also with thine heart, to stand to my Lord's ordinance?"

William. And I said, "Sir, have I not told you here, how that I heard a Master of Divinity say that, in such a case, it is all one to touch a book, and to swear by a book?"

Archbishop. And the Archbishop said, "There is no Master of Divinity in England so great, that if he hold this opinion before me, but I shall punish him as I shall do thee, except thou swear as I shall charge thee!"

William. And I said, " Sir, is not CHRYSOSTOM an ententif Doctor ? "

Archbishop. And the Archbishop said, " Yea ! "

William. And I said, " If CHRYSOSTOM proveth him worthy great blame that bringeth forth a book to swear upon, it must needs follow that he is more to blame that sweareth on that book ! "

Archbishop. And the Archbishop said, " If CHRYSOSTOM meant according to the ordinance of Holy Church, we will accept him ! "

A Clerk. And then said a Clerk to me, " Is not the Word of GOD, and GOD Himself *equipollent*, that is, of one authority ? "

William. And I said, " Yea ! "

A Clerk. Then he said to me, " Why wilt thou not swear, then, by the Gospel of GOD, that is, GOD's Word ; since it is all one to swear by the Word of GOD and by GOD Himself ? "

William. And I said, " Sir, since I may not, now, otherwise be believed but by swearing, I perceive, as AUGUSTINE saith, that it is not speedful that ye, that should be my brethren, should not believe me : therefore I am ready, by the Word of GOD (as the LORD commanded me by His Word), to swear."

A Clerk. Then the Clerk said to me, " Lay, then, thine hand upon the book, touching the Holy Gospel of GOD ; and take thy charge ! "

William. And I said, " Sir, I understand that the Holy Gospel of GOD may not be touched with man's hands ! "

A Clerk. And the Clerk said I fonded [*fooled*], and that I said not truth.

William. And I asked this Clerk, " Whether it were more to read the Gospel, or to touch the Gospel ? "

A Clerk. And he said, " It was more to read the Gospel ! "

William. Then I said, " Sir, by authority of Saint JEROME, the Gospel is not the Gospel for [*through*] reading of the letter, but for the belief that men have in the Word of GOD ; that it is the Gospel that we believe, and not the letter we read : for because the letter that is touched with man's hand is not the Gospel, but the sentence that is verily believed in man's heart is the Gospel. For so Saint JEROME saith, *The Gospel, that is the virtue of GOD's Word is not in the* *leaves of the book, but it is in the root of reason. Neither the Gospel,* he saith, *is in the writing above of the letters; but the Gospel is in the marking of the sentence of Scriptures.*

"This sentence approveth Saint PAUL, saying thus, *The Kingdom of GOD is not in word, but in virtue.* And DAVID saith, *The voice of the LORD, that is, His Word, is in virtue.* And, after, DAVID saith, *Through the Word of GOD, the heavens were formed; and in the Spirit of His mouth is all the virtue of them.* And I pray you, Sir, understand ye well how DAVID saith that, *in the Spirit of the mouth of the LORD is all the virtue of angels and of men"*?

A Clerk. And the Clerk said to me, "Thou wouldst make us to fond with thee! Say we not that the Gospels are written in the *Mass* book?"

William. And I said, "Sir, though men use [*are accustomed*] to say thus, yet it is unperfect speech. For the principal part of a thing is properly the whole thing: for, lo, man's soul that may not now be seen here, nor touched with any sensible thing, is properly Man! And all the virtue of a tree is in the root thereof, that may not be seen; for do away with the root, and the tree is destroyed! And, Sir, as ye said to me, right now, GOD and His Word are of one authority; and, Sir, Saint JEROME witnesseth that CHRIST, Very GOD and Very Man, is hid in the letter of his Law; thus also, Sir, the Gospel is hid in the letter!

"For, Sir, as it is full likely many divers men and women here in the earth touched CHRIST, and saw him, and knew his bodily person; which neither touched, nor saw, nor knew ghostly his Godhead: right thus, Sir, many men now touch, and see, and write, and read the Scriptures of GOD's Law, which neither touch, see, nor read effectually the Gospel. For as the Godhead of CHRIST, that is, the virtue of GOD, is known by the virtue through belief; so is the Gospel, that is CHRIST's Word!"

A Clerk. And a Clerk said to me, "These be full misty matters and unsavoury, that thou showest here to us!"

William. And I said, "Sir, if ye, that are Masters, know not plainly this sentence, ye may sore dread that the Kingdom of Heaven be taken from you! as it was from the Princes of Priests and from the Elders of the Jews."

A Clerk (? Malveren). And then a Clerk, as I guess

MALVEREN, said to me, "Thou knowest not thine equivocations! for the 'Kingdom of Heaven' hath diverse under-
standings. What callest thou the 'Kingdom of Heaven' in
this sentence, that thou shewest here?"

William. And I said, "Sir, by good reason, and sentence
of Doctors, the Realm of Heaven is called here, the understanding of GOD's Word."

A Clerk. And a Clerk said to me, "From whom, thinkest
thou, that this understanding is taken away?"

William. And I said, "Sir, by authority of CHRIST
himself, the effectual understanding of CHRIST's word is
taken away from all them chiefly which are great-lettered
[*learned*] men, and presume to understand high things, and
will be holden wise men, and desire mastership and high
state and dignity: but they will not conform them to the
living and teaching of CHRIST and of His Apostles."

Archbishop. Then the Archbishop said, "Well, well,
thou wilt judge thy sovereigns! By God! the King [*HENRY
IV.*] doeth not his duty, but he suffer thee to be condemned!"

A Clerk. ND then another Clerk said to me, "Why,
on Friday last, that was [*August* 5, 1407],
counselledst thou a man of my Lord's, that
he should not shrive him to Man, but
only to GOD?"

And with this asking, I was abashed; and then, by and
by, I knew that I was surely betrayed of a man that came
to me in prison [? *at Saltwood Castle*] on the Friday before,
communing with me in this matter of confession: and,
certain, by his words, I thought that this man came then to
me of full fervent and charitable will. But now I know, he
came to tempt me and to accuse me. GOD forgive him, if
it be His holy will!

And with all mine heart, when I had thought thus, I said
to this Clerk, "Sir, I pray you that ye would fetch this man
hither! and all the words, as near as I can repeat them,
which that I spake to him on Friday in the prison, I will
rehearse now here, before you all, and before him."

Archbishop. And, as I guess, the Archbishop then said
to me, "They that are now here, suffice to repeat them. How
saidest thou to him?"

William. And I said, "Sir, that man came and asked me of divers things; and after his asking, I answered him, as I understood that good was. And, as he shewed to me by his words, he was sorry for his living in Court, and right heavy for his own vicious living, and also for the viciousness of other men, and specially of priests' evil living; and herefore, he said to me with a sorrowful heart, as I guessed, that he purposed fully, within short time, for to leave the Court, and busy him to know GOD's Law, and to conform all his life hereafter.

"And when he had said to me these words, and others more, which I would rehearse and [*if*] he were present, he prayed me to hear his confession.

"And I said to him, 'Sir, wherefore come ye to me, to be confessed of me? Ye wot well that the Archbishop putteth and holdeth me here, as one unworthy either to give or to take any Sacrament of Holy Church!'

"And he said to me, 'Brother, I wot well, and so wot many others more, that you and such others are wrongfully vexed; and herefore I will common [*commune*] with you the more gladly.'

"And I said to him, 'Certain, I wot well that many men of this Court [*i.e., the Archbishop's*], and specially Priests of this household [*Chaplains*], would be full evil a paid, both with you and me, if they wist that ye were confessed of me!'

"And he said that he cared not therefore, for he had full little affection in them! and, as methought, he spake these words and many others of so good will and of so high desire for to have known and done the pleasant Will of GOD.

"And I said then to him, as with my foresaid Protestation, I say to you now here, 'Sir, I counsel you for to absent you from all evil company, and to draw you to them that love and busy them to know and to keep the precepts of GOD; and then the good Spirit of GOD will move you for to occupy busily all your wits in gathering together of all your sins, as far as ye can bethink you; shaming greatly of them, and sorrowing heartily for them. Yea, Sir, the HOLY GHOST will then put in your heart a good will and a fervent desire for to take and to hold a good purpose, to hate ever and to fly, after your cunning and power, all occasion of sin: and so then wisdom shall come to you from above, lightening with divers beams of grace and of heavenly desire all your

wits, informing you how ye shall trust stedfastly in the mercy
of the LORD, [ac]knowledging to Him only all your vicious
living, praying to Him ever devoutly of charitable counsel
and continuance, hoping without doubt that if ye continue
thus busying you faithfully to know and keep his biddings,
that He will, for He only may, forgive you all your sins!'

"And this man said then to me, 'Though GOD forgive
men their sins, yet it behoveth men to be assoiled [*absolved*]
of priests, and to do the penance that they enjoin them!'

"And I said to him, 'Sir, it is all one to assoil men of
their sins, and to forgive men their sins: wherefore since it
pertaineth only to GOD to forgive sin, it sufficeth in this
case, to counsel men and women for to leave their sin, and
to comfort them that busy them thus to do, for to hope
stedfastly in the mercy of GOD. And againward, priests
ought to tell sharply to customable sinners, that if they will
not make an end of their sin, but continue in divers sins
while that they may sin, all such deserve pain without
end. And herefore priests should ever busy them to live well
and holily, and to teach the people busily and truly the
Word of GOD; shewing to all folk, in open preaching and in
privy counselling, that the LORD GOD only forgiveth sin.
And therefore those priests that take upon them to assoil
men of their sins, blaspheme GOD; since that it pertaineth
only to the LORD to assoil men of all their sins. For, no
doubt, a thousand years after that CHRIST was man, no
priest of CHRIST durst take upon him to teach the people,
neither privily nor apertly, that they behoved needs to come
to be assoiled of them; as priests do now. But by authority
of CHRIST's word, priests bound indured [*hardened*] customable sinners to everlasting pains, [those] which, in no time of
their living, would busy them faithfully to know the biddings
of GOD, nor to keep them. And, again, all they that would
occupy all their wits to hate and to flee all occasion of sin,
dreading over all things to offend GOD, and loving for to
please Him continually; to these men and women, priests
shewed how the LORD assoileth them of their sins. And
thus CHRIST promised to confirm in heaven, all the binding
and loosing that priests, by authority of his Word, bind men
in sin that are indured therein; or loose them out of sin here
upon earth that are verily repentant.'

"And this man hearing these words, said that he 'might well in conscience consent to this sentence. But,' he said, 'is it not needful to the lay people that cannot thus do, to go shrive them to priests?'

"And I said, 'If a man feel himself so distroubled with any sin, that he cannot by his own wit, avoid this sin without counsel of them that are herein wiser than he; in such a case, the counsel of a good priest is full necessary. And if a good priest fail, as they do now commonly, in such a case; Saint AUGUSTINE saith that a man may lefully comon [*lawfully commune*] and take counsel of a virtuous secular man. But, certain, that man or woman is overladen and too beastly, which cannot bring their own sins into their mind, busying them night and day for to hate and for to forsake all their sins, doing a sigh for them, after their cunning and power. And, Sir, full accordingly to this sentence, upon mid-Lenton Sunday, two years [*March* 29, 1405], as I guess, now agone, I heard a Monk of Feversham, that men called MOREDOM, preach at Canterbury, at the Cross within Christchurch Abbey, saying thus of Confession: *As through the suggestion of the Fiend, without counsel of any other body than of themselves, many men and women can imagine and find means and ways enough to come to pride, to theft, to lechery, and to other divers vices: in contrary wise*, this Monk said, *since the LORD GOD is more ready to forgive sin than the Fiend is or may be of power to move anybody to sin, then whoever will shame and sorrow heartily for their sins, [ac]knowledging them faithfully to GOD, amending them after their power and cunning, without counsel of any other body than of GOD and himself, through the grace of GOD, all such men and women may find sufficient means to come to GOD's mercy, and so to be clean assoiled of all their sins.*' This sentence I said, Sir, to this man of yours, and the self words, as near as I can guess."

Archbishop. And the Archbishop said, "Holy Church approveth not this learning."

William. And I said, "Sir, Holy Church, of which CHRIST is head in heaven and in earth, must needs approve this sentence. For, lo, hereby all men and women may, if they will, be sufficiently taught to know and to keep the commandments of GOD, and to hate and to fly continually all occasion of sin, and to love and to seek virtues busily,

and to believe in GOD stably, and to trust in His mercy
stedfastly, and so to come to perfect charity and continue
therein perseverantly: and more, the LORD asketh not of
any man here now in this life.   And, certain, since JESUS
CHRIST died upon the cross wilfully to make men free; Men
of the Church are too bold and too busy to make men thrall!
binding them 'under the pains of endless curse,' as they say, to
do many observances and ordinances, which neither the living
nor the teaching of CHRIST, nor of his Apostles approveth."

A Clerk. And a Clerk said then to me, " Thou shewest
plainly here thy deceit, which thou hast learned of them that
travail to sow popil [*tares*] among wheat! But I counsel thee to
go away clean from this learning, and submit thee lowly to
my Lord, and thou shalt find him yet to be gracious to thee!"

Another Clerk. And as fast, another Clerk said to me,
" How wast thou so bold at Paul's Cross in London, to stand
there hard, with thy tippet [*cape*] bounden about thine head,
and to reprove in his sermon, the worthy Clerk ALKERTON,
drawing away all, that thou mightest! Yea, and the same
day at afternoon, thou meeting that worthy Doctor in Watling street, calledst him, 'False flatterer, and hypocrite!'"

William. And I said, " Sir, I think certainly, that then
was no man nor woman that hated verily sin and loved
virtues, hearing the sermon of the Clerk of Oxford, and also
ALKERTON'S sermon, but they said, and might justly say, that
ALKERTON reproved the Clerk untruly, and slandered him
wrongfully and uncharitably. For, no doubt, if the living and
teaching of CHRIST chiefly and his Apostles be true, nobody
that loveth GOD and His Law will blame any sentence that
the Clerk then preached there; since, by authority of GOD's
Word, and by approved Saints and Doctors, and by open
reason, this Clerk approved all things clearly that he preached
there."

A Clerk. And a Clerk of the Archbishop said to me, " His
sermon was false, and that he sheweth openly, since he dare
not stand forth and defend his preaching, that he then
preached there."

William. And I said, " Sir, I think that he purposeth to
stand stedfastly thereby, or else he slandereth foully himself
and many others that have great trust that he will stand by
the truth of the Gospel. For I wot well his sermon is writ-

ten both in Latin and in English; and many men have it, and they set great price thereby. And, Sir, if ye were present with the Archbishop [*i.e., of CANTERBURY, in whose presence he was then standing*] at Lambeth, when this Clerk appeared; and were at his Answer before the Archbishop : ye wot well that this Clerk denied not there his sermon; but, two days, he maintained it before the Archbishop and his Clerks."

Archbishop or a Clerk. And then the Archbishop, or one of his Clerks said (I wot not which of them!), " That harlot [*at this time applied to men also*] shall be met with, for that sermon. For no man but he, and thou, and such other false harlots, praiseth any such preaching."

Archbishop. And then the Archbishop said, "Your cursed sect is busy, and it joyeth right greatly to contrary and to destroy the privilege and freedom of Holy Church."

William. And I said, "Sir, I know no men travail so busily as this sect doth, which you reprove, to make rest and peace in Holy Church. For pride, covetousness, and simony which distrouble most Holy Church, this sect hateth and flyeth, and travaileth busily to move all other men in like manner unto meekness and wilful poverty and charity, and free ministring of the sacraments : this sect loveth, and useth, and is full busy to move all other folks, thus to do. For these virtues owe all members of Holy Church to their head, CHRIST."

A Clerk. Then a Clerk said to the Archbishop, " Sir, it is far day, and ye have far to ride to-night; therefore make an end with him, for he will none make! But the more, Sir, that ye busy you for to draw him towards you, the more con- tumax [*contumacious*] he is made, and the further from you."

Malveren. And then MALVEREN said to me, " WILLIAM! kneel down, and pray my Lord, of grace! and leave all thy fantasies, and become a child of Holy Church!"

William. And I said, " Sir, I have prayed the Archbishop oft, and yet I pray him, for the love of CHRIST! that he will leave his indignation that he hath against me; and that he will suffer me, after my cunning and power, for to do mine office of priesthood, as I am charged of GOD to do it. For I covet nought else, but to serve my GOD to His pleasing, in the state that I stand in, and have taken me to."

Archbishop. And the Archbishop said to me, "If, of good heart, thou wilt submit thee now, here, meekly to be

ruled, from this time forth by my counsel, obeying meekly
and wilfully to mine ordinance, thou shalt find it most profitable and best to thee for to do thus. Therefore, tarry thou
me no longer! Grant to do this, that I have said to thee
now, here, shortly; or deny it utterly!"

William. And I said to the Archbishop, "Sir, owe [*ought*]
we to believe that JESUS CHRIST was and is Very GOD and
Very Man?"

Archbishop. And the Archbishop said, "Yea!"

William. And I said, "Sir, owe we to believe that all
CHRIST's living and his teaching is true in every point?"

Archbishop. And he said, "Yea!"

William. And I said, "Sir, owe we to believe that the
living of the Apostles and the teaching of CHRIST and of all
Prophets are true, which are written in the *Bible* for the
health and salvation of GOD's people?"

Archbishop. And he said, "Yea!"

William. And I said, "Sir, owe all Christian men and
women, after their cunning and power, for to conform their
living to the teaching specially of CHRIST; and also to the
teaching and living of his Apostles and of Prophets, in all
things that are pleasant to GOD, and edification to His
Church?"

Archbishop. And he said, "Yea!"

William. And I said, "Sir, ought the doctrine, the bidding,
or the counsel of anybody to be accepted or obeyed unto,
except this counsel, these biddings, or this counsel may be
granted and affirmed by CHRIST's living and his teaching,
or by the living and teaching of his Apostles and Prophets?"

Archbishop. And the Archbishop said to me, "Other
doctrine ought not to be accepted, nor we owe not to obey to
any man's bidding or counsel; except we can perceive that
this bidding or counsel accordeth with the bidding and
teaching of CHRIST and of his Apostles and Prophets?"

William. And I said, "Sir, are not all the learning and
biddings and counsels of Holy Church means and healthful
remedies to know, and to withstand the privy suggestions
and the apert temptations of the Fiend; and also ways and
healthful remedies to slay pride and all other deadly sins and
the branches of them; and sovereign means to purchase

L   12

grace, for to withstand and overcome all fleshly lusts and movings?"

Archbishop. And the Archbishop said, "Yea!"

William. And I said, "Sir, whatsoever thing ye or any other body bid or counsel me to do ; according to this foresaid learning, after my cunning and power, through the help of GOD, I will meekly, with all mine heart, obey thereto!"

Archbishop. And the Archbishop said to me, "Submit thee then, now, here, meekly and wilfully to the ordinance of Holy Church, which I shall shew to thee!"

William. And I said, "Sir, according as I have here, now before you, rehearsed, I will now be ready to obey full gladly to CHRIST, the Head of all Holy Church, and to the learning and biddings and counsels of every pleasing member of Him."

Archbishop. Then the Archbishop striking with his hand fiercely upon a cupboard, spake to me, with a great spirit, saying, "By Jesu! but if thou leave such additions, obliging thee now here without any exception to mine ordinance, ere that I go out of this place, I shall make thee as sure as any thief that is in the prison of Lantern. Advise thee now, what thou wilt do!" And then, as if he had been angered, he went from the cupboard where he stood, to a window.

And then MALVEREN and another Clerk came nearer me, and they spake to me many words full pleasantly, and another while they menaced me and counselled full busily to submit me, or else they said I should not escape punishing over measure ; for they said I should be degraded, cursed, and burned, and so then damned!

Malveren and a Clerk. "But now," they said, "thou mayest eschew all these mischiefs, if thou will submit thee wilfully and meekly to this worthy Prelate, that hath cure of thy soul! And for the pity of CHRIST!" said they, "bethink thee, how great clerks [PHILIP DE REPINGTON] the Bishop of LINCOLN, HEREFORD, and PURVEY were, and yet are; and also B[OWTON] that is a well understanding man : which also have forsaken and revoked all the learning and opinions that thou and such others hold! Wherefore, since each of them is mickle wiser than thou art ; we counsel thee for the best, that, by the example of these four Clerks, thou follow them, submitting thee as they did!"

A Clerk. And one of the [Arch]bishop's Clerks said, then,

there, that " he heard NICHOLAS HEREFORD say, that ' since
he forsook and revoked all the learning and opinions of the
Lollards, he hath had mickle greater favour and more delight
to hold against them ; than ever he had to hold with them,
while he held with them. ' "

Malveren. And therefore MALVEREN said to me, " I understand and [*if*] thou wilt take thee to a priest, and shrive
thee clean, forsake all such opinions, and take thy penance of
my Lord here, for the holding and teaching of them, within
short time thou shalt be greatly comforted in this doing ! "

William. And I said to the Clerks, that thus busily counselled me to follow these foresaid men, " Sirs, if these men, of
whom ye counsel me to take example, had forsaken benefices
of temporal profit and of worldly worship, so that they had
absented them and eschewed from all occasions of covetousness and of fleshly lusts; and had taken them to simple living
and wilful poverty : they had herein given good example to
me and many others to have followed them. But now, since
all these four men have slanderously and shamefully done
the contrary, consenting to receive and to have and to hold
temporal benefices, living now more worldly and more fleshly
than they did before, conforming them to the manners of this
world ; I forsake them herein, and in all their foresaid slanderous doing !

" For I purpose, with the help of GOD into remission of
all my sins and of my foul cursed living, to hate and to fly
privily and apertly, to follow these men ! teaching and counselling whomsoever that I may, for to fly and eschew the way
that they have chosen to go in, which will lead them to the
worst end, if, in convenient time, they repent them not, verily
forsaking and revoking openly the slander that they have put,
and every day yet put to CHRIST's Church. For, certain,
so open blasphemy and slander, as they have spoken and done
in their revoking and forsaking of the Truth, ought not, nor
may not, privily be amended duly. Wherefore, Sirs, I pray
you that ye busy you not for to move me to follow these men
in revoking and forsaking of the Truth and Soothfastness !
as they have done, and yet do; wherein by open evidence, they
stir GOD to great wroth, and not only against themselves,
but also against all them that favour them or consent to them
herein, or that comoneth [*communeth*] with them, except it be

for their amendment. For whereas these men first were pursued of enemies, now they have obliged them by oath for to slander and pursue CHRIST in his members! Wherefore, as I trust stedfastly in the goodness of GOD, the worldly covetousness, and the lusty living, and the sliding from the truth of these runagates [*renegades*] shall be to me, and to many other men and women, an example and an evidence to stand the more stiffly by the Truth of CHRIST.

"For, certain, right many men and women do mark and abhor the foulness and cowardice of these aforesaid untrue men, how that they are overcome, and stopped with benefices, and withdrawn from the truth of GOD's Word, forsaking utterly to suffer therefore bodily persecution. For by this unfaithful doing and apostasy, of them specially that are great lettered men, and have [ac]knowledged openly the truth; and now either for pleasure or displeasure of tyrants have taken hire and temporal wages, to forsake the Truth and to hold against it, slandering and pursuing them that covet to follow CHRIST in the way of righteousness: many men and women therefore are now moved. But many more, through the grace of GOD, shall be moved hereby, for to learn the Truth of GOD, and to do thereafter, and to stand boldly thereby."

Archbishop. Then the Archbishop said to his Clerks, "Busy you no longer about him! for he, and others such as he is, are confeder[at]ed so together, that they will not swear to be obedient, and to submit them to Prelates of Holy Church. For now, since I stood here, his fellow sent me word that *he will not swear, and that he* [WILLIAM of Thorpe] *counselled him that he should not swear to me.* But, losell! in that thing that in thee is, thou hast busied thee to lose this young man; but, blessed be GOD! thou shalt not have thy purpose of him! For he hath forsaken all thy learning, submitting him to be buxom [*submissive*] and obedient to the ordinance of Holy Church; and weepeth full bitterly, and curseth thee full heartily for the venomous teaching which thou hast shewed to him, counselling him to do thereafter. And for thy false counselling of many others and him, thou hast great cause to be right sorry! For, long time, thou hast busied thee to pervert whomsoever thou mightest! Therefore as many deaths thou art worthy of, as thou hast given evil counsels. And therefore, by Jesu! thou shalt go thither where NICHOLAS HEREFORD and JOHN PURVEY were harboured! and I undertake, ere this day eight days, thou shalt be right glad for to do what thing that ever I bid thee do!

"And, losell! I shall assay if can make thee there, as sorrowful as, it was told me, thou wast glad of my last going out of England [*in* 1397]. By St. Thomas! I shall turn thy joy into sorrow!"

William. And I said, "Sir, there can nobody prove lawfully that I joyed ever of the manner of your going out of this land [*the Archbishop had been banished*]. But, Sir, to say the sooth, I was joyful when ye were gone! for [ROBERT DE BRAYBROOKE] the Bishop of LONDON (in whose prison ye left me!) found in me no cause for to hold me longer in his prison; but, at the request of my friends, he delivered me to them, asking of me no manner of submitting."

Archbishop. Then the Archbishop said to me, "Wherefore that I yede [*went*] out of England is unknown to thee! But be this thing well known to thee! that GOD, as I wot well, hath called me again and brought me into this land, for to destroy thee and the false sect that thou art of! as, by God! I shall pursue you so narrowly that I shall not leave a step of you in this land!"

William. And I said to the Archbishop, "Sir, the holy prophet JEREMY said to the false prophet HANANIAH, *When the word*, that is, the prophecy, *of a prophet is known or fulfilled; then it shall be known that the LORD sent the prophet in truth!*"

Archbishop. And the Archbishop, as if he had not been pleased with my saying, turned him away-ward, hither and thither, and said, "By God! I shall set on thy shins a pair of perlis [? *pearls*], that thou shalt be glad to change thy voice!"

These and many more wondrous and convicious [*railing*] words were spoken to me; menacing me and all others of the same sect, for to be punished and destroyed to the uttermost.

And the Archbishop called then to him, a Clerk; and rounded with him [*whispered in his ear*], and that Clerk went forth: and soon he brought in the Constable of Saltwood Castle, and the Archbishop rounded a good while with him. And then the Constable went forth, and then came in divers secular [*laymen*] ; and they scorned me on every side, and menaced me greatly. And some counselled the Archbishop to burn me by and by [*at once*] : and some others counselled him to drown me in the sea, for it is near [at] hand there.

A Clerk. And a Clerk standing besides me there, kneeled down to the Archbishop, praying him that he would deliver me to him for to say *Matins* with him ; and he would undertake that, within three days, I should not resist anything that was commanded me to do, of my Prelate.

And the Archbishop said that he would ordain for me himself.

And then, after, came in again the Constable and spake privily to the Archbishop.

And then the Archbishop commanded the Constable to lead me forth thence, with him : and so he did.

And when we were gone forth thence, we were sent after again.

And when I came in again before the Archbishop, a Clerk bade me kneel down, and ask grace, and submit me lowly, and I should find it for the best.

William. And I said then to the Archbishop, "Sir, as I have said to you, divers times, to-day, I will wilfully and lowly obey and submit me to be ordained ever, after my cunning and power, to GOD and His Law, and to every member of Holy Church ; as far forth as I can perceive that these members accord with their head, CHRIST, and will teach me, rule me, or chastise me by authority specially of GOD's Law."

Archbishop. And the Archbishop said, "I wist well, he would not, without such additions, submit him ! "

And then, I was rebuked, scorned, and menaced on every side ; and yet, after this, divers persons cried upon me to kneel down and submit me : but I stood still, and spake no word.

And then there was spoken of me and to me many great words ; and I stood, and heard them menace, curse, and scorn me : but I said nothing.

Archbishop. Then a while after, the Archbishop said to me, "Wilt thou not submit thee to the ordinance of Holy Church ? "

William. And I said, " Sir, I will full gladly submit me, as I have shewed you before."

And then, the Archbishop bade the Constable to have me forth thence in haste.

And so then I was led forth, and brought into a foul unhonest prison, where I came never before. But, thanked be GOD ! when all men were gone forth then from me, and had sparred [*barred*] fast the prison door after them, by and by [*immediately*] after, I therein by myself busied me to think on GOD, and to thank Him of His goodness.

And I was then greatly comforted in all my wits, not only for that I was then delivered, for a time, from the sight, from the hearing, from the presence, from the scorning, and from the menacing of my enemies : but much more I rejoiced in the LORD, because that through His grace, He kept me so, both among the flattering specially, and among the menacing of mine adversaries, that without heaviness and anguish of my conscience, I passed away from them. For as a tree laid upon another tree overthwart or on cross wise, so was the Archbishop and his three Clerks always contrary to me, and I to them.

Now, good GOD ! (for Thine holy name and for the praising of Thy most blessed name, make us one together), if it be Thy will, by authority of thy Word that is true perfect charity : and else not ! And that it may thus be, all that this writing read or hear, pray heartily to the LORD GOD ! that He (for His great goodness that cannot be with tongue expressed) grant to us and to all others, that in the same wise and for the same cause specially, or for any other cause be at [a] distance, to be knit and made
One in true Faith, in stedfast Hope, and
in perfect Charity.
Amen.

❧ Thus endeth the Examination of Master William Thorpe.

And hereafter followeth his Testament.

ATTHEW, an Apostle of CHRIST and his gospeller, witnesseth truly in the Holy Gospel, the most holy living and the most wholesome teaching of CHRIST. He rehearseth how that CHRIST likeneth them that hear his words and keep them, to a wise man that buildeth his house upon a stone, that is a stable and a sad [firm] ground.

This house is man's soul, in whom CHRIST delighteth to dwell, if it be grounded, that is, stablished, faithfully in his living, and in his true teaching, adorned or made fair with divers virtues, which CHRIST used and taught without any meddling of any error, as are chiefly the conditions of charity.

This foresaid stone is CHRIST, upon which every faithful soul must be builded, since upon none other ground than upon CHRIST's living and his teaching, nobody may make any building or housing wherein CHRIST will come and dwell. This sentence witnesseth PAUL to the Corinthians, shewing them that nobody may set any other ground than is set, that is, CHRIST's living and his teaching.

And because that all men and women should give all their business here in this life to build them virtuously upon this sure foundation, Saint PAUL [ac]knowledging the fervent desire and the good will of the people of Ephesus, wrote to them comfortably, saying, Now ye are not strangers, guests, nor yet comelings, but ye are the citizens and of the household of GOD, builded above upon the foundament of the Apostles and Prophets. In which foundament, every building that is builded and made through the grace of GOD, it increaseth or groweth into a holy temple; that is, everybody that is *grounded and builded faithfully in the teaching and living of* CHRIST *is therethrough made the holy temple of* GOD.

This is the stable ground and stedfast stone, CHRIST *! which is the sure corner-stone fast joining and holding mightily together two walls.* For *through* CHRIST JESU, *mean or middle Person of the Trinity, the Father of Heaven is piteous or mercifully joined and made one together to Mankind : and through dread to offend* GOD, *and fervent love to please him, men be unseparably made one to* GOD, *and defended surely under His protection.*

Also this foresaid stone CHRIST *was figured by the square stones of which the Temple of* GOD *was made.* For *as a square stone, wheresoever it is cast or laid, it abideth and lieth stably ; so* CHRIST *and every faithful member of his Church, by example of him, abideth and dwelleth stably in true faith and in all other heavenly virtues, in all adversities that they suffer in this Valley of Tears.* For, *lo, when these foresaid square stones were hewen and wrought for to be laid in the walls or pillars of* GOD's *Temple, none noise or stroke of the workmen was heard.* Certain, *this silence in working of this stone figureth* CHRIST *chiefly, and his faithful members, which by example of him have been, and yet are, and ever to the world's end shall be, so meek and patient in every adversity, that no sound nor yet any grudging shall any lime be perceived in them.*

Nevertheless this chief and most worshipful corner-stone, which only is ground of all virtues, proud beggars reproved ! but this despite and reproof CHRIST *suffered most meekly in his own person, for to give example of all meekness and patience to all his faithful followers.* Certain, *this world is now so full of proud beggars which are named priests ; but the very office of working of priesthood which* CHRIST *approveth true, and accepteth, is far from the multitude of priests that now reign in this world.*

For, from the highest priest to the lowest, all (as who say) study, that is, they imagine and travail busily how they may please this world and their flesh. This sentence *and many such others lependeth upon them, if it be well considered ; either* GOD *the Father of heaven hath deceived all mankind by the living specially and teaching of* JESUS CHRIST, *and by the living and teaching of his Apostles and Prophets; all else all the Popes that have been since I had any knowledge or discretion, with all the College of Cardinals, Archbishops, and Bishops, Monks, Canons, and Friars, with all the contagious flock of the comminalty of priesthood, which have, all my life-time and mickle longer, reigned and yet reign and increase damnably from sin into sin, have been and yet be proud obstinate heretics, covetous simoners* [traffickers in ecclesiastical preferments], *and defouled adulterers in the ministering of the Sacraments, and especially in the ministering of the Sacrament of the Altar.*

For, as their works shew (whereto CHRIST *biddeth us take heed!) the highest priests and Prelates of this priesthood challenge and occupy* [hold] *unlawfully temporal lordships. And for temporal favour and mede, they sell and give benefices to unworthy and unable persons; yea, these simoners sell sin! suffering men and women in every degree and estate, to lie and continue, from year to year, in divers vices slanderously. And thus, by evil example of high priests in the Church, lower priests under them are not only suffered, but they are maintained to sell full dear to the people for temporal mede, all the Sacraments. And thus all this foresaid priesthood is blown so high, and borne up in pride and vainglory of their estate and dignity, and so blinded with worldly covetousness, that they disdain to follow* CHRIST *in very meekness and wilful poverty, living holily, and preaching* GOD's *Word truly, freely, and continually; taking their livelihood at the free vill of the people, of their pure almose* [alms], *where and when, they suffice not (for their true and busy preaching) to get their sustenance with their hands.*

To this true sentence, grounded on CHRIST's *own living and teaching of his Apostles; these foresaid worldly and fleshly priests will not consent effectually. But, as their works and also their words shew, boldly and unshamefastly these foresaid named priests and Prelates covet, and enforce them mightily and busily, that all Holy Scripture were expounded and drawn according to* their *manners, and to* their *ungrounded* [unwarranted] *usages and findings.*

For they will not (since they hold it but folly and madness !) conform their manners to the pure and simple living of CHRIST *and his Apostles, nor they will not follow freely their learning. Wherefore all the Emperors and Kings, and all other lords and ladies, and all the common people in every degree and state, which have before time known or might have known ; and also all they that now yet know or might know this foresaid witness of priesthood ; and would not, nor yet will enforce them, after their cunning and power, to withstand charitably the foresaid enemies and traitors of* CHRIST *and his Church : all these strive, with* ANTICHRIST, *against* JESU *! And they shall bear the indignation of* GOD *Almighty without end, if in convenient time they amend them not, and repent them verily ; doing therefore due mourning and sorrow, after their cunning and power.*

For through presumptions and negligence of priests and Prelates (not of the Church of CHRIST, *but occupying their prelacy, unduly in the Church, and also by flattering and false covetousness of other divers named priests), lousengers, and lounderers are wrongfully made and called Hermits ; and have leave to defraud poor and needy creatures of their livelihood, and to live by their false winning and begging in sloth and other divers vices. And also of these Prelates, these cokir noses [?] are suffered to live in pride and hypocrisy, and to defoul themselves both bodily and ghostly.*

Also by the suffering and counsel of these foresaid Prelates and of other priests, are made vain, both Brotherhoods and Sisterhoods, full of pride and envy ; which are full contrary to the Brotherhood of CHRIST, *since they are cause of mickle dissension : and they multiply and sustained it uncharitably, for in lusty eating, and drinking unmeasurably and out of time, they exercise themselves. Also this vain confederacy of Brotherhoods is permitted to be of one clothing, and to hold together. And in all these ungrounded and unlawful doings, priests are partners and great meddlers and counsellors.*

And over this viciousness, hermits and pardoners, ankers [anchorites], *and strange beggars are licensed and admitted of*

Prelates and priests for to beguile the people with flatterings and leasings [falsehoods] *slanderously, against all good reason and true belief; and so to increase divers vices in themselves, and also among all them that accept them or consent to them.*

And thus, the viciousness of these forenamed priests and Prelates, has been long time, and yet is, and shall be cause of wars, both within the realm and without.

And, in the same wise, these unable [useless] *priests have been, and yet are, and shall be, the chief cause of pestilence of men, and murrain of beasts, and of bareness of the earth, and of all other mischiefs, to the time that Lords and Commons able them through grace for to know and to keep the Commandments of GOD, enforcing them then faithfully and charitably by one assent, for to redress and make one, this foresaid priesthood to the wilful poor, meek, and innocent living and teaching, specially of* CHRIST *and his Apostles.*

Therefore all they that know, or might know the viciousness that reigneth now cursedly in these priests and in their learning, if they suffice not to withstand this contagious viciousness: let them pray to the LORD *heartily for the health of his Church! abstaining them prudently from these endured* [hardened] *enemies of* CHRIST *and his people, and from all their Sacraments! since to them all that know them, or may know, they are but fleshly deeds and false: as Saint* CYPRIAN *witnesseth in the first Question of* Decrees *and in the first* Cause. Ca. Si quis inquit.

For as this Saint, and great Doctors witness there, that not only vicious priests, but also all they that favour them or consent to them in their viciousness, shall together perish with them, if they amend them not duly: as all they perished that consented to DATHAN *and* ABIRAM. *For nothing were more confusion to these foresaid vicious priests, than to eschew them prudently in all their unlawful Sacraments, while they continue in their sinful living slanderously, as they have long time done and yet do. And nobody need to be afraid, though death did follow by any wise or other, for to die out of this world without taking of any Sacrament of these foresaid* CHRIST's *enemies: since* CHRIST *will not fail for to minister himself all lawful and heal-ful sacraments, and necessary at all time ; and especially at the end, to all them that are in true faith, in steadfast hope, and in perfect charity.*

But yet some mad fools say, for to eschew slander they will be shriven once a year and comuned [receive the Sacrament] *of their proper priests ; though they know them defouled with slanderous vices. No doubt, but all they that thus do or consent, privily or apertly, to such doing, are culpable of great sin ; since St. PAUL witnesseth that not only they that do evil are worthy of death and damnation, but also they that consent to evil doers. Also, as their slanderous works witness, these foresaid vicious priests despise and cast from them heavenly cunning that is given of the HOLY GHOST. Wherefore the LORD throweth all such despisers from Him, that they use nor do any priesthood to Him. No doubt then, all they that wittingly or wilfully take, or consent that any other body should take any Sacrament of any such named priest, sinneth openly and damnably against all the Trinity, and are unable to any Sacrament of health.*

And that this foresaid sentence [opinion] *is altogether true unto remission of all my sinful living, trusting steadfastly in the mercy of GOD, I offer to Him my soul !*

And to prove also this foresaid sentence true, with the help of GOD, I purpose fully to suffer meekly and gladly my most wretched body to be tormented, where GOD will ! and of whom He will ! how He will and when He will ! and as long as He will ! and what temporal pain He will ! and death ! to the praising of His name, and to the edification of His Church. And I, that am most unworthy and wretched caitiff, shall now, through the special grace of GOD, make to Him pleasant sacrifice of my most sinful and unworthy body.

I BESEECH *heartily all folk that read or hear this end of my purposed Testament, that, through the grace of GOD, they dispose verily and virtuously all their wits, and able, in like manner, all their members for to understand truly and to keep faithfully, charitably, and continually all*

the commandments of GOD, and so then to pray devoutly to all the blessed Trinity, that I may have grace with wisdom and prudence from above, to end my life here, in this foresaid Truth and for this
Cause in true faith
and steadfast hope
and in perfect
charity,
A M E N .

ERE endeth, sir [*the Reverend*] WILLIAM THORPE'S *Testament* on the Friday after the Rood Day [*Holy Rood-day, or Exaltation of the Holy Cross*, falls on Sept. 14th], and the twenty [? *nineteenth*] day of September, in the year of our Lord a thousand four hundred and sixty.

And on the Sunday [*August 7th*] next after the feast of Saint PETER that we called Lammas Day [*August 1st*] in the year of our Lord a thousand four hundred and seven, the said sir WILLIAM THORPE was accused of these points, before written in this book, before THOMAS ARUNDELL, Archbishop of CANTERBURY, as it is said before.

And so was it then betwixt the Day of his Accusing, and the Day that this was written three and fifty years; and as mickle more as from the Lammas
[*August 1st*] to the Woodmas
[*September 19th*].

Behold the end !

❡ The strength of a tale is in its end.

Here followeth
The Examination of the
Lord Cobham.

[The following is but an abridgement of the Story of Sir JOHN OLD-
CASTLE : respecting which, Miss L. TOULMIN SMITH has recently pub-
lished, in the *Anglia* for April 1882, THOMAS OCCLEVE's Ballad against
Lord COBHAM and the Lollards, in 1415.]

¶ The Belief of the Lord Cobham.

E IT known to all men! that in the year of
our LORD a thousand four hundred and
thirteen, in the first year of King HENRY
the FIFTH; the King gave to [THOMAS
ARUNDELL] the Bishop of CANTERBURY,
leave to correct the Lord COBHAM.

And because no man durst summon him
personally, the Archbishop set up a Citation
on his Cathedral Church door on the Wednesday [*September*
6, 1413] next before the nativity of our Lady [*September 8th*] in
the foresaid year: and that Citation was taken down by the
friends of the Lord COBHAM.

And, after that, the Bishop set up another on our Lady
Day [*September 8, 1413*] ; which also was rent down.

And because he came not to answer on the day assigned
in the Citation, the Bishop cursed him for contumacy.

And the Lord COBHAM seeing all this malice purposed
against him, wrote this *Belief* that followeth, with his own
hand ; and noted [*signed*] it himself; and also answered to
Four Points put against him by the Bishop: and he went to
the King, supposing to get of him good favour and lordship.

¶ The Belief.

*BELIEVE in GOD the Father Almighty, Maker of
heaven and earth ; and in JESU CHRIST His only
Son our Lord, which was conceived of the HOLY
GHOST, born of the Virgin MARY, and suffered
death under PONTIUS PILATE, crucified, dead, and buried. He*

went down to hells. The third day He rose again from death. He ascended up into heavens. He sitteth on the right hand of GOD, the Father Almighty. From thence, He is to come to judge the quick and dead.

I believe in the HOLY GHOST, all Holy Church, the Communion of Saints, forgiveness of sins, uprising of flesh, and everlasting life. Amen.

AND for to declare more plainly my soothfastness in the belief of Holy Church, I believe faithfully and verily, that there is but one GOD Almighty; and in this Godhead and of this Godhead be Three Persons, the Father, the Son, and the HOLY GHOST ; and these Three Persons be the same GOD Almighty.

Furthermore, I believe that the Second Person of this most blessed Trinity, in most convenient time before ordained, took flesh and blood of the most blessed Virgin, our Lady Saint MARY, for the redemption and salvation of mankind; that was lost before, for ADAM's sin.

And I believe that JESU CHRIST our Lord, which is both GOD and Man, is head of all Holy Church ; and that all those that be, and shall be saved, be members of this most Holy Church. Which Holy Church is departed [divided] in three parts. Of the which, one part is now in Heaven; that is to say, the saints that in this life live accordingly with the most blessed Law of CHRIST and his living, despising and forsaking the Devil and his works, the prosperities of this world, and the foul lust of the flesh.

The second part is in Purgatory, abiding the mercy of GOD, and purging them there of their sins; of the which they have been truly confessed in deed, or else in will to have been.

The third part of this Church is here in Earth, the which is called the Fighting Church ; for it fighteth, every day and night, against the temptation of the Devil, the prosperity of this false failing world, and the proud rebellion of the flesh against the soul. This Church is departed [divided] by the most blessed ordinance of GOD *into three Estates; that is to say, Priesthood, Knighthood, and Commons : to every Estate of the which, GOD gave charge that one should help another, and none destroy other.*

As to Priests, they should be most holy and least worldly ; and truly living as near as they could, after the example of CHRIST *and his Apostles. And all their business should be, day and night, in holy example of living, and true preaching and teaching of GOD's Law to both the other parts. And also they should be most meek, most serviceable, and most lovely in spirit, both to GOD and man.*

In the second part of this Church, that is Knighthood, be con-tained all that bear the sword by the law of Office : which should maintain GOD's Law to be preached and taught to the people ; and principally the Gospel of CHRIST *; and truly to live thereafter. The which part should rather put themselves to peril of death, than to suffer any Law or Constitution* [referring to the Constitutions of ARUNDEL in 1408] *to be made of man, wherethrough the free-dom of GOD's Law might be letted to be preached and taught to the people, or whereof any error or heresy might grow in the Church. For I suppose fully that there may come none heresy nor error among the people, but by false Laws, Constitutions, or teachings contrary to* CHRIST's *Law, or by false leasings* [lies].

Also the second part should defend the common people from tyrants, oppressors, and extortioners : and maintain the Clergy, doing truly their office, in preaching, teaching, praying, and freely ministering the Sacraments of Holy Church. And if this Clergy be negligent in doing this office, this second part of the Church ought, by their office that they have taken of GOD, to constrain the Clergy in due wise, to do their office in the form that GOD hath ordained to be done.

The third part of this Fighting Church oweth [ought] *to bear good will to Lords and Priests, truly to do their bodily labour in tilling the earth, and with their true merchandise doing their duties that they owe both to Knighthood and to Priesthood, as GOD's Law limiteth ; keeping faithfully the commandments of GOD.*

Moreover, I believe all the Sacraments of Holy Church for to be meedful and profitable to all that shall be saved; taking them after the intent that GOD and Holy Church have ordained.

And for as mickle as I am slandered falsely in my Belief in the Sacrament of the Altar, I do all Christian men to wit, that I believe verily that the most blessed Sacrament of the Altar is very CHRIST's body in form of bread; the same body that was born of the blessed Virgin our Lady Saint MARY, done on the cross, dead, buried, and on the third day rose from death to life, the which body is now glorified in heaven.

Also I believe that all GOD's Law is true; and who that liveth contrary to this blessed Law, and so continueth to his life's end, and dieth so breaking the holy commandments of GOD, that he shall be damned into everlasting pains. And he that will learn this most blessed Law, and live thereafter, keeping these holy commandments of GOD, and endeth in charity shall have everlasting bliss.

Also I understand that this followeth of Belief, that our Lord JESU CHRIST (that is both GOD and Man) asketh no more here in earth, but that he obey to him after the form of his Law, in truly keeping of it. And if any Prelate of the Church ask more obedience than this, of any man living; he exalteth himself, in that, above CHRIST: and so he is an open Antichrist.

Also these points I hold as of Belief in especial.

And in general, I believe all that GOD wills that I believe, praying, at the reverence of Almighty GOD, to you my liege Lord [HENRY V.] that this Belief might be examined by the wisest and truest Clerks of your realm: and if it be truth, that it might be confirmed, and I to be holden for a true Christian man; and if it be false, that it might be damned [condemned], and I taught a better Belief by GOD's Law; and I will gladly obey thereto.

This foresaid Belief, the Lord COBHAM wrote; and took it with him, and offered it to the King [HENRY V.], for to see: and the King would not receive it, but bade him take it to them that should be his judges

And then the Lord of COBHAM offered to bring before the

King, to purge him of all error and heresy, that they would put against him, a hundred Knights and Squires.

And also he offered to fight with any man, Christian or heathen, that would say he were false in his belief; except the King and his brethren.

And after, he said "He would submit him to all manner [of] correction, that any man would correct him, after GOD's Law."

And notwithstanding all this, the King suffered him to be summoned personally, in his own [*the King's*] chamber.

And the Lord of COBHAM said to the King, that he had appealed to the Pope from the Archbishop; and therefore, he said, "he ought not to take him for his judge": and so he had there his Appeal ready written, and shewed to the King.

And therewith the King was more angry, and said, "He should not pursue his appeal : but rather he should be in ward till his appeal were admitted, and then (would he or not !) he should be his judge ! "

And thus nothing of all this was allowed; but, because he would not swear to submit him to the Church, and take what penance the Archbishop would enjoin him, he was arrested, and sent to the Tower of London to keep his day that the [arch]bishop assigned him in the King's Chamber.

And then he made the *Belief* aforesaid, with the *Answer* to *Four Points* that now follow, to be written in two parts of an Indenture.

And when he came to answer; he gave that one part to the [arch]bishop, and that other part he kept to himself.

The Indenture of the Lord Cobham.

, *JOHN OLDCASTLE Knight, and Lord of COBHAM, will that all Christian men wit, how that THOMAS of ARUNDELL, Archbishop of CANTERBURY hath not only laid it to my charge maliciously, but also very untruly, by his Letter and his Seal written against me in most slanderous wise, that I should otherwise feel and teach of the Sacraments of the Holy Church; assigning in special the Sacrament of the Altar, the Sacrament of Penance, and also in Worshipping of Images, and in Going on Pilgrimages, otherwise*

*than feeleth and teacheth the universal Holy Church. I take Al-
mighty GOD to witness, that it hath been, and now is, and ever,
with the help of GOD, shall be, mine intent and my will to believe
faithfully and truly in all the Sacraments that ever GOD ordained
to be done in Holy Church.*

And, moreover, for to declare me in these points aforesaid.

*I believe that the most worshipful Sacrament of the Altar is very
CHRIST's body in form of bread : the same body that was born of
the blessed Virgin our Lady Saint MARY, done on the cross, dead
and buried, and the third day rose from death to life ; the which
body is now glorified in heaven.*

*Also as for the Sacrament of Penance, I believe that it is need-
ful to every man that shall be saved, to forsake sin, and to do due
penance for sin before done, with true confession, very contrition,
and due satisfaction, as GOD's Law limiteth and teacheth ; and
else, may he not be saved ; which penance I desire all men to do.*

*And as for Images, I understand that they be not of Belief, but
they were ordained (since Belief was given of CHRIST) by sufferance of the Church for to be Kalenders to laymen, to represent and
bring to mind the Passion of our Lord JESU CHRIST, and [the]
martyrdom and good living of other Saints. And that who so it
be, that doeth the worship to dead images that is due to GOD; or
putteth hope, faith, or trust in help of them as he should do to GOD ;
or hath affection in one more than in another : he doth in that, the
great sin of Idolatry.*

*Also I suppose this fully, that every man in this earth is a
Pilgrim towards Bliss or towards Pains. And he that knoweth not,
nor will not know, nor keep the holy commandments of GOD in
his living (albeit that he goeth on pilgrimage in all parts of the
world), and he die so, he shall be damned. And he that knoweth the
holy commandments of GOD and keepeth them to his end, he shall
be saved ; though he never in his life, go on pilgrimage as men use
[are accustomed] now to Canterbury, or to Rome, or to any other
place.*

This *Belief* indented, containing the foresaid *Belief* with these foresaid *Answers*, he took to the Bishops when he came to answer [*in the Chapter House of St. Paul's*] on the Saturday next before Michaelmas in the year beforesaid [*September 23, 1413*].

And whatsoever the Bishops asked him, he bade them look what his Bill said thereto ; and thereby he would stand to the death. Other answer gave he not that day : but the Bishops were not quieted herewith.

And the Archbishop bade him take avisement [*counsel*] till Monday [*September 25th*] next following, to answer to this point:

If there remained material bread in the Sacrament of the Altar, after the words of consecration ?

And in the meantime, he perceived that the uttermost malice was purposed against him, howsoever he answered : therefore he put his life in GOD's hand, and answered thus, as followeth.

This is the judgement and sentence given upon Sir JOHN OLDCASTLE Knight and Lord of COBHAM, the Monday [September 25th] *next before Michaelmas Day, at the Friar Preachers's* [the Dominican Friary within Ludgate] *in London, in the year of our Lord, a thousand, four hundred and thirteen.*

[THOMAS ARUNDELL] the Archbishop of CANTERBURY, [RICHARD CLIFFORD] the Bishop of LONDON, [HENRY BEAUFORT] the Bishop of WINCHESTER, [BENEDICT NICOLLS] the Bishop of BANGOR; Master JOHN WITNAM, Master JOHN WHITEHEAD [*both of New College, Oxford*], Doctors of Divinity; Master PHILIP MORGAN, Master HENRY WARE, Master JOHN KEMP, Doctors of [Canon] Law; and sir [*Rev.*] ROBERT WOMBEWELL, Vicar of St. Lawrence in the Jewry; Master JOHN STEVENS, Master JAMES COLE, Notaries : with the Four Orders of Friars, and many other Clerks, deeming and convicting him for an heretic and a cursed man.

The Archbishop made all these Clerks, both Religious and Secular, to swear upon a book, that they should not, for love or favour of the one party, nor for any envy or hatred of the other party, say, nor witness but the truth.

And the two foresaid Notaries were sworn also to write and

to witness the words and process that were to be said on both the parties, and to say the sooth if it otherwise were.

After this, the Lord of COBHAM came, and was brought before them all, to his Examination, and to his Answer.

Then the Archbishop said to him, " Lord of COBHAM, ye be advised well enough of the words and Process that were said to you, upon Saturday last past, in the Chapter House of Paul's: the which Process were now too long to rehearse. Then I proffered to have assoiled [absolve] you (for ye were accursed!) of your contumacy and disobedience to Holy Church."

Then said the Lord COBHAM forthwith, "GOD saith, *Maledicam benedictionibus vestris,* that is to say, ' I shall curse your blessings ! ' "

Then said the Archbishop, " Sir, then I proffered to have assoiled you, if ye would have asked it; and yet I do the same ! "

Then said the Lord of COBHAM, " Nay, forsooth, I trespassed never against you ! and therefore will I not do it."

And with that, he kneeled down on the pavement, and held up his hands and said, " I shrive me to GOD ! and to you all, Sirs ! that, in my youth, I have sinned greatly and grievously in lechery and in pride, and hurt many men, and done many other horrible sins ; Good Lord ! I cry Thee, mercy ! "

And therewith weepingly, he stood up again and said, "Here, for the breaking of GOD's Law and His commandments, ye cursed me not! but for your own laws and traditions, above GOD's Law : and therefore it shall be destroyed."

Then the Archbishop examined the Lord of his *Belief.* And the Lord of COBHAM said, "I believe fully in all GOD's Law, and I believe that it is all true ! and I believe all that GOD wills that I believe."

Then the Archbishop examined him of the Sacrament of the Altar, how he believed therein ?

The Lord of COBHAM said, "CHRIST upon Shere [*or Shrive or Maunday*] Thursday [*the day before Good Friday*] at night, sitting with his disciples at the Supper, after that he had supped, he took bread and giving thanks to the Father, he blessed it and brake it, and gave it to his disciples saying,

Take, and eat ye of this, all ! This is my body that shall be betrayed for you ! Do you this, in the remembrance of me. This I believe!" said he.

Then the Archbishop asked him, "If it were bread after the consecration, and the sacramental words said?"

The Lord of COBHAM said, "I believe that the Sacrament of the Altar is very CHRIST'S body in form of bread ; the same body that was born of the Virgin MARY, done on the cross, dead and buried, and the third day rose from death to life : which body is now glorified in heaven."

Then said one of the Doctors of the Law, "After the sacramental words said, there remaineth no bread but the body of CHRIST!"

Then the Lord of COBHAM said to one, Master JOHN WHITEHEAD, "You said to me in the Castle of Cowling [*Lord COBHAM's home*], that the host sacred was not CHRIST'S body: but I said, 'It was CHRIST'S body!' though Seculars and Friars hold each one against other in this opinion."

Then said they, "We say all that it is GOD'S body!"

And they asked him, "Whether it were material bread after the consecration?"

Then said the Lord, "I believe it is CHRIST'S body in form of bread. Sir, believe ye not thus?"

And the Archbishop said, "Yea!"

Then the Doctors asked him, "Whether it were only CHRIST'S body after the consecration, and no bread?"

And he said to them, "It is CHRIST'S body and bread. For right as CHRIST was here in manhood, and the godhead hid in the manhood : so I believe verily that CHRIST'S flesh and his blood is hid there in the form of bread."

Then they smiled each on other, deeming him taken in heresy ; and said, "It is an heresy!"

The Archbishop asked him, "What bread it was?" and the Clerks also, "Whether it were material or not?"

Then the Lord said, "The Gospel speaketh not of this term *material*; and therefore I will not! but say, it is CHRIST'S body and bread! For the Gospel saith, *Ego sum panis vivus qui de cœlo descendi*, that is to say, "I am quick bread that came down from heaven." For as our Lord JESUS CHRIST is Very GOD and Very Man; so the most blessed Sacrament of the Altar is CHRIST'S body and bread.

Then they said, "It is an heresy, to say that it is bread after the consecration and the sacramental words said, but only CHRIST's body."

The Lord said, "Saint PAUL the Apostle was as wise as ye be! and he called it *bread*; where he saith thus *The bread that we break, is it not the partaking of the body of the LORD?*"

Then they said, "PAUL must be otherwise understanded; for it is an heresy to say, that it is bread after the consecration, but only CHRIST's body: for it is against the determination of the Church."

Then they asked him, "Whether he believed not in the determination of the Church?"

And he said, "No, forsooth! but I believe all GOD's Law, and all that GOD wills that I believe; but not in your law nor in your determination: for ye be no part of Holy Church, as openly your deeds shew; but very Antichrists, contrary to GOD's law. For ye have made laws for your covetousness."

"This," they said, "was heresy: not for to believe in the determination of the Church."

Then the Archbishop asked him, "What was Holy Church?"

He said, "I believe that Holy Church is the number of all them that shall be saved; of whom CHRIST is head: of the which Church, one part is in Heaven, another in Purgatory, and the third here in Earth. This part here, standeth in three degrees and estates, Priesthood, Knighthood, and the Comminalty, as I said plainly in my *Belief*."

Then the Archbishop said to him, "Wot you who is of this Church? It is doubt to you who is thereof? Ye should not judge!"

The Lord said, "*Operibus credite! justum judicium judicate!*" that is to say, "Believe ye the works! judge ye rightful judgement!"

Also he said to them all, "Where find ye by GOD's Law, that ye should set thus upon any man, or any man's death, as ye do? But ANNAS and CAIAPHAS sat and judged CHRIST; and so do you!"

Then said they, "Yes, Sir, CHRIST judged JUDAS!"

The Lord of COBHAM said, "No, CHRIST judged not JUDAS!

but he judged himself, and went and hanged himself: but CHRIST said, *Woe to him*, as he doth to many of you! For since the venom was shed into the Church; ye followed never CHRIST, nor ye stood never in perfection of GOD's Law!"

Then the Archbishop asked him, "What was that venom?" The Lord said, "The lordships and possessions. For then, cried an angel, 'Woe! woe! woe! This day is venom shed into the Church of GOD!' For before that time, there many martyrs of Popes; and since I can tell of none! but, sooth it is, since that time one hath put down another, and one hath slain another, and one hath cursed another, as the Chronicles tell; also of much more cursedness."

Also he said, "CHRIST was meek, and the Pope is proud. CHRIST was poor and forgave; the Pope is rich and a man-slayer, as it is openly proved. And thus this is the nest of Antichrist, and out of this nest cometh Antichrist's disciples, of whom these Monks and Friars be the tail."

Then said [RICHARD DODINGTON] Prior of the Friars Augustines, "Sir, why say ye so?"

And the Lord of COBHAM said, "For as ye be Pharisees, "divided," and divided in habit [*dress*]; so ye make division among the people. And thus these friars and monks with such others be the members of the nest of Antichrist."

And he said, "CHRIST saith, *Woe be to you, Scribes and Pharisees, hypocrites! for ye close up the Kingdom of Heaven before men: for, sooth, ye enter not yourselves! nor ye will not suffer them that would, to enter in!* And thus, ye be the disciples of Antichrist! For ye will not suffer GOD's Law to go through, nor to be taught and preached of good priests; which will speak against your sins, and reprove them: but of such that be flatterers, which sustain you in your sins and cursedness."

Then said the Archbishop, "By our Lady! Sir, there shall no such preach, that preacheth dissension and division, if GOD will!"

Then said the Lord of COBHAM to the Archbishop, "CHRIST saith that *there shall be so great tribulation, as never was since the beginning.* And this shall be in your days! and by you! for ye have slain many men, and shall more hereafter: but CHRIST saith, *Except that those days were shortened, no flesh should be saved* : but hastily GOD will short[en] your days ! Furthermore, Bishops, Priests, and Deacons be grounded in GOD's Law : but not these other Religious [*Monks and Friars*] as far as I can wit."

Then a Doctor of Law, one Master JOHN KEMP, put to him these four Points that follow :

"*The faith and determination of Holy Church touching the blessed Sacrament of the Altar is this. That after the sacramental words be said of a priest in his* Mass, *the material bread that was before, is turned into* CHRIST'*s body, and the material wine that was before, is turned into* CHRIST'*s very blood : and so there remaineth in the Sacrament of the Altar, no material bread nor material wine ; the which were there, before the saying of the sacramental words.* Sir, believe you this ? "

The Lord of COBHAM said, " This is not my belief. For my belief is, as I said to you before, that the worshipful Sacrament of the Altar is very CHRIST's body in form of bread."

Then said the Archbishop, " Sir JOHN! ye must say otherwise ! "

The Lord of COBHAM said, " Nay, if GOD will ! but that it is CHRIST's body in form of bread, as all the common belief is."

The Doctor [JOHN KEMP] said, " The second is this, *The Holy Church hath determined that every Christian man living bodily upon the earth oweth* [ought] *to be shriven to a priest ordained by the Church, if he may come to him.* Sir, what say ye to this ? "

The Lord answered and said, " A sick man and sore wounded had need to have a sure Leech and a true, knowing his cure ; and therefore a man should be principally shriven to GOD ; and else his confession is nought. And a man should rather go and be counselled with a good priest that knoweth GOD's Law, and liveth thereafter ; than with his own priest, if he were an evil man, or with any other such."

The Doctor said, " The Third is this, CHRIST *ordained Saint* PETER *to be his Vicar in earth, whose See is the Church of Rome ; ordaining and granting that the same power that he gave to* PETER *should succeed to all* PETER'S *successors, the which we call now the Popes of Rome : by whose power in the Church particularly and specially, be ordained Prelates as Archbishops, Bishops, and other degrees; to whom Christian men owe* [ought] *to obey after the law of the Church of Rome.* This is the determination of the Church."

To this, he answered and said, "Who that followeth next PETER in living, is next him in succession : but your living refuseth poor PETER'S living, and many other Popes that were martyrs in Rome that followed PETER in manner of living; whose conditions ye have clean forsaken, all the world may know it well!"

The Doctor said, "The fourth point is this. *Holy Church hath determined that it is meedful to a Christian man, to go on pilgrimages to holy places; and there especially to worship holy relics of Saints, Apostles, Martyrs, Confessors, and all Saints approved by the Church of Rome.*"

To this, he said, "It were enough to bury Saints fair in the earth; but now Saints that be dead, be compelled to beg for covetousness! the which in their life, hated covetousness and begging. But I say to you all, and know it for a truth, that with your shrines and idols, and your feigned absolutions and indulgences, and your temporalities, ye draw to you all the richesse of this world."

"Why Sir," said one of the Clerks, "will ye not worship images?"

"What worship?" said the Lord.

Then said Friar [THOMAS] PALMER [Warden of the Minorites], "Sir, ye will worship the Cross of CHRIST that he died on?"

"Where is it?" said the Lord.

The Friar said, "I put case, Sir, that it were here before you!"

The Lord said, "This is a ready man! to put to me a question of a thing, that they wot never where it is? And yet I ask you, What worship?"

A Clerk said, "Such worship as PAUL speaketh of, that is this, *GOD forbid me to joy, but in the cross of our Lord JESU CHRIST.*"

Then said the Lord, and spread his arms abroad, "This is a very cross!"

Then said the [Henry Beauclerc] Bishop of London, "Sir, ye wot well! that he died on a material cross."

Then said the Lord, "Our salvation come in only by him that died on the cross, and by the material cross. And, well I wot, that this was the cross that Paul joyed on, that is, in the Passion of our LORD Jesu Christ."

The Archbishop said, "Sir John! ye must submit you to the ordinance of the Church!"

The Lord said, "I wot not whereto?"

Then the Archbishop read a bill of his judgement, and convicted him for a heretic.

After the reading of the bill, the Lord said, "Though ye judge my body, I hope to GOD! that He will save my soul!" and he said that he "would stand to the death, by these things beforesaid; with the help of Jesu!"

And then he said to all the people, "Sirs, for GOD's love! be well ware of these men! for they will beguile you else! and lead you blindlings into hell, and themselves also! For Christ saith, 'If one blind man lead another, both fall into the ditch!'"

And after this, thus he prayed for his enemies, and said, "LORD GOD! I beseech thee, forgive my pursuers! if it be thy will!"

And then he was led again to the Tower of London: and thus was the end.

WHILE the Lord of Cobham was in the Tower, he sent out privily to his friends; and they, at his desire, informed and writ this bill that followeth next, commending it to the people, that they should cease the slanders and leasings that his enemies made on him.

FOR as mickle as Sir JOHN OLDCASTLE, Knight and
Lord of COBHAM, is untruly convicted and prisoned,
and falsely reported and slandered among the people
by his adversaries, that he should otherwise
feel and speak of the Sacraments of Holy
Church, and especially of the blessed
Sacrament of the Altar, than
was written in his Belief,
which was indented
and taken to the
Clergy, and set
up in divers
open places
in the city of
London: Known
be it to all the world,
that he never varied in any
point therefrom; but this is plainly
his Belief, that all the Sacraments of
Holy Church be profitable and meedful to
all them that shall be saved, taking them after
the intent that GOD and Holy Church hath
ordained. Furthermore he believeth
that the blessed Sacrament of the
Altar is verily and
truly CHRIST's
body in form
of bread.

Truth long-hid now is disclosed.

Praised be GOD! Amen.

On Translating the Bible.

[Chapter xv. of the Prologue to the second recension of the Wycliffite Version. Attributed to JOHN PURVEY.]

On Translating the Bible.

[*Chapter xv. of the Prologue to the second recension of the Wycliffite Version. Attributed to* JOHN PURVEY.]

OR as much as Christ saith that the gospel shall be preached in all the world, and David saith of the apostles and their preaching, "the sound of them yede out into each land, and the words of them yeden out into the ends of the world," and eft David saith, "the Lord shall tell in the scriptures of peoples, and of these princes that were in it," that is, in holy church, and as Jerome saith on that verse, "holy writ is the scripture of peoples, for it is made, that all peoples should know it," and the princes *How every man should con and keep the scripture, and holy writ is the scripture of peoples, as Jerome saith.* of the church, that were therein, be the apostles, that had authority to write holy writ, for by that same that the apostles wrote their scriptures by authority, and confirming of the Holy Ghost, it is holy scripture, and faith of Christian men, and this dignity hath no man after them, be he never so holy, never so cunning, as Jerome witnesseth on that verse. Also, Christ saith of the Jews that cried "Hosanna" to him in the temple, that though they were still, stones should cry, and by stones he understandeth heathen men, that worshipped stones for their gods. And we English men be come of heathen men, therefore we be understood by these stones, that should cry holy writ, and as Jews, that is interpreted knowledging, signify clerks, that should knowledge to God, by repentance of sins, and by voice of God's hearing, so our lewd men, suing the corner-stone Christ, may be signified by stones, that be hard and abiding in the foundation ; for though covetous clerks be wood by simony, heresy

and many other sins, and despise and stop holy writ, as
much as they may, yet the lewd people crieth after holy
writ, to con it, and keep it, with great cost and peril of their
life. For these reasons and other, with common charity to
save all men in our realm, which God would have saved, a
simple creature hath translated the bible out of Latin into
English. First, this simple creature had much travail, with
divers fellows and helpers, to gather many old bibles, and
other doctors, and common gloses, and to make one Latin
bible some deal true ; and then to study it of the new, the text
with the glose, and other doctors, as he might get, and
specially Lyra[1] on the Old Testament, that helped full
much in this work ; the third time to counsel with old
grammarians and old divines, of hard words, and hard
sentences, how they might best be understood and translated ; the fourth time to translate as clearly as he could to
the sentence, and to have many good fellows and cunning
at the correcting of the translation. First, it is to know,
that the best translating is out of Latin into English, to
translate after the sentence, and not only after the words, so
that the sentence be as open, either opener, in English as
in Latin, and go not far from the letter ; and if the letter
may not be sued in the translating, let the sentence ever be
whole and open, for the words owe to serve to the intent
and sentence, and else the words be superfluous either false.
In translating into English, many resolutions may make the
sentence open, as an ablative case absolute may be resolved
into these three words, with covenable verb, *the while, for,
if*, as grammarians say ; as thus, *the master reading, I stand,*
may be resolved thus, *while the master readeth, I stand,* either
if the master readeth, etc., either *for the master,* etc. ; and
sometimes it will accord well with the sentence to be
resolved into *when,* either into *afterward,* thus *when the
master read, I stood,* either *after the master read, I stood ;* and
sometime it may well be resolved into a verb of the same
tense, as other be in the same reason, and into this word
et, that is, *and* in English, as thus, *arescentibus hominibus
prae timore,* that is, *and men shall wax dry for dread.* Also
a participle of a present tense, either preterite, of active
voice, either passive, may be resolved into a verb of the

---

[1] *Nicolaus de Lyra.*

same tense, and a conjunction copulative, as thus, *dicens*, that is, *saying*, may be resolved thus, *and saith*, either *that saith ;* and this will, in many places, make the sentence open, where to English it after the word, would be dark and doubtful. Also a relative, *which*, may be resolved into his antecedent with a conjunction copulative, as thus, *which runneth, and he runneth.* Also when a word is once set in a reason, it may be set forth as oft as it is understood, either as oft as reason and need ask ; and this word *autem* either *vero*, may stand for *forsooth*, either for *but*, and thus I use commonly ; and sometimes it may stand for *and*, as old grammarians say. Also when rightful construction is letted by relation, I resolve it openly, thus, where this reason, *Dominum formidabunt adversarii ejus*, should be Englished thus by the letter, *the Lord his adversaries shall dread*, I English it thus by resolution, *the adversaries of the Lord shall dread him ;* and so of other reasons that be like. At the beginning I purposed, with God's help, to make the sentence as true and open in English as it is in Latin, either more true and more open than it is in Latin ; and I pray, for charity and for common profit of Christian souls, that if any wise man find any default of the truth of translation, let him set in the true sentence and open of holy writ, but look that he examine truly his Latin bible, for no doubt he shall find full many bibles in Latin full false, if he look, many, namely new; and the common Latin bibles have more need to be corrected, as many as I have seen in my life, than hath the English bible late translated ; and where the Hebrew, by witness of Jerome, of Lyra, and other expositors discordeth from our Latin bibles, I have set in the margin, by manner of a glose, what the Hebrew hath, and how it is understood in some place; and I did this most in the Psalter, that of all our books discordeth most from Hebrew ; for the church readeth not the Psalter by the last translation of Jerome out of Hebrew into Latin, but another translation of other men, that had much less cunning and holiness than Jerome had ; and in full few books the church readeth the translation of Jerome, as it may be proved by the proper originals of Jerome, which he glosed. And whether I have translated as openly or openlier in English as in Latin, let wise men deem, that know well

both languages, and know well the sentence of holy scripture.   And whether I have done thus, or nay, ne doubt, they
that con well the sentence of holy writ and English together, and will travail, with God's grace, thereabout, may
make the bible as true and as open, yea, and openlier in
English than it is in Latin.   And no doubt to a simple
man, with God's grace and great travail, men might expound
much openlier and shortlier the bible in English, than the
old great doctors han expounded it in Latin, and much
sharplier and groundlier than many late postillators, either
expositors, han done.   But God, of his great mercy, give
to us grace to live well, and to say the truth in covenable
manner, and acceptable to God and his people, and to spill
not our time, be it short, be it long, at God's ordinance.
But some, that seem wise and holy, say thus, if men now
were as holy as Jerome was, they might translate out of
Latin into English, as he did out of Hebrew and out of
Greek into Latin, and else they should not translate now,
as them thinketh, for default of holiness and of cunning.
Though this replication seem colourable, it hath no good
ground, neither reason, neither charity, for why this replica-
cion is more against saint Jerome, and against the first
seventy translators, and against holy church, than against
simple men, that translate now into English; for saint Jerome
was not so holy as the apostles and evangelists, whose books
he translated into Latin, neither had he so high gifts of the
Holy Ghost as they had ; and much more the seventy translators were not so holy as Moses and the prophets, and
specially David, neither they had so great gifts of God, as
Moses and the prophets had.   Furthermore holy church
approveth, not only the true translation of mean Christian
men, steadfast in Christian faith, but also of open heretics,
that did away many mysteries of Jesus Christ by guileful
translation, as Jerome witnesseth in a prologue on Job, and
in the prologue of Daniel.   Much more let the Church of
England approve the true and whole translation of simple
men, that would for no good in earth, by their witting and
power, put away the least truth, yea, the least letter, either
tittle, of holy writ, that beareth substance, either charge.
And dispute they not of the holiness of men now living in
this deadly life, for they con not thereon, and it is reserved

only to God's doom. If they know any notable default by the translators, either helpers of them, let them blame the default by charity and mercy, and let them never damn a thing that may be done lawfully by God's law, as wearing of a good cloth for a time, either riding on a horse for a great journey, when they wit not wherefore it is done; for such things may be done of simple men, with as great charity and virtue, as some, that hold them great and wise, can ride in a gilt saddle, either use cushions and beds and cloths of gold and of silk, with other vanities of the world. God grant pity, mercy, and charity, and love of common profit, and put away such foolish dooms, that be against reason and charity. Yet worldly clerks ask greatly what spirit maketh idiots hardy to translate now the bible into English, since the four great doctors durst never do this? This replication, is so lewd, that it needeth no answer, no but stillness, either courteous scorn; for the great doctors were none English men, neither they were conversant among English men, neither in case they could the language of English, but they ceased never till they had holy writ in their mother tongue, of their own people. For Jerome, that was a Latin man of birth, translated the Bible, both out of Hebrew and out of Greek, into Latin, and expounded full much thereto; and Austin, and many more Latins expounded the bible, for many parts, in Latin, to Latin men, among which they dwelt, and Latin was a common language to their people about Rome, and beyond, and on this half, as English is common language to our people, and yet this day the common people in Italy speak Latin corrupt, as true men say, that han been in Italy; and the number of translators out of Greek into Latin passeth man's knowing, as Austin witnesseth in the 2nd book of Christian Teaching, and saith thus, "the translators out of Hebrew into Greek may be numbered, but Latin translators, either they that translated into Latin, may not be numbered in any manner." For in the first times of faith, each man, as a Greek book came to him, and he seemed to himself to have some cunning of Greek and of Latin, was hardy to translate; and this thing helped more than letted understanding, if readers be not negligent, forwhy the beholding of many books hath

showed oft, either declared, some darker sentences. This
saith Austin there. Therefore Grosted saith, that it was
God's will, that divers men translated, and that divers
translations be in the church, for where one said darkly, one
either more said openly. Lord God! since at the beginning
of faith so many men translated into Latin, and to great
profit of Latin men, let one simple creature of God translate
into English, for profit of English men; for if worldly
clerks look well their chronicles and books, they should find,
that Bede translated the bible, and expounded much in
Saxon, that was English, either common language of this
land, in his time; and not only Bede, but also King Alured,
that founded Oxford, translated in his last days the
beginning of the Psalter into Saxon, and would more, if he
had lived longer. Also French men, Beemers[1] and Bretons
have the bible, and other books of devotion and of exposition, translated in their mother language; why should
not English men have the same in their mother language, I
can not wit, no but for falseness and negligence of clerks,
either for our people is not worthy to have so great grace
and gift of God, in pain of their old sins. God for his
mercy amend these evil causes, and make our people to
have, and con, and keep truly holy writ, to life and death!

But in translating of words equivocal, that is, that hath
many significations under one letter, may lightly be peril, for
Austin saith in the 2nd book of Christian Teaching, that if
equivocal words be not translated into the sense, either
understanding, of the author, it is error; as in that place of
the Psalm, *the feet of them be swift to shed out blood*, the
Greek word is equivocal to *sharp* and *swift*, and he that
translated *sharp feet*, erred, and a book that hath *sharp feet*,
is false, and must be amended; as that sentence *unkind
young trees shall not give deep roots*, oweth to be thus,
plantings of aoutrry shall not give deep roots. Austin saith
this there. Therefore a translator hath great need to study
well the sentence, both before and after, and look that such
equivocal words accord with the sentence, and he hath need
to live a clean life, and be full devout in prayers, and have
not his wit occupied about worldly things, that the Holy
Spirit, author of wisdom, and cunning, and truth, dress him

[1] Bohemians.

in his work, and suffer him not for to err. Also this word *ex*
signifieth sometimes *of,* and sometimes it signifieth *by,* as
Jerome saith; and this word *enim* signifieth commonly *forsooth,* and, as Jerome saith, it signifieth *cause thus, for why*;
and this word *secundum* is taken for *after,* as many men say,
and commonly, but it signifieth well *by,* either *up,* thus *by
your word,* either *up your word.* Many such adverbs, con-
junctions, and prepositions be set oft one for another, and at
free choice of authors sometimes; and now they shall be
taken as it accordeth best to the sentence. By this manner,
with good living and great travail, men may come to true
and clear translating, and true understanding of holy writ,
seem it never so hard at the beginning. God grant to us
all grace to con well, and keep well holy writ, and suffer
joyfully some pain for it at the last! Amen.

Dialogue between a L ORD *and*

a C LERK *upon Translation.*

[From T REVISA's Translation of H IGDEN's
Polychronicon.]

Dialogue between a Lord and a Clerk upon Translation.

From Trevisa's Translation of Higden's *Polychronicon.*

 HE LORD.—Sith the time that the great and high tower of Babylon was builded, men have spoken with divers tongues, in such wise that divers men be strange to other and understand not others' speech. Speech is not known but if it be learned ; common learning of speech is by hearing, and so alway he that is deaf is alway dumb, for he may not hear speech for to learn. So men of far countries and lands that have divers specches, if neither of them have learned others' language, neither of them wot what other meaneth. Though they meet and have great need of information and of lore of talking and of speech, be the need never so great, neither of them understandeth other's speech no more than gagling of geese. For jangle that one never so fast, that other is never the wiser, though he shrew him instead of 'good-morrow'! This is a great mischief that followeth now mankind ; but God of His mercy and grace hath ordained double remedy. One is that some man learneth and knoweth many divers speeches, and so between strange men, of the which neither understandeth other's speech, such a man may be mean and tell either what other will mean. That other remedy is that one language is learned, used, and known in many nations and lands. And so Latin is learned, known, and used, specially on this half Greece, in all the nations and lands of

Europe.   Therefore clerks, of their goodness and courtesy, make and write their books in Latin, for their writing and books should be understood in divers nations and lands. And so Ranulphus, monk of Chester (Ralph Higden), wrote in Latin his books of Chronicles, that describeth the world about in length and in breadth, and maketh mention and mind of doings and deeds of marvels and wonders, and reckoneth the years to his last days from the first making of heaven and of earth.   And so therein is great and noble information and lore to them that can therein read and understand.   Therefore I would have these books of Chronicles translated out of Latin into English, for the more men should them understand and have thereof cunning, information and lore.

THE CLERK.—These books of Chronicles be written in Latin, and Latin is used and understood on this half Greece in all the nations and lands of Europe.   And commonly English is not so wide understood, ne known; and the English translation should no man understand but English men alone; then how should the more men understand the Chronicles, though they were translated out of Latin, that is so wide used and known, into English, that is not used and known but of English men alone?

THE LORD.—This question and doubt is easy to assail. For if these Chronicles were translated out of Latin into English, then by that so many the more men should understand them as understand English, and no Latin.

THE CLERK.—Ye can speak, read, and understand Latin; then it needeth not to have such an English translation.

THE LORD.—I deny this argument; for though I can speak, read, and understand Latin, there is much Latin in these books of Chronicles that I can not understand, neither thou, without studying, avisement, and looking of other books.   Also, though it were not needful for me, it is needful for other men that understand no Latin.

THE CLERK.—Men that understand no Latin may learn and understand.

THE LORD.—Not all; for some may not for other manner business, some for age, some for default of wit, some for default of chattel, other of friends to find them to school, and some for other divers defaults and lets.

THE CLERK.—It needeth not that all such know the Chronicles.

THE LORD.—Speak not too straitly of thing that needeth ; for straitly to speak of thing that needeth, only thing that is, and may not fail, needeth to be. And so it needeth that God be, for God is, and may not fail. And, so for to speak, no man needeth for to know the Chronicles, for it might and may be that no man them knoweth. Otherwise to speak of thing that needeth ; somewhat needeth for to sustain or to have other things thereby, and so meat and drink needeth for keeping and sustenance of life. And, so for to speak, no man needeth for to know the Chronicles. But in the third manner to speak of thing that needeth, all that is profitable needeth, and, so for to speak, all men need to know the Chronicles.

THE CLERK.—Then they that understand no Latin may ask and be informed and ytaught of them that understand Latin.

THE LORD.—Thou speakest wonderly, for the lewd man wots not what he should ask, and namely of lore of deeds that come never in his mind ; nor wots of whom commonly he should ask. Also, not all men that understand Latin have such books to inform lewd men ; also some can not, and some may not, have while, and so it needeth to have an English translation.

THE CLERK.—The Latin is both good and fair, therefore it needeth not to have an English translation.

THE LORD.—The reason is worthy to be plunged in a pludde and laid in powder of lewdness and of shame. It might well be that thou makest only in mirth and in game.

THE CLERK.—The reason must stand but it be assoiled.

THE LORD.—A blear-eyed man, but he were all blind of wit, might see the solution of this reason ; and though he were blind he might grope the solution, but if his feeling him failed. For if this reason were aught worth, by such manner arguing men might prove that the three score and ten interpreters, and Aquila, Symachus, Theodocion, and Origines were lewdly occupied when they translated holy writ out of Hebrew into Greek ; and also that Saint Jerome was lewdly occupied when he translated holy writ out of Hebrew into Latin, for the Hebrew is both good and fair and y-written by inspiration of the Holy Ghost ; and all these for their translations be highly praised of all Holy Church. Then the foresaid lewd reason is worthy to be powdered, laid a-water and y-soused. Also holy writ in Latin is both good and fair, and yet for to make a sermon of holy writ all in Latin to men that can English and no Latin, it were a lewd deed, for they be never the wiser for the Latin, but it be told them in English what it is to mean ; and it may not be told in English what the Latin is to mean without translation out of Latin into English. Then it needeth to have an English translation, and for to keep it in mind that it be not forgeten, it is better that such a translation be made and written than said and not written. And so this foresaid lewd reason should move no man that hath any wit to leave the making of English translation.

The CLERK—A great deal of these books standeth much by holy writ, by holy doctors, and by philosophy ; then these books should not be translated into English.

The LORD—It is wonder that thou makest so feeble arguments, and hast gone so long to school. Aristotle's books and other books also of logic and of philosophy were translated out of Greek into Latin. Also at praying of King Charles, John Scott translated Deny's books out of Greek into Latin, and then out of Latin into French ; then what hath English trespassed that it might not be translated into English ? Also King Alured, that founded the University of Oxford, translated the best laws into English tongue, and a great deal of the Psalter out of Latin into English, and caused Wyrefrith, Bishop of Worcester, to translate Saint Gregory's books, the dialogues, out of Latin into Saxon. Also Caedmon of Whitby was inspired of the Holy Ghost, and made wonder poesies in English nigh of all the stories of holy writ. Also the holy man Beda translated St. John's gospel out of Latin into English. Also thou wotest where the Apocalypse is written in the walls and roof of a chapel, both in Latin and in French. Also the gospel, and prophecy, and the right faith of holy church must be taught and preached to English men that can no Latin. Then the gospel, and prophecy, and the right faith of holy church must be told them in English, and that is not done but by English translation, for such

English preaching is very translation, and such English preaching is good and needful; then English translation is good and needful.

The CLERK—If a translation were made that might be amended in any point, some men it would blame.

The LORD—If men blame that is not worthy to be blamed, then they be to blame. Clerks know well enough that no sinful man doth so well that it ne might do better, ne make so good a translation that he ne might be better. Therefore Origines made two translations, and Jerome translated thrice the Psalter. I desire not translation of these the best that might be, for that were an idle desire for any man that is now alive, but I would have a skilful translation, that might be known and understood.

The CLERK—Whether is you liefer have, a translation of these chronicles in rhyme or in prose?

The LORD—In prose, for commonly prose is more clear than rhyme, more easy and more plain to know and understand.

The CLERK—Then God grant us grace grathly to gin, wit and wisdom wisely to work, might and mind of right meaning to make translation trusty and true, pleasing to the Trinity, three persons and one God, in majesty, that ever was and ever shall be, and made heaven and earth, and light for to shine, and departed light and darkness, and called light, day, and darkness, night; and so was made eventide and morrowtide one day, that had no morrowtide. The second day He made the firmament between waters, and departed waters that were under the firmament fro the waters that were above the firmament, and called the firmament heaven. The third day He gathered waters that be under the firmament into one place and made the earth unheled, and named the gathering of waters, seas, and dry earth, land; and made trees and grass. The fourth day he made sun and moon and stars, and set them in the firmament of heaven there for to shine, and to be tokens and signs to depart times and years, night and day. The fifth day He made fowls and birds in the air, and fishes in the water. The sixth day He made beasts of the land, and man of the earth, and put them in Paradise, for he should work and wone therein. But man brake God's hest and fell into

sin, and was put out of Paradise into woe and sorrow.
worthy to be damned to the pain of hell without any end.
But the Holy Trinity had mercy of man, and the Father
sent the Son, and the Holy Ghost alight on a maid, and the
Son took flesh and blood of that blissful maid, and died on
the Rood to save mankind, and arose the third day, glorious
and blissful, and taught his disciples, and ascended into
heaven when it was time ; and shall come at the day of
Doom and deem quick and dead.   Then all they that be
written in the Book of Life shall wend with Him into the
bliss of heaven, and be there in body and soul, and see and
know His Godhead and Manhood in joy without any end.

Thus endeth the Dialogue.

The Epistle of Sir John Trevisa, Chaplain unto Lord Thomas of Barkley, upon the translation of Polychronicon into our English tongue.

EALTH and worship to my worthy and worshipful Lord Sir Thomas, Lord of Barkley! I, John Trevisa, your priest and beadsman, obedient and buxom to work your will, hold in heart, think in thought, and mean in mind your needful meaning and speech that ye spake and said, that ye would have English translation of Ranulphus of Chester's books of chronicles. Therefore I will fond to take that travail, and make English translation of the same books, as God granteth me grace, for blame of backbiters will I not blinne; for envy of enemies, for evil spiting and speech of evil speakers will I not leave to do this deed; for travail will I not spare. Comfort I have in meedful making and pleasing to God, and in knowing that I wot that it is your will for to make this translation clear and plain to be known and understood. In some place I shall set word for word, and active for active, and passive for passive, a-row right as it standeth, without changing of the order of words. But in some place I must change the order of words, and set active for passive, and again-ward. And in some place I must set a reason for a word, and tell what it meaneth. But for all such changing, the meaning shall stand and not be changed. But some words and names of countries, of lands, of cities,

of waters, of rivers, of mountains and hills, of persons, and of places, must be set and stand for themselves in their own kind, as Asia, Europe, Africa, and Syria, Mount Atlas, Sindi, and Oreb, Marach, Jordan, and Arnon, Bethlehem, Nazareth, Jerusalem, and Damascus, Hannibal, Rasin, Ahasuerus, and Cyrus, and many such words and names. If any man make of these books of chronicles a better English translation, and more profitable, God do him meed! And because ye make me do this meedful deed, He that quiteth all good deeds quite your meed in the bliss of heaven, in wealth and liking, with all the holy saints of mankind and the nine orders of angels; as Angels, Arch-angels, Principates, Potestates, Virtutes, Dominations, Thrones, Cherubim and Seraphim, to see God in his blissful face, in joy without any end.   Amen.

Thus endeth he his epistle.

Certain

Prefaces and Epilogues by

WILLIAM CAXTON.

1475-1490.

WILLIAM CAXTON.

The Recuyell of the Histories of Troy.

Title and Prologue to Book I.

ERE beginneth the volume entitled and named the Recuyell of the Histories of Troy, composed and drawn out of divers books of Latin into French by the right venerable person and worshipful man, Raoul le Feure, priest and chaplain unto the right noble, glorious, and mighty prince in his time, Philip, Duke of Burgundy, of Brabant, etc., in the year of the Incarnation of our Lord God a thousand four hundred sixty and four, and translated and drawn out of French into English by William Caxton, mercer, of the city of London, at the commandment of the right high, mighty, and virtuous Princess, his redoubted Lady, Margaret, by the grace of God Duchess of Burgundy, of Lotrylk, of Brabant, etc.; which said translation and work was begun in Bruges in the County of Flanders, the first day of March, the year of the Incarnation of our said Lord God a thousand four hundred sixty and eight, and ended and finished in the holy city of Cologne the 19th day of September, the year of our said Lord God a thousand four hundred sixty and eleven, etc.

And on that other side of this leaf followeth the prologue.

When I remember that every man is bounden by the commandment and counsel of the wise man to eschew sloth and idleness, which is mother and nourisher of vices, and ought to put myself unto virtuous occupation and business, then I, having no great charge of occupation, following the said counsel took a French book, and read therein many strange and marvellous histories, wherein I had great pleasure and delight, as well for the novelty of the same as for the fair language of French, which was in prose so well and compendiously set and written, which methought I understood the sentence and substance of every matter. And for so much as this book was new and late made and drawn into French, and never had seen it in our English tongue, I thought in myself it should be a good business to translate it into our English, to the end that it might be had as well in the royaume of England as in other lands, and also for to pass therewith the time, and thus concluded in myself to begin this said work. And forthwith took pen and ink, and began boldly to run forth as blind Bayard in this present work, which is named "The Recuyell of the Trojan Histories." And afterward when I remembered myself of my simpleness and unperfectness that I had in both languages, that is to wit in French and in English, for in France was I never, and was born and learned my English in Kent, in the Weald, where I doubt not is spoken as broad and rude English as in any place of England; and have continued by the space of 30 years for the most part in the countries of Brabant, Flanders, Holland, and Zealand. And thus when all these things came before me, after that I had made and written five or six quires I fell in despair of this work, and purposed no more to have continued therein, and those quires laid apart, and in two years after laboured no more in this work, and was fully in will to have left it, till on a time it fortuned that the right high, excellent, and right virtuous princess, my right redoubted Lady, my Lady Margaret, by the grace of God sister unto the King of England and of France, my sovereign lord, Duchess of Burgundy, of Lotryk, of Brabant, of Limburg, and of Luxembourg, Countess of Flanders, of Artois, and of Burgundy, Palatine of Hainault, of Holland, of Zealand and of Namur, Marquesse of the Holy Empire, Lady of Frisia, of Salins and of Mechlin, sent for me to speak with her good Grace of divers matters, among the which I let her Highness have knowledge of the foresaid beginning

of this work, which anon commanded me to show the said
five or six quires to her said Grace; and when she had seen
them anon she found a default in my English, which she
commanded me to amend, and moreover commanded me
straitly to continue and make an end of the residue then
not translated; whose dreadful commandment I durst in
no wise disobey, because I am a servant unto her said
Grace and receive of her yearly fee and other many good
and great benefits, (and also hope many more to receive of
her Highness), but forthwith went and laboured in the said
translation after my simple and poor cunning, also nigh as
I can following my author, meekly beseeching the boun-
teous Highness of my said Lady that of her benevolence
list to accept and take in gree this simple and rude work
here following; and if there be anything written or said to
her pleasure, I shall think my labour well employed, and
whereas there is default that she arette it to the simpleness of my cunning which is full small in this behalf; and
require and pray all them that shall read this said work to
correct it, and to hold me excused of the rude and simple
translation.

And thus I end my prologue.

Epilogue to Book II.

Thus endeth the second book of the Recule of the
Histories of Troy. Which bookes were late translated
into French out of Latin by the labour of the venerable
person Raoul le Feure, priest, as afore is said; and by me
indigne and unworthy, translated into this rude English
by the commandment of my said redoubted Lady, Duchess
of Burgundy. And for as much as I suppose the said two
books be not had before this time in our English language,
therefore I had the better will to accomplish this said
work; which work was begun in Bruges and continued in
Ghent and finished in Cologne, in the time of the troublous
world, and of the great divisions being and reigning, as well
in the royaumes of England and France as in all other
places universally through the world; that is to wit the year
of our Lord a thousand four hundred seventy one. And as

for the third book, which treateth of the general and last destruction of Troy, it needeth not to translate it into English, for as much as that worshipful and religious man, Dan John Lidgate, monk of Bury, did translate it but late ; after whose work I fear to take upon me, that am not worthy to bear his penner and ink-horn after him, to meddle me in that work. But yet for as much as I am bound to contemplate my said Lady's good grace, and also that his work is in rhyme and as far as I know it is not had in prose in our tongue, and also, peradventure, he translated after some other author than this is ; and yet for as much as divers men be of divers desires, some to read in rhyme and metre and some in prose; and also because that I have now good leisure, being in Cologne, and have none other thing to do at this time ; in eschewing of idleness, mother of all vices, I have delibered in myself for the contemplation of my said redoubted lady to take this labour in hand, by the sufferance and help of Almighty God; whom I meekly supplye to give me grace to accomplish it to the pleasure of her that is causer thereof, and that she receive it in gree of me, her faithful, true, and most humble servant, etc.

Epilogue to Book III.

Thus end I this book, which I have translated after mine Author as nigh as God hath given me cunning, to whom be given the laud and praising. And for as much as in the writing of the same my pen is worn, my hand weary and not steadfast, mine eyne dimmed with overmuch looking on the white paper, and my courage not so prone and ready to labour as it hath been, and that age creepeth on me daily and feebleth all the body, and also because I have promised to divers gentlemen and to my friends to address to them as hastily as I might this said book, therefore I have practised and learned at my great charge and dispense to ordain this said book in print, after the manner and form as ye may here see, and is not written with pen and ink as other books be, to the end that every man may have them at once. For all the books of this story, named

" The Recule of the Histories of Troy" thus imprinted as ye here see, were begun in one day and also finished in one day, which book I have presented to my said redoubted Lady, as afore is said. And she hath well accepted it, and largely rewarded me, wherefore I beseech Almighty God to reward her everlasting bliss after this life, praying her said Grace and all them that shall read this book not to disdain the simple and rude work, neither to reply against the saying of the matters touched in this book, though it accord not unto the translation of others which have written it. For divers men have made divers books which in all points accord not, as Dictes, Dares, and Homer. For Dictes and Homer, as Greeks, say and write favourably for the Greeks, and give to them more worship than to the Trojans; and Dares writeth otherwise than they do. And also as for the proper names, it is no wonder that they accord not, for some one name in these days have divers equivocations after the countries that they dwell in; but all accord in conclusion the general destruction of that noble city of Troy, and the death of so many noble princes, as kings, dukes, earls, barons, knights, and common people, and the ruin irreparable of that city that never since was re-edified; which may be example to all men during the world how dreadful and jeopardous it is to begin a war, and what harms, losses, and death followeth. Therefore the Apostle saith : " All that is written is written to our doctrine," which doctrine for the common weal I beseech God may be taken in such place and time as shall be most needful in increasing of peace, love, and charity ; which grant us He that suffered for the same to be crucified on the rood tree. And say we all Amen for charity !

Dictes and Sayings of the Philosophers.

First edition (1477). Epilogue.

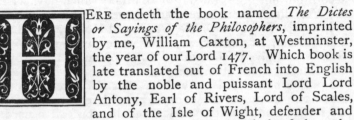ERE endeth the book named *The Dictes or Sayings of the Philosophers*, imprinted by me, William Caxton, at Westminster, the year of our Lord 1477. Which book is late translated out of French into English by the noble and puissant Lord Lord Antony, Earl of Rivers, Lord of Scales, and of the Isle of Wight, defender and director of the siege apostolic for our holy father the Pope in this royaume of England, and governor of my Lord Prince of Wales. And it is so that at such time as he had accomplished this said work, it liked him to send it to me in certain quires to oversee, which forthwith I saw, and found therein many great, notable, and wise sayings of the philosophers, according unto the books made in French which I had often before read; but certainly I had seen none in English until that time. And so afterward I came unto my said Lord, and told him how I had read and seen his book, and that he had done a meritorious deed in the labour of the translation thereof into our English tongue, wherein he had deserved a singular laud and thanks, &c. Then my said Lord desired me to oversee it, and where I should find fault to correct it; whereon I answered unto his Lordship that I could not amend it, but if I should so presume I might apaire it, for it was right well and cunningly made and translated into right good and fair English. Notwithstanding, he willed me to oversee it, and shewed me divers things, which, as seemed to him, might be left out, as divers letters missives sent from Alexander to Darius and Aristotle, and each to other, which letters were little appertinent unto dictes and sayings aforesaid, foras-

much as they specify of other matters. And also desired me, that done, to put the said book in imprint. And thus obeying his request and commandment, I have put me in devoir to oversee this his said book, and behold as nigh as I could how it accordeth with the original, being in French. And I find nothing discordant therein, save only in the dictes and sayings of Socrates, wherein I find that my said Lord hath left out certain and divers conclusions touching women. Whereof I marvel that my Lord hath not written them, ne what hath moved him so to do, ne what cause he had at that time; but I suppose that some fair lady hath desired him to leave it out of his book; or else he was amorous on some noble lady, for whose love he would not set it in his book; or else for the very affection, love, and good will that he hath unto all ladies and gentlewomen, he thought that Socrates spared the sooth and wrote of women more than truth; which I cannot think that so true a man and so noble a philosopher as Socrates was should write otherwise than truth. For if he had made fault in writing of women, he ought not, ne should not, be believed in his other dictes and sayings. But I perceive that my said Lord knoweth verily that such defaults be not had ne found in the women born and dwelling in these parts ne regions of the world. Socrates was a Greek, born in a far country from hence, which country is all of other conditions than this is, and men and women of other nature than they be here in this country. For I wot well, of whatsoever condition women be in Greece, the women of this country be right good, wise, pleasant, humble, discreet, sober, chaste, obedient to their husbands, true, secret, steadfast, ever busy, and never idle, attemperate in speaking, and virtuous in all their works—or at least should be so. For which causes so evident my said Lord, as I suppose, thought it was not of necessity to set in his book the sayings of his author Socrates touching women. But forasmuch as I had commandment of my said Lord to correct and amend where I should find fault, and other find I none save that he hath left out these dictes and sayings of the women of Greece, therefore in accomplishing his commandment—forasmuch as I am not certain whether it was in my Lord's copy or not, or else, peradventure, that the wind had blown over the leaf at the time of translation

of his book—I purpose to write those same sayings of that
Greek Socrates, which wrote of the women of Greece and
nothing of them of this royaume, whom, I suppose, he never
knew; for if he had, I dare plainly say that he would have
reserved them specially in his said dictes. Always not
presuming to put and set them in my said Lord's book but
in the end apart in the rehearsal of the works, humbly
requiring all them that shall read this little rehearsal, that
if they find any fault to arette it to Socrates, and not to me,
which writeth as hereafter followeth.

Socrates said that women be the apparels to catch men,
but they take none but them that will be poor or else them
that know them not. And he said that there is none so
great empechement unto a man as ignorance and women.
And he saw a woman that bare fire, of whom he said that
the hotter bore the colder. And he saw a woman sick, of
whom he said that the evil resteth and dwelleth with the
evil. And he saw a woman brought to the justice, and
many other women followed her weeping, of whom he said
the evil be sorry and angry because the evil shall perish.
And he saw a young maid that learned to write, of whom
he said that men multiplied evil upon evil. And he said
that the ignorance of a man is known in three things, that
is to wit, when he hath no thought to use reason; when
he cannot refrain his covetise; and when he is governed
by the counsel of women, in that he knoweth that they know
not. And he said unto his disciples: "Will ye that I enseign
and teach you how ye shall now escape from all evil?"
And they answered, "Yea." And then he said to them,
"For whatsoever thing that it be, keep you and be well
ware that ye obey not women." Who answered to him
again, "And what sayest thou by our good mothers, and
of our sisters?" He said to them, "Suffice you with that
I have said to you, for all be semblable in malice." And
he said, "Whosoever will acquire and get science, let him
never put him in the governance of a woman." And he saw
a woman that made her fresh and gay, to whom he said,
"Thou resemblest the fire; for the more wood is laid to
the fire the more will it burn, and the greater is the heat."
And on a time one asked him what him semed of women;
he answered that the women resemble a tree called Edelfla,

which is the fairest tree to behold and see that may be, but within it is full of venom. And they said to him and demanded wherefore he blamed so women? and that he himself had not come into this world, ne none other men also, without them. He answered, "The woman is like unto a tree named Chassoygnet, on which tree there be many things sharp and pricking, which hurt and prick them that approach unto it; and yet, nevertheless, that same tree bringeth forth good dates and sweet." And they demanded him why he fled from the women? And he answered, "Forasmuch as I see them flee and eschew the good and commonly do evil." And a woman said to him, "Wilt thou have any other woman than me?" And he answered to her, "Art not ashamed to offer thyself to him that demandeth nor desireth thee not?"

So, these be the dictes and sayings of the philosopher Socrates, which he wrote in his book; and certainly he wrote no worse than afore is rehearsed. And forasmuch as it is accordant that his dictes and sayings should be had as well as others', therefore I have set it in the end of this book. And also some persons, peradventure, that have read this book in French would have arette a great default in me that I had not done my devoir in visiting and overseeing of my Lord's book according to his desire. And some other also, haply, might have supposed that Socrates had written much more ill of women than here afore is specified, wherefore in satisfying of all parties, and also for excuse of the said Socrates, I have set these said dictes and sayings apart in the end of this book, to the intent that if my said lord or any other person, whatsoever he or she be that shall read or hear it, that if they be not well pleased withal, that they with a pen race it out, or else rend the leaf out of the book. Humbly requiring and beseeching my said lord to take no displeasure on me so presuming, but to pardon whereas he shall find fault; and that it please him to take the labour of the imprinting in gree and thanks, which gladly have done my diligence in the accomplishing of his desire and commandment; in which I am bounden so to do for the good reward that I have received of his said lordship; whom I beseech Almighty God to increase and to continue in his virtuous disposition in this world, and after this life to live everlastingly in Heaven. Amen.

Boethius de Consolatione Philosophiae.

Epilogue (1478).

THUS endeth this book, which is named "The Book of Consolation of Philosophy," which that Boecius made for his comfort and consolation, he being in exile for the common and public weal, having great heaviness and thoughtes, and in manner of despair, rehearsing in the said book how Philosophy appeared to him shewing the mutability of this transitory life, and also informing how fortune and hap should be understood, with the predestination and prescience of God as much as may and is possible to be known naturally, as afore is said in this said book. Which Boecius was an excellent author of divers books, craftily and curiously made in prose and metre; and also had translated divers books out of Greek into Latin, and had been senator of that noble and famous city Rome; and also his two sons senators for their prudence and wisdom. And forasmuch as he withstood to his power the tyranny of Theodoric, then Emperor, and would have defended the said city and senate from his wicked hands, whereupon he was convicted and put in prison; in which prison he made this foresaid book of consolation for his singular comfort. And forasmuch as the style of it is hard and difficult to be understood of simple persons, therefore the worshipful father and first founder and embellisher of ornate eloquence in our English, I mean Master Geoffrey Chaucer, hath translated this said work out of Latin into our usual and mother tongue, following the Latin as nigh as is possible to be understood; wherein in mine opinion he hath deserved a perpetual laud and thank of all this noble royaume of England, and especially of them that shall read and understand it. For in the said book they may see what this transitory and mutable world is, and whereto every man living in it ought to intend. Then forasmuch as this said book so translated is rare and not spread ne known as it is digne and worthy, for the erudition and learning as such as be ignorant and not knowing of it, at request of a singular friend and gossip of mine, I, William Caxton, have done my devoir and pain to imprint it in form as is here afore made; in hoping that it shall profit much people to the weal and health of their souls, and for to learn to have and keep the better patience in adversities. And furthermore I desire and require you that of your charity ye would pray for the soul of the said worshipful man Geoffrey Chaucer, first translator of this said book into English, and embellisher in making the said language ornate and fair, which shall endure perpetually; and therefore he ought eternally to be remembered, of whom the body and corpse lieth buried in the Abbey of Westminster beside London, to-fore the chapel of Saint Benedict, by whose sepulchre is written on a table hanging on a pillar his Epitaph, made by a Poet Laureate, whereof the copy followeth &c.

Epitaphium Galfridi Chaucer. per
poetam laureatum Stephanum surigonum
Mediolanensem in decretis licenciatum.

Pyerides muse si possunt numina fletus
   Fundere, diuinas atque rigare genas,
Galfridi vatis Chaucer crudelia fata
   Plangite; sit lacrimis abstinuisse nefas.
Uos coluit viuens: at vos celebrate sepultum;
   Reddatur merito gracia digna viro.
Grande decus vobis, en docti musa Maronis
   Qua didicit melius lingua latina loqui.
Grande nouumque decus Chaucer famamque parauit;
   Heu quantum fuerat prisca britanna rudis.
Reddidit insignem maternis versibus, vt iam
   Aurea splendescat, ferrea facta prius.

Hunc latuisse virum nil si tot opuscula vertes
  Dixeris, egregiis quae decorata modis.
Socratis ingenium. vel fontes philosophie
  Quitquid et arcani dogmata sacra ferunt
Et quascunque velis tenuit dignissimus artes
  Hic vates, paruo conditus hoc tumulo.
Ah laudis quantum preclara britannia perdis
  Dum rapuit tantum mors odiosa virum.
Crudeles parcae, crudelia fila sorores !
  Non tamen extincto corpore fama perit
Uiuet in eternum, viuent dum scripta poetæ,
  Uiuant eterno tot monimenta die.
Si qua bonos tangit pietas, si carmine dignus
  Carmina qui cecinit tot cumulata modis,
Haec sibi marmoreo scribantur verba sepulchro,
  Haec maneat laudis sarcina summa suae :
Galfridus Chaucer vates et fama poesis
  Materne, hac sacra sum tumulatus humo.

Post obitum Caxton voluit te viuere cura
  Willelmi, Chaucer, clare poeta, tui :
Nam tua non solum compressit opuscula formis,
  Has quoque sed laudes iussit hic esse tuas.

Golden Legend.

First Edition (1483). Prologue.

HE Holy and blessed doctor Saint Jerome saith this authority, "Do always some good work to the end that the devil find thee not Idle." And the holy doctor Saint Austin saith in the book of the labour of monks, that no man strong or mighty to labour ought to be idle; for which cause when I had performed and accomplished divers works and histories translated out of French into English at the request of certain lords, ladies, and gentlemen, as the Recuyel of the History of Troy, the Book of the Chess, the History of Jason, the history of the Mirror of the World, the 15 books of Metamorphoses in which be contained the fables of Ovid, and the History of Godfrey of Boulogne in the conquest of Jerusalem, with other divers works and books, I ne wist what work to begin and put forth after the said works to-fore made. And forasmuch as idleness is so much blamed, as saith Saint Bernard, the mellifluous doctor, that she is mother of lies and step-dame of virtues, and it is she that overthroweth strong men into sin, quencheth virtue, nourisheth pride, and maketh the way ready to go to hell; and John Cassiodorus saith that the thought of him that is idle thinketh on none other thing but on licorous meats and viands for his belly; and the holy Saint Bernard aforesaid saith in an epistle, when the time shall come that it shall behove us to render and give accounts of our idle time, what reason may we render or what answer shall we give when in idleness is none excuse; and Prosper saith that whosoever liveth in idleness liveth in manner of a dumb beast. And because I have seen the authorities that blame and despise so much idleness, and also know well that it is one of the capital and deadly sins much hateful unto God, therefore I have concluded and firmly purposed in myself no more to be idle, but will apply myself to labour and such occupation as I have been accustomed to do. And forasmuch as Saint Austin aforesaid saith upon a psalm that good work ought not to be done for fear of pain, but for the love of righteousness, and that it be of very and sovereign franchise, and because me-seemeth to be a sovereign weal to incite and exhort men and women to keep them from sloth and idleness, and to let to be understood to such people as be not lettered the nativities, the lives, the passions, the miracles, and the death of the holy saints, and also some other notorious deeds and acts of times past, I have submised myself to translate into English the legend of Saints, which is called *Legenda Aurea* in Latin, that is to say, the *Golden Legend*; for in like wise as gold is most noble above all other metals, in like wise is this legend holden most noble above all other works. Against me here might some persons say that this legend hath been translated before, and truth it is; but forasmuch as I had by me a legend in French, another in Latin, and the third in English, which varied in many and divers places, and also many histories were comprised in the two other books which were not in the English book; and therefore I have written one out of the said three books, which I have ordered otherwise than the said English legend is, which was so to-fore made, beseeching all them that shall see or hear it read to pardon me where I have erred or made fault, which, if any be, is of ignorance and against my will; and submit it wholly of such as can and may, to correct it, humbly beseeching them so to do, and in so doing they shall deserve a singular laud and merit; and I shall pray for them unto Almighty God that He of His benign grace reward them, etc., and that it profit to all them that shall read or hear it read, and may increase in them virtue, and expel vice and sin, that by the example of the holy saints amend their living here in this short life, that by their merits they and I may come to everlasting life and bliss in Heaven. Amen.

Caton (1483).

Prologue.

ERE beginneth the prologue or proem of the book called *Caton*, which book hath been translated into English by Master Benet Burgh, late Archdeacon of Colchester, and high canon of St. Stephen's at Westminster, which ful craftily hath made it in ballad royal for the erudition of my lord Bousher, son and heir at that time to my lord the Earl of Essex. And because of late came to my hand a book of the said Cato in French, which rehearseth many a fair learning and notable examples, I have translated it out of French into English, as all along hereafter shall appear, which I present unto the city of London.

Unto the noble, ancient, and renowned city, the city of London, in England, I, William Caxton, citizen and conjury of the same, and of the fraternity and fellowship of the mercery, owe of right my service and good will, and of very duty am bounden naturally to assist, aid, and counsel, as far forth as I can to my power, as to my mother of whom I have received my nurture and living, and shall pray for the good prosperity and policy of the same during my life. For, as me-seemeth, it is of great need, because I have known it in my young age much more wealthy, prosperous, and richer, than it is at this day. And the cause is that there is almost none that intendeth to the common weal, but only every man for his singular profit. Oh! when I remember the noble Romans, that for the common weal of the city of Rome they spent not only their moveable goods but they put their bodies and lives in jeopardy and to the death, as by many a noble example we may see in the acts of Romans, as of the two noble Scipios, African and Asian, Actilius, and many others. And among all others the noble Cato, author and maker of this book, which he hath left for to remain ever to all the people for to learn in it and to know how every man ought to rule and govern him in this life, as well for the life temporal as for the life spiritual. And as in my judgement it is the best book for to be taught to young children in school, and also to people of every age, it is full convenient if it be well understood. And because I see that the children that be born within the said city increase, and profit not like their fathers and elders, but for the most part after that they be come to their perfect years of discretion and ripeness of age, how well that their fathers have left to them great quantity of goods yet scarcely among ten two thrive, [whereas] I have seen and known in other lands in divers cities that of one name and lineage successively have endured prosperously many heirs, yea, a five or six hundred years, and some a thousand; and in this noble city of London it can unneth continue unto the third heir or scarcely to the second,—O blessed Lord, when I remember this I am all abashed ; I cannot judge the cause, but fairer ne wiser ne better spoken children in their youth be nowhere than there be in London, but at their full ripening there is no kernel ne good corn found, but chaff for the most part. I wot well there be many noble and wise, and prove well and be better and richer than ever were their fathers. And to the end that many might come to honour and worship, I intend to translate this said book of Cato, in which I doubt not, and if they will read it and understand they shall much the better con rule themselves thereby ; for among all other books this is a singular book, and may well be called the regiment or governance of the body and soul.

There was a noble clerk named Pogius of Florence, and was secretary to Pope Eugene and also to Pope Nicholas, which had in the city of Florence a noble and well-stuffed library which all noble strangers coming to Florence desired to see ; and therein they found many noble and rare books. And when they had asked of him which was the best book of them all, and that he reputed for best, he said that he held Cato glosed for the best book of his library. Then since that he that was so noble a clerk held this book for the best, doubtless it must follow that this is a noble book and a virtuous, and such one that a man may eschew all vices and ensue virtue. Then to the end that this said book may profit unto the hearers of it, I beseech Almighty God that I may achieve and accomplish it unto his laud and glory, and to the erudition and learning of them that be ignorant, that they may thereby profit and be the better. And I require and beseech all such that find fault or error, that of their charity they correct and amend it, and I shall heartily pray for them to Almighty God, that he reward them.

Aesop. (1483).

Epilogue.

Now then I will finish all these fables with this tale that followeth, which a worshipful priest and a parson told me lately. He said that there were dwelling in Oxford two priests, both masters of art, of whom that one was quick and could put himself forth, and that other was a good simple priest. And so it happened that the master that was pert and quick, was anon promoted to a benefice or twain, and after to prebends and for to be a dean of a great prince's chapel, supposing and weening that his fellow the simple priest should never have been promoted, but be alway an Annual, or at the most a parish priest, So after long time that this worshipful man, this dean, came riding into a good parish with a ten or twelve horses, like a prelate, and came into the church of the said parish, and found there this good simple man sometime his fellow, which came and welcomed him lowly; and that other bad him "good morrow, master John," and took him slightly by the hand, and asked him where he dwelt. And the good man said, "In this parish." "How," said he, "are ye here a soul priest or a parish priest?" "Nay, sir," said he, "for lack of a better, though I be not able ne worthy, I am parson and curate of this parish." And then that other availed his bonnet and said, "Master parson, I pray you to be not displeased; I had supposed ye had not been beneficed; but master," said he, "I pray you what is this benefice worth to you a year?" "Forsooth," said the good simple man, "I wot never, for I make never accounts thereof how well I have had it four or five years." "And know ye not," said he, "what it is worth? it should seem a good benefice." "No, forsooth" said he, "but I wot well what it shall be worth to me." "Why" said he, "what shall it be worth?" "Forsooth" said he, "if I do my true diligence in the cure of my parishioners in preaching and teaching, and do my part longing to my cure, I shall have heaven therefore; and if their souls be lost, or any of them by my default, I shall be punished therefore, and hereof am I sure." And with that word the rich dean was abashed, and thought he should do the better and take more heed to his cures and benefices than he had done. This was a good answer of a good priest and an honest. And herewith I finish this book, translated and printed by me, William Caxton, at Westminster in the Abbey, and finished the 26th day of March, the year of our Lord 1484, and the first year of the reign of King Richard the Third.

Chaucer's Canterbury Tales.
Second Edition. (1484).
Proem.

REAT thanks, laud, and honour ought to be given unto the clerks, poets, and historiographs that have written many noble books of wisedom of the lives, passions, and miracles of holy saints, of histories of noble and famous acts and faites, and of the chronicles since the beginning of the creation of the world unto this present time, by which we be daily informed and have knowledge of many things of whom we should not have known if they had not left to us their monuments written. Among whom and in especial before all others, we ought to give a singular laud unto that noble and great philosopher Geoffrey Chaucer, the which for his ornate writing in our tongue may well have the name of a laureate poet. For to-fore that he by labour embellished, ornated, and made fair our English, in this realm was had rude speech and incongruous, as yet it appeareth by old books, which at this day ought not to have place ne be compared among, ne to, his beauteous volumes and ornate writings, of whom he made many books and treatises of many a noble history, as well in metre as in rhyme and prose; and them so craftily made that he comprehended his matters in short, quick, and high sentences, eschewing prolixity, casting away the chaff of superfluity, and shewing the picked grain of sentence uttered by crafty and sugared eloquence; of whom among all others of his books I purpose to print, by the grace of God, the book of the tales of Canterbury, in which I find many a noble history of every state and degree; first rehearsing the conditions and the array of each of them as properly as possible is to be said.

And after their tales which be of nobleness, wisdom, gentleness, mirth, and also of very holiness and virtue, wherein he finisheth this said book, which book I have diligently overseen and duly examined, to that end it be made according unto his own making. For I find many of the said books which writers have abridged it, and many things left out; and in some place have set certain verses that he never made ne set in his book; of which books so incorrect was one brought to me, 6 years past, which I supposed had been very true and correct; and according to the same I did do imprint a certain number of them, which anon were sold to many and divers gentlemen, of whom one gentleman came to me and said that this book was not according in many place unto the book that Geoffrey Chaucer had made. To whom I answered that I had made it according to my copy, and by me was nothing added ne minished. Then he said he knew a book which his father had and much loved, that was very true and according unto his own first book by him made; and said more, if I would imprint it again he would get me the same book for a copy, howbeit he wist well that his father would not gladly depart from it. To whom I said, in case that he could get me such a book, true and correct, yet I would once endeavour me to imprint it again for to satisfy the author, whereas before by ignorance I erred in hurting and defaming his book in divers places, in setting in some things that he never said ne made, and leaving out many things that he made which be requisite to be set in it. And thus we fell at accord, and he full gently got of his father the said book and delivered it to me, by which I have corrected my book, as hereafter, all along by the aid of Almighty God, shall follow; whom I humbly beseech to give me grace and aid to achieve and accomplish to his laud, honour, and glory; and that all ye that shall in this book read or hear, will of your charity among your deeds of mercy remember the soul of the said Geoffrey Chaucer, first author and maker of this book. And also that all we that shall see and read therein may so take and understand the good and virtuous tales, that it may so profit unto the health of our souls that after this short and transitory life we may come to everlasting life in Heaven. Amen.

By WILLIAM CAXTON.

Malory's King Arthur. (1485).

Prologue.

FTER that I had accomplished and finished divers histories, as well of contemplation as of other historical and worldly acts of great conquerors and princes, and also certain books of ensamples and doctrine, many noble and divers gentlemen of this realm of England came and demanded me many and oft times wherefore that I have not done made and printed the noble history of the Saint Graal, and of the most renowned Christian King, first and chief of the three best Christian and worthy, Arthur, which ought most to be remembered among us Englishmen before all other Christian Kings. For it is notoyrly known through the universal world that there be nine worthy and the best that ever were; that is to wit three Paynims, three Jews, and three Christian men. As for the Paynims, they were to-fore the Incarnation of Christ, which were named—the first, Hector of Troy, of whom the history is come both in ballad and in prose—the second, Alexander the Great ; and the third, Julius Caesar, Emperor of Rome, of whom the histories be well known and had. And as for the three Jews, which also were before the Incarnation of our Lord of whom the first was Duke Joshua, which brought the children of Israel into the land of behest; the second, David, King of Jerusalem; and the third Judas Maccabæus ; of these three the Bible rehearseth all their noble histories and acts. And since the said Incarnation have been three noble Christian men, installed and admitted through the universal world into

the number of the nine best and worthy, of whom was first the noble Arthur, whose noble acts I purpose to write in this present book here following. The second was Charlemagne, or Charles the Great, of whom the history is had in many places both in French and English; and the third and last was Godfrey of Boulogne, of whose acts and life I made a book unto the excellent prince and king of noble memory, King Edward the Fourth. The said noble gentlemen instantly required me to print the history of the said noble king and conqueror, King Arthur, and of his knights, with the history of the Saint Graal, and of the death and ending of the said Arthur, affirming that I ought rather to print his acts and noble feats than of Godfrey of Boulogne or any of the other eight, considering that he was a man born within this realm, and king and emperor of the same; and that there be in French divers and many noble volumes of his acts, and also of his knights. To whom I answered that divers men hold opinion that there was no such Arthur, and that all such books as be made of him be but feigned and fables, because that some chronicles make of him no mention, ne remember him nothing, ne of his knights; whereto they answered, and one in special said, that in him that should say or think that there was never such a king called Arthur, might well be aretted great folly and blindness; for he said that there were many evidences of the contrary. First ye may see his sepulchre in the monastery of Glastonbury; and also in 'Polychronicon,' in the fifth book, the sixth chapter, and in the seventh book, the twenty-third chapter, where his body was buried, and after found and translated into the said monastery. Ye shall see also in the history of Boccaccio, in his book 'De casu principum,' part of his noble acts and also of his fall. Also Galfridus in his British book recounteth his life, and in divers places of England many remembrances be yet of him, and shall remain perpetually, and also of his knights. First in the Abbey of Westminster at Saint Edward's shrine remaineth the print of his seal in red wax closed in beryl, in which is written 'Patricius Arthurus, Britanniae Galliae Germaniae Daciae Imperator.' Item, in the castle of Dover ye may see Gawain's skull and Caradoc's mantle; at Winchester the round table; in other places Lancelot's sword, and many other things. Then all these things considered, there can no man reasonably gainsay but here was a king of this land named Arthur ; for in all places, Christian and heathen, he is reputed and taken for one of the nine worthy, and the first of the three Christian men. And also he is more spoken of beyond the sea ; more books made of his noble acts than there be in England, as well in Dutch, Italian, Spanish, and Greek as in French ; and yet of record remain in witness of him in Wales in the town of Camelot the great stones and marvellous works of iron lying under the ground, and royal vaults, which divers now living hath seen. Wherefore it is a marvel why he is no more renowned in his own country, save only it accordeth to the word of God, which saith that no man is accepted for a prophet in his own country. Then all these things aforesaid alleged, I could not well deny but that there was such a noble king named Arthur, and reputed one of the nine worthy, and first and chief of the Christian men ; and many noble volumes be made of him and of his noble knights in French, which I have seen and read beyond the sea, which be not had in our maternal tongue, but in Welsh be many, and also in French, and some in English, but nowhere nigh all. Wherefore such as have lately been drawn out briefly into English, I have, after the simple cunning that God hath sent to me, under the favour and correction of all noble lords and gentlemen, emprised to imprint a book of the noble histories of the said King Arthur and of certain of his knights, after a copy unto me delivered, which copy Sir Thomas Mallory did take out of certain books of French and reduced it into English. And I according to my copy have down set it in print, to the intent that noble men may see and learn the noble acts of chivalry, the gentle and virtuous deeds that some knights used in those days, by which they came to honour, and how they that were vicious were punished and oft put to shame and rebuke ; humbly beseeching all noble lords and ladies and all other estates, of what estate or degree they be of, that shall see and read in this said book and work, that they take the good and honest acts in their remembrance and to follow the same, wherein they shall find many joyous and pleasant histories and noble and renowned acts of humanity, gentleness, and chivalry. For herein may be seen noble chivalry, courtesy, humanity, friendliness, hardyhood, love, friendship, cowardice, murder, hate, virtue, and sin.   Do after the good and leave the evil, and it shall bring you to good fame and renown.   And for to pass the time this book shall be pleasant to read in ; but for to give faith and believe that all is true that is contained herein, ye be at your liberty.   But all is written for our doctrine, and for to beware that we fall not to vice ne sin, but to exercise and follow virtue, by which we may come and attain to good fame and renown in this life, and after this short and transitory life to come unto everlasting bliss in heaven ; the which He grant us that reigneth in Heaven, the Blessed Trinity.   Amen.

Then to proceed forth in this said book which I direct unto all noble princes, lords and ladies, gentlemen or gentlewomen, that desire to read or hear read of the noble and joyous history of the great conqueror and excellent king, King Arthur, sometime King of this noble realm then called Britain, I, William Caxton, simple person, present this book following, which I have emprised to imprint. And treateth of the noble acts, feats of arms, of chivalry, prowess, hardihood, humanity, love, courtesy, and very gentleness, with many wonderful histories and adventures. And for to understand briefly the contents of this volume, I have divided it into 21 books, and every book chaptered, as hereafter shall by God's grace follow.   The first book shall treat how Uther Pendragon begat the noble conqueror, King Arthur, and containeth 28 chapters.   The second book treateth of Balyn the noble knight, and containeth 19 chapters.   The third book treateth of the marriage of King Arthur to Queen Guinevere, with other matters, and containeth 15 chapters.   The fourth book how Merlin was assotted, and of war made to King Atthur, and containeth 29 chapters.   The fifth book treateth of the conquest of Lucius the emperor, and containeth 12 chapters.   The sixth book treateth of Sir Lancelot and Sir Lionel, and marvellous adventures, and containeth 18 chapters.   The seventh book treateth of a noble knight called Sir Gareth, and named by Sir Kay 'Beaumains,' and containeth 36 chapters.   The eighth book treateth of the birth of Sir Tristram the noble knight, and of his acts, and containeth

41 chapters. The ninth book treateth of a knight named
by Sir Kay, ' Le cote mal taillé,' and also of Sir Tristram,
and containeth 44 chapters. The tenth book treateth of
Sir Tristram, and other marvellous adventures, and containeth 83 chapters. The eleventh book treateth of Sir
Lancelot and Sir Galahad, and containeth 14 chapters.
The twelfth book treateth of Sir Lancelot and his madness,
and containeth 14 chapters. The thirteenth book treateth
how Galahad came first to King Arthur's court, and the
quest how the Sangreal was begun, and containeth 20
chapters. The fourteenth book treateth of the quest of the
Sangreal, and containeth 10 chapters. The fifteenth book
treateth of Sir Lancelot, and containeth 6 chapters. The
sixteenth book treateth of Sir Boris and Sir Lionel his
brother, and containeth 17 chapters. The seventeenth book
treateth of the Sangreal, and containeth 23 chapters. The
eighteenth book treateth of Sir Lancelot and the Queen,
and containeth 25 chapters. The nineteenth book treateth
of Queen Guinevere, and Lancelot, and containeth 13
chapters. The twentieth book treateth of the piteous death
of Arthur, and containeth 22 chapters. The twenty-first
book treateth of his last departing, and how Sir Lancelot
came to revenge his death, and containeth 13 chapters.
The sum is 21 books, which contain the sum of five hundred
and seven chapters, as more plainly shall follow hereafter.

Eneydos (1490).

Prologue.

FTER divers work made, translated, and achieved, having no work in hand, I sitting in my study whereas lay many divers pamphlets and books, happened that to my hand came a little book in French, which lately was translated out of Latin by some noble clerk of France, which book is named *Aeneidos*, made in Latin by that noble poet and great clerk, Virgil. Which book I saw over, and read therein how, after the general destruction of the great Troy, Aeneas departed, bearing his old father Anchises upon his shoulders, his little son Iulus on his hand, his wife with much other people following, and how he shipped and departed, with all the history of his adventures that he had ere he came to the achievement of his conquest of Italy, as all along shall be shewed in his present book. In which book I had great pleasure because of the fair and honest terms and words in French; which I never saw before like, ne none so pleasant ne so well ordered; which book as seemed to me should be much requisite to noble men to see, as well for the eloquence as the histories. How well that many hundred years past was the said book of *Aeneidos*, with other works, made and learned daily in schools, especially in Italy and other places; which history the said Virgil made in metre. And when I had advised me in this said book, I delibered and concluded to translate it into English; and forthwith took a pen and ink and wrote a leaf or twain, which I oversaw again to correct it. And when I saw the fair and strange terms therein, I doubted that it should not please some gentlemen

which late blamed me, saying that in my translations I
had over curious terms, which could not be understood of
common people, and desired me to use old and homely
terms in my translations. And fain would I satisfy every
man, and so to do took an old book and read therein, and
certainly the English was so rude and broad that I could
not well understood it. And also my Lord Abbot of Westminster did do show to me lately certain evidences written
in old English, for to reduce it into our English now used.
And certainly it was written in such wise that it was more
like to Dutch than English, I could not reduce ne bring it
to be understood. And certainly our language now used
varieth far from that which was used and spoken when I
was born. For we Englishmen be born under the domina-
tion of the moon, which is never steadfast but ever wavering,
waxing one season and waneth and decreaseth another season.
And that common English that is spoken in one shire
varieth from another, insomuch that in my days happened
that certain merchants were in a ship in Thames for to
have sailed over the sea into Zealand, and for lack of
wind they tarried at Foreland, and went to land for to
refresh them. And one of them named Sheffield, a mercer,
came into a house and asked for meat, and especially he
asked after eggs; and the goodwife answered that she
could speak no French, and the merchant was angry, for he
also could speak no French, but would have had eggs, and
she understood him not. And then at last another said,
that he would have "eyren"; then the goodwife said that
she understood him well. Lo, what should a man in these
days now write, eggs or eyren? Certainly it is hard to
please every man because of diversity and change of language. For in these days every man that is in any reputation in his country will utter his communication and matters
in such manners and terms that few men shall understand
them. And some honest and great clerks have been with
me and desired me to write the most curious terms that I
could find; and thus between plain, rude and curious I
stand abashed. But in my judgment the common terms
that be daily used be lighter to be understood than the old
and ancient English. And forasmuch as this present book
is not for a rude uplandish man to labour therein ne read it,

but only for a clerk and a noble gentleman that feeleth and understandeth in feats of arms, in love and in noble chivalry. Therefore in a mean between both I have reduced and translated this said book into our English, not over-rude ne curious ; but in such terms as shall be understood, by God's grace, according to my copy. And if any man will intermit in reading of it, and findeth such terms that he cannot understand, let him go read and learn Virgil or the pistles of Ovid, and there he shall see and understand lightly all, if he have a good reader and informer. For this book is not for every rude and uncunning man to see, but to clerks and very gentlemen that understand gentleness and science. Then I pray all them that shall read in this little treatise to hold me for excused for the translating of it, for I acknowledge myself ignorant of cunning to emprise on me so high and noble a work. But I pray Master John Skelton, late created poet laureate in the University of Oxenford, to oversee and correct this said book, and to address and expound, wherever shall be found fault, to them that shall require it.

For him I know for sufficient to expound and English every difficulty that is therein ; for he hath lately translated the Epistles of Tully, and the book of Diodorus Siculus, and divers other works out of Latin into English, not in rude and old language, but in polished and ornate terms craftily, as he that hath read Virgil, Ovid, Tully, and all the other noble poets and orators to me unknown. And also he hath read the nine Muses, and understands their musical sciences, and to whom of them each science is appropred. I suppose he hath drunken of Helicon's well. Then I pray him and such others to correct, add, or minish whereas he or they shall find fault; for I have but followed my copy in French as nigh as to me is possible. And if any word be said therein well, I am glad ; and if otherwise, I submit my said book to their correction. Which book I present unto the high born, my to-coming natural and sovereign lord Arthur, by the grace of God Prince of Wales, Duke of Cornwall and Earl of Chester, first-begotten son and heir unto our most dread natural and sovereign lord and most Christian King, Henry the VII., by the grace of God King of England and of France, and lord of Ireland; beseeching his noble Grace to receive it in thank of me his most humble subject and servant. And I shall pray unto Almighty God for his prosperous increasing in virtue, wisdom, and humanity, that he may be equal with the most renowned of all his noble progenitors; and so to live in this present life that after this transitory life he and we all may come to everlasting life in Heaven. Amen.

A Miracle Play of the Nativity.

[The Pageant of the Shearmen and
Tailors, from the Coventry
Corpus Christi Plays.]

A Miracle Play of the Nativity.

[The Pageant of the Shearmen and Tailors, from the Coventry Corpus Christi Plays.]

SAYE.   The Sovereign that seeth every
    secret,
    He save you all and make you perfect
      and strong,
    And give us grace with His mercy for to
      meet!
    For now in great misery mankind is
      bound;
The serpent hath given us so mortal a wound
That no creature is able us for to release
Till the right Unction of Judah doth cease.

Then shall much mirth and joy increase,
    And the right root in Israel spring,
That shall bring forth the grain of holiness;
    And out of danger He shall us bring
    Into that region where He is King
Which above all other far doth abound,
And that cruel Satan he shall confound.

Wherefore I come here upon this ground
    To comfort every creature of birth;
For I, Isaye the prophet, hath found
    Many sweet matters whereof we may make mirth
      On this same wise;
For, though that Adam he deemed to death
With all his childer, as Abel and Seth,
Yet Ecce virgo concipiet,—
    Lo where a remedy shall rise.

Behold, a maid shall conceive a child
  And get us more grace than ever men had,
And her maidenhood nothing defiled.
She is deputed to bear the Son, Almighty God.
  Lo! sovereignties, now may you be glad.
For of this maiden all we may be fain;
  For Adam, that now lies in sorrows full sad,
Her glorious birth shall redeem him again
    From bondage and thrall.
  Now be merry every mon,
  For this deed briefly in Israel shall be done,
  And before the Father in throne,
    That shall glad us all.

More of this matter fain would I move,
  But longer time I have not here for to dwell.
That Lord that is merciful his mercy so in us may prove
  For to save our souls from the darkness of hell;
    And to His bliss
      He us bring
    As He is
      Both Lord and King
      And shall be everlasting
      In secula seculorum, Amen.
        [*Exit* ISAIAH ; *enter* GABRIEL *to* MARY.]

GABRIEL.   Hail, Mary, full of grace!
  Our Lord God is with thee ;
Above all women that ever was,
  Lady, blessed mote thou be!

MARY.   Almighty Father and King of bliss,
  From all disease thou save me now!
For inwardly my spirits troubled is,
  That I am amazed and know not how.

GABRIEL.   Dread thee nothing, maiden, of this;
  From heaven above hither am I sent
Of embassage from that King of bliss
  Unto thee, Lady and Virgin reverent!
  Saluting thee here as most excellent,

Whose virtue above all other doth abound.
Wherefore in thee grace shall be found ;
For thou shalt conceive upon this ground
   The Second Person of God in throne ;
   He will be born of thee alone;
      Without sin thou shalt him see.
   Thy grace and thy goodness will never be gone,
      But ever to live in virginity.

MARY.   I marvel sore how that may be.
   Man's company knew I never yet,
Nor never to do, cast I me,
   While that our Lord sendeth me my wit.

GABRIEL.   The Holy Ghost in thee shall light,
   And shadow thy soul so with virtue
From the Father that is on height.
   These words, turtle, they be full true.

This child that of thee shall be born
   Is the Second Person in Trinity ;
He shall save that was forlorn,
   And the fiend's power destroy shall He.

These words, Lady, full true they been,
   And further, Lady, here in thine own lineage
Behold Elizabeth, thy cousin clean,
   The which was barren and past all age,

And now with child she hath been
Six months and more, as shall be seen ;
   Wherefore, discomfort thee not, Mary !
   For to God impossible nothing may be.

MARY.   Now, and it be that Lord's will
   Of my body to be born and for to be,
His high pleasures for to fulfil
   As his own handmaid I submit me.

GABRIEL.   Now blessed be the time set
   That thou wast born in thy degree !
For now is the knot surely knit,
   And God conceived in Trinity.

Now farewell, Lady of mightes most!
　Unto the Godhead I thee beteach.
MARY.　That Lord thee guide in every coast,
　And lowly He lead me and be my leech!
　　*Here the angel departeth, and Joseph cometh in and
　　saith:*

JOSEPH.　Mary, my wife so dear,
How do ye, dame, and what cheer
　Is with you this tide?
MARY.　Truly, husband, I am here
　Our Lord's will for to abide.

JOSEPH.　What! I trow that we be all shent!
Say, woman; who hath been here sith I went,
　To rage with thee?
MARY.　Sir, here was neither man nor man's even,
But only the sond of our Lord God in heaven.
JOSEPH.　Say not so, woman; for shame, let be!

Ye be with child so wonders great,
Ye need no more thereof to treat,
　Against all right.
Forsooth, this child, dame, is not mine.
Alas, that ever with mine eyne
　I should see this sight!

Tell me, woman; whose is this child?
MARY.　None but yours, husband so mild,
　And that shall be seen, [i-wis].
JOSEPH.　But mine? alas! alas! why say ye so?
Well-away! woman, now may I go,
　Beguiled, as many another is.

MARY.　Nay, truly, sir, ye be not beguiled,
Nor yet with spot of sin I am not defiled;
　Trust it well, husband.
JOSEPH.　Husband, in faith! and that a-cold!
Ah! well-away, Joseph, as thou art old!
　Like a fool now may I stand
　　And truss.

But, in faith, Mary, thou art in sin ;
So much as I have cherished thee, dame, and all thy
    kin,
    Behind my back to serve me thus !

All old men, example take by me,—
How I am beguiled here may you see !—
    To wed so young a child.
Now farewell, Mary, I leave thee here alone,—
[Woe] worth thee, dame, and thy works each one !—
    For I will no more be beguiled
        For friend nor foe.
    Now of this deed I am so dull,
    And of my life I am so full,
        No further may I go.
                    [*Lies down to sleep* ; *to him enters an Angel.*]

FIRST ANGEL.   Arise up, Joseph, and go home again
    Unto Mary, thy wife, that is so free.
To comfort her look that thou be fain,
    For, Joseph, a clean maiden is she :
She hath conceived without any train
    The Second Person in Trinity ;
Jesu shall be his name, certain,
    And all this world save shall He ;
        Be not aghast.
JOSEPH.   Now, Lord, I thank thee with heart full sad,
For of these tidings I am so glad
    That all my care away is cast ;
    Wherefore to Mary I will in haste.
                    [*Returns to* MARY.]

Ah ! Mary, Mary, I kneel full low ;
    Forgive me, sweet wife, here in this land !
Mercy, Mary ! for now I know
    Of your good governance and how it doth stand.

    Though that I did thee mis-name,
Mercy Mary ! while I live,
Will I never sweet wife thee grieve
    In earnest nor in game.

MARY.   Now, that Lord in Heaven, sir, He you forgive!
And I do forgive you in His name
For evermore.
JOSEPH.   Now truly, sweet wife, to you I say the same.

But now to Bethlehem must I wind,
And show myself, so full of care;
And I to leave you, thus great, behind,—
God wot, the while, dame, how you should fare.

MARY.   Nay, hardily, husband, dread ye nothing;
For I will walk with you on the way.
I trust in God, Almighty King,
To speed right well in our journey.

JOSEPH.   Now, I thank you, Mary, of your goodness,
That ye my words will not blame;
And sith that to Bethlehem we shall us dress,
Go we together in God's holy name.
[*They set out and travel awhile.*]

Now to Bethlehem have we leagues three;
The day is nigh spent, it draweth toward night;
Fain at your ease, dame, I would that ye should be,
For you groan all wearily, it seemeth in my sight.

MARY.   God have mercy, Joseph, my spouse so dear;
All prophets hereto doth bear witness,
The weary time now draweth near
That my child will be born, which is King of bliss.

Unto some place, Joseph, hendly me lead,
That I might rest me with grace in this tide.
The light of the Father over us both spread,
And the grace of my Son with us here abide!

JOSEPH.   Lo! blessed Mary, here shall ye lend,
Chief chosen of our Lord and cleanest in degree;
And I, for help to town will I wend.
Is not this the best, dame? what say ye?

MARY.   God have mercy, Joseph, my husband so meek!
And heartily I pray you, go now from me.
JOSEPH.   That shall be done in haste, Mary so sweet!
The comfort of the Holy Ghost leave I with thee.

Now to Bethlehem straight will I wend
   To get some help for Mary so free.
Some help of women God may me send,
   That Mary, full of grace, pleased may be.
[*In another part of the place a shepherd begins to speak.*]

FIRST PASTOR. Now God, that art in Trinity,
Thou save my fellows and me!
For I know not where my sheep nor they be,
   This night it is so cold.
Now is it nigh the midst of the night;
These weathers are dark and dim of light,
That of them can I have no sight,
   Standing here on this wold.

But now to make their heartes light,
Now will I full right
   Stand upon this lo,
And to them cry with all my might,—
   Full well my voice they know:
   What ho! fellows! ho! ho! ho!
   [*Two other shepherds appear (in the street).*]

SECOND PASTOR. Hark, Sim, hark! I hear our brother
   on the lo.
This is his voice, right well I know;
Therefore toward him let us go,
   And follow his voice aright.
See, Sim, see, where he doth stand!
I am right glad we have him fand!
Brother where hast thou been so lang,
   And it is so cold this night?

FIRST PASTOR. Eh! friends, there came a pirie of wind
   with a mist suddenly,
That forth of my ways went I
And great heaviness then made I!
   And was full sore afright.
Then forth to go wist I not whither,
But travelled on this lo hither and thither;
I was so weary of this cold weather
   That near past was my might.

THIRD PASTOR.   Brethren now we be past that fright,
And it is far within the night,
Full soon will spring the daylight,
　　　It draweth full near the tide.
Here awhile let us rest,
And repast ourselves of the best;
Till that the sun rise in the east
　　　Let us all here abide.

There the shepherds draws forth their meat and doth eat and drink and as they drink, they find the star and say thus:

THIRD PASTOR.   Brethren, look up and behold!
　　What thing is yonder that shineth so bright?
As long as ever I have watched my fold,
　　　Yet saw I never such a sight
　　　　In field.
Aha! now is come the time that old fathers hath told,
That in the winter's night so cold,
A child of maiden born be He would
　　In whom all prophecies shall be fulfilled.

FIRST PASTOR.   Truth it is without nay,
So said the prophet Isaye,
　　That a child should be born of a maid so bright
In winter nigh the shortest day,
　　Or else in the midst of the night.

SECOND PASTOR.   Loved be God, most of might,
That our grace is to see that sight;
Pray we to Him as it is right,
　　　If that His will it be,
That we may have knowledge of this signification
And why it appeareth on this fashion;
And ever to Him let us give laudation,
　　　In earth while that we be.

　　There the Angels sing " Gloria in excelsis Deo."

THIRD PASTOR.   Hark! They sing above in the clouds
　　clear!
Heard I never of so merry a quere.
Now, gentle brethren, draw we near
　　　To hear their harmony.

FIRST PASTOR.—Brother, mirth and solace is come us
   among ;
For by the sweetness of their song,
God's Son is come, whom we have looked for long,
   As signifieth this star that we do see.
SECOND PASTOR.   "Glory, gloria in excelsis," that was
   their song ;
   How say ye, fellows, said they not thus ?
FIRST PASTOR.   That is well said ; now go we hence
To worship that child of high magnificence,
And that we may sing in His presence
   "Et in terra pax hominibus."
There the shepherds sings " As I out rode," and Joseph saith :

JOSEPH.   Now, Lord, this noise that I do hear,
   With this great solemnity,
Greatly amended hath my cheer ;
   I trust high news shortly will be.
   There the Angels sing " Gloria in excelsis" again.

MARY.   Ah! Joseph, husband, come hither anon ;
   My child is born that is King of bliss.
JOSEPH.   Now welcome to me, the maker of mon,
With all the homage that I con ;
   Thy sweet mouth here will I kiss.
MARY.   Ah! Joseph, husband, my child waxeth cold,
   And we have no fire to warm him with.
JOSEPH.   Now in mine arms I shall him fold,
   King of all kings by field and by frith ;
He might have had better, and Himself would,
   Than the breathing of these beasts to warm him with.

MARY.   Now, Joseph, my husband, fetch hither my child,
   The Maker of man, and high King of bliss.
JOSEPH.   That shall be done anon, Mary so mild,
   For the breathing of these beasts hath warmed [Him]
      well, i-wis.
               [Angels appear to the shepherds.]

FIRST ANGEL.   Herd-men hend,
Dread ye nothing

Of this star that ye do see;
For this same morn
God's Son is born
In Bethlehem of a maiden free.

SECOND ANGEL.   Hie you thither in haste;
It is His will ye shall Him see
Lying in a crib of poor repast,
Yet of David's line come is He.
[*The Shepherds approach and worship the Babe.*]

FIRST PASTOR.   Hail, maid, mother, and wife so mild!
As the angel said, so have we fand.
I have nothing to present with thy child
But my pipe; hold, hold, take it in thy hand;
Wherein much pleasure that I have fand;
And now, to honour thy glorious birth,
Thou shalt it have to make thee mirth:

SECOND PASTOR.   Now, hail be thou, child, and thy dame!
For in a poor lodging here art thou laid,
So the angel said and told us thy name;
Hold, take thou here my hat on thy head!
And now of one thing thou art well sped,
For weather thou hast no need to complain,
For wind, ne sun, hail, snow and rain.

THIRD PASTOR.   Hail be thou, Lord over water and lands!
For thy coming all we may make mirth.
Have here my mittens to put on thy hands,
Other treasure have I none to present thee with.

MARY.   Now, herdmen hend,
For your coming,
To my child shall I pray,
As He is heaven King,
To grant you His blessing,
And to His bliss that ye may wend
At your last day.
There the shepherds singeth again and goth forth of the place,
and the two prophets cometh in and saith thus:

FIRST PROPHET. Novels, novels,
Of wonderful marvels
Very high and diffuse unto the hearing!
As Scripture tells,
These strange novels
    To you I bring.

SECOND PROPHET. Now heartily, sir, I desire to know,
If it would please you for to show
    Of what manner a thing.
    FIRST PROPHET. Very mystical unto your hearing,—
Of the nativity of a King.

SECOND PROPHET. Of a King? Whence should he come?
    FIRST PROPHET. From that region royal and mighty
        mansion,
The Seed celestial and heavenly wisdom,
    The Second Person and God's own Son,
For our sake now is man become.

This goodly sphere
Descended here
Into a Virgin clear,
    She undefiled.

.   .   .   .   .
By whose work obscure
Our frail nature
    Is now beguiled.
    SECOND PROPHET. Why, hath she a child?

FIRST PROPHET. Eh! trust it well;
    And never-the-less
Yet is she a maiden even as she was,
And her Son the King of Israel.

SECOND PROPHET. A wonderful marvel
    How that may be,
And far doth excell
    All our capacity:
    How that the Trinity,
        Of so high regality,
    Should joined be
        Unto our mortality!

FIRST PROPHET.   Of his own great mercy,
  As ye shall see the exposition,
Through whose humanity
All Adam's progeny
  Redeemed shall be out of perdition.

Sith man did offend,
Who should amend
  But the said man, and none other?
For the which cause He
Incarnate would be
  And live in misery as man's own brother.

SECOND PROPHET.   Sir, unto the Deity,
I believe perfectly,
  Impossible to be there is nothing;
Howbeit this wark
Unto me is dark
  In the operation or working.
FIRST PROPHET.   What more reprief
Is unto belief
  Than to be doubting?

SECOND PROPHET.   Yet doubts oft-times hath derivation.
FIRST PROPHET.   That is by the means of communication
Of truths to have a due probation
    By the same doubts reasoning.
  SECOND PROPHET.   Then to you this one thing:
Of what noble and high lineage is she
That might this veritable prince's mother be?

FIRST PROPHET.   Undoubted she is come of high parage,
Of the house of David and Solomon the sage;
And one of the same line joined to her by marriage;
    Of whose tribe
    We do subscribe
This child's lineage.

SECOND PROPHET.   And why in that wise?
FIRST PROPHET.   For it was the guise
  To count the parent on the man's line,
  And not on the feminine,
    Amongst us here in Israel.

SECOND PROPHET. Yet can I not espy by no wise
How this child born should be without nature's
  prejudice.
FIRST PROPHET. Nay, no prejudice unto nature, I dare
  well say;
For the King of nature may
  Have all at His own will.
  Did not the power of God
  Make Aaron's rod
Bear fruit in one day?

SECOND PROPHET. Truth it is indeed.
FIRST PROPHET. Then look you and read.
SECOND PROPHET. Ah! I perceive the seed
  Whereupon that you spake.
It was for our need
  That He frail nature did take,
And His blood He should shed
  Amends for to make
    For our transgression;
  As it is said in prophecy
  That of the line of Judee
  Should spring a right Messee
  By whom all we
    Shall have redemption.

FIRST PROPHET. Sir, now is the time come,
And the date thereof run,
  Of Ilis nativity.
  SECOND PROPHET. Yet I beseech you heartily
    That ye would show me how
  That this strange novelty
    Were brought unto you.

FIRST PROPHET. This other night so cold,
Hereby upon a wold,
Shepherds watching their fold,
  In the night so far
  To them appeared a star,
  And ever it drew them nar;

Which star they did behold
Brighter, they say, in fold,
  Than the sun so clear
  In his midday sphere,
And they these tidings told.

SECOND PROPHET.   What, secretly?
FIRST PROPHET.   Nay, nay, hardily;
  They made thereof no counsel;
For they sang as loud
As ever they could,
  Praising the King of Israel.

SECOND PROPHET.   Yet do I marvel
  In what pile or castle
    These herdmen did Him see.

FIRST PROPHET.   Neither in halls nor yet in bowers
  Born would He not be,
Neither in castles nor yet in towers
  That seemly were to see;

But at His Father's will,
The prophecy to fulfil,
  Betwixt an ox and an ass
  Jesu, this King, born he was.
Heaven He bring us till!

SECOND PROPHET.   Sir, ah! but when these shepherds
    had seen him there,
Into what place did they repair?
FIRST PROPHET.   Forth they went and glad they were,
  Going they did sing;
With mirth and solace they made good cheer
  For joy of that new tiding;

And after, as I heard them tell,
He rewarded them full well:
He grant them heaven therein to dwell;
  In are they gone with joy and mirth,
And their song it is "Noël."

There the prophets goeth forth and HEROD *cometh in,
and the messenger.*

NUNTIUS.   Faites paix, dominies, barons de grande renom!
Paix, seigneurs, chevaliers de noble puissance!
Paix, gentils hommes, compagnons petits et grands!
Je vous command de garder, trestous, silence!
Paix, tant que votre noble Roi seit ici present!
Que nulle personne ici non fasse point de difference,
N' ici harde de frapper; mais gardez toute patience,—
Mais gardez [a] votre seigneur toute reverence;
Car il est votre Roi tout puissant.
Au nom de lui, paix tous! je vous command,
Et le roi Herod le grand-diable vous emporte!

HEROD.   Qui statis in Jude et Rex Israel,
   And the mightiest conqueror that ever walked on ground;
For I am even he that made both heaven and hell,
   And of my mighty power holdeth up this world round.
   Magog and Madroke, both them did I confound,
And with this bright brand their bones I brake asunder,
That all the wide world on those raps did wonder.

I am the cause of this great light and thunder;
   It is through my fury that they such noise doth make.
My fearful countenance the clouds so doth encumber
   That off-times for dread thereof the very earth doth quake.
   Look, when I with malice this bright brand doth shake,
All the whole world from the north to the south
I may them destroy with one word of my mouth!

To recount unto you mine innumerable substance,
   That were too much for any tongue to tell;
For all the whole Orient is under mine obedience,
   And prince am I of Purgatory and chief captain of hell;
   And those tyrannous traitors by force may I compel,
Mine enemies to vanquish and even to dust them drive,
And with a twinkle of mine eye not one to be left alive.

Behold my countenance and my colour,
   Brighter than the sun in the midst of the day.
Where can you have a more greater succour
   Than to behold my person that is so gay?
   My falcon and my fashion, with my gorgeous array—
He that had the grace alway thereon to think,
Live he might alway without either meat or drink.

And this my triumphant fame most highliest doth abound
   Throughout this world in all regions abroad,
Resembling the favour of that most mighty Mahound;
   From Jupiter by descent and cousin to the great God,
   And named the most renowned King Herod,
Which that all princes hath under subjection,
And all their whole power under my protection.

And therefore, my herald, here, called Calchas,
   Warn thou every port that no ships arrive,
Nor also alien stranger through my realm pass,
   But they for their truage do pay marks five.
     Now speed thee forth hastily,
     For they that will the contrary,
     Upon a gallows hanged shall be,
And, by Mahound, of me they get no grace.

NUNTIUS.   Now, lord and master, in all the hast
   Thy worthy will it shall be wrought,
And thy royal countries shall be past.
   In as short time as can be throught.

HEROD.   Now shall our regions throughout be sought
   In every place both east and west;
If any caitiffs to me be brought,
   It shall be nothing for their best.
   And the while that I do rest,
Trumpets, viols, and other harmony
Shall bless the waking of my majesty.
   Here HEROD *goeth away and the three kings speaketh in the
     street.*

FIRST REX.   Now blessed be God of his sweet sond,
   For yonder a fair bright star I do see!
Now is he comen us among,
   As the prophet said that it should be.

A said there should a babe be born,
   Coming of the root of Jesse,
To save mankind that was forlorn;
   And truly comen now is He.

Reverence and worship to Him will I do,
  As God and man, that all made of nought.
All the prophets accorded and said even so,
  That with his precious blood mankind should be bought.

He grant me grace,
  By yonder star that I see,
And into that place
  Bring me,
That I may Him worship with humility
And see His glorious face.

SECOND REX. Out of my way I deem that I am,
  For tokens of this country can I none see;
Now God, that on earth madest man,
  Send me some knowledge where that I be!

Yonder, me-thinks, a fair bright star I see,
  The which betokeneth the birth of a child
That hither is come to make man free ;
  He born of a maid, and she nothing defiled.

To worship that child is mine intent;
  Forth now will I take my way.
I trust some company God hath me sent,
  For yonder I see a king labour on the way;

Toward him now will I ride.
  Hark! comely King, I you pray,
Into what coast will ye this tide
  Or whither lies your journey?

FIRST REX. To seek a child is mine intent,
Of whom the prophetes hath meant ;
The time is come, now is he sent,
  By yonder star here may [I] see.
SECOND REX.—Sir, I pray you, with your license,
To ride with you unto His presence ;
To Him will I offer frankincense,
  For the Head of all Holy Church shall He be.

THIRD REX.   I ride wandering in wayes wide,
    Over mountains and dales ; I wot not where I am.
Now, King of all Kings, send me such guide
    That I might have knowledge of this country's name.

Ah! yonder I see a sight, by seeming all afar,
    The which betokens some news, as I trow;
As, me-think, a child pearing in a star.
    I trust He be come that shall defend us from woe.

Two Kings yonder I see,
    And to them will I ride
For to have their company ;
    I trust they will me abide.
Hail comely Kings and gent !
Good sirs, I pray you, whither are ye meant?

FIRST REX.   To seek a child is our intent,
    Which betokens yonder star, as ye may see.
SECOND REX.   To Him I purpose this present.
    THIRD REX.   Sirs, I pray you, and that right humbly,
    With you that I may ride in company.
To Almighty God now pray we
That His precious person we may see.

Here HEROD *cometh in again and the messenger saith:*

NUNTIUS.—Hail, lord most of might!
    Thy commandement is right;
    Into thy land is come this night
        Three kings, and with them a great company.
    HEROD.   What make those kings in this country?
    NUNTIUS.   To seek a king and a child, they say.
        HEROD.   Of what age should he be?
        NUNTIUS.   Scant twelve days old fully.

HEROD.   And was he so late born?
NUNTIUS.   Eh, sir, so they showed me, this same day
    in the morn.
HEROD.   Now, in pain of death bring them me beforn.

And therefore, herald, now hie thee in haste,
In all speed that thou were dight,
   Or that those kings the country be past;
Look thou bring them all three before my sight.

And in Jerusalem inquire more of that child;
But I warn thee that thy words be mild,
For there must thou heed and craft wield
How to fordo his power, and those three kings shall be
   beguiled.

NUNTIUS. Lord, I am ready at your bidding,
To serve thee as my lord and king;
For joy thereof, lo, how I spring
With light heart and fresh gambolling,
   Aloft here on this mould!

HEROD. Then speed thee forth hastily,
And look that thou bear thee evenly;
And also, I pray thee heartily,
That thou do commend me
   Both to young and old.

              [*The* Messenger *goes to the* Kings.]

NUNTIUS. Hail, sir kings, in your degree!
  Herod, king of these countries wide,
Desireth to speak with you all three,
  And for your coming he doth abide.

FIRST REX. Sir, at his will we be right bain.
  Hie us, brethren, unto that lord's place;
To speak with him we would be fain;
  That child that we seek, He grant us of His grace!

              [*They go to* HEROD.]

NUNTIUS. Hail, lord without peer!
These three kings here have we brought.
HEROD. Now welcome, sir kings, all in-fere!
But of my bright blee, sirs, abash ye not!

Sir kings, as I understand,
A star hath guided you into my land,
Wherein great hearting ye have found
    By reason of her beams bright.

Wherefore I pray you heartily
The very truth that ye would certify,
How long it is surely
    Since of that star you had first sight.

First Rex.   Sir king, the very truth to say,
    And for to show you as it is best,
This same is even the twelfth day
    Sith it appeared to us to be west.

Herod.   Brethren, then is there no more to say,
But with heart and will keep ye your journey,
And come home by me this same way,
    Of your news that I might know.

You shall triumph in this country,
And with great concord banquet with me,
And that child myself then will I see,
    And honour him also.

Second Rex.   Sir, your commandment we will fulfil,
And humbly obey ourself theretill.
He that wieldeth all things at will
    The ready way us teach,
Sir King, that we may pass your land in peace!
Herod.   Yes, and walk softly even at your own ease.

Your passport for a hundred days
    Here shall you have of clear command,
Our realm to labour any ways
    Here shall you have by special grant.

Third Rex.   Now farewell, king of high degree!
    Humbly of you our leave we take.
Herod.   Then adieu, sir kings all three!
And while I live be bold of me.
There is nothing in this country
    But for your own ye shall it take.
                    [*Exeunt the* Three Kings.]

Now these three kings are gone on their way ;
　Unwisely and unwittily have they all wrought.
When they come again they shall die that same day,
　And thus these vile wretches to death they shall be
　　brought.
　　　Such is my liking.
He that against my laws will hold,
Be he king or kaiser never so bold,
I shall them cast into cares cold,
　And to death I shall them bring.
*There Herod goeth his ways and the three kings come in
again.*

FIRST REX. O blessed God, much is thy might !
Where is this star that gave us light?

SECOND REX. Now kneel we down here in this
　presence,
Beseeching that Lord of high magnificence
That we may see his high excellence,
　If that his sweet will be.

THIRD REX. Yonder, brother, I see the star,
Whereby I know He is not far ;
Therefore, lords, go we nar
　Into this poor place.
　There the Three Kings *goes in to the josen, to* MARY
　and her Child.

FIRST REX. Hail, Lord, that all this world hath
　wrought !
Hail, God and man together in-fere !
For thou hast made all thing of nought,
　Albeit that Thou liest poorly here.
A cupfull [of] gold here have I thee brought,
　In tokening Thou art without peer.

SECOND REX. Hail be Thou, Lord of high magnifi-
　cence !
　In tokening of priesthood and dignity of office,
To Thee I offer a cupfull of incense,
　For it behoveth thee to have such sacrifice.

THIRD REX.   Hail be Thou, Lord long looked for!
  I have brought Thee myrrh for mortality,
In tokening Thou shalt mankind restore
  To life by Thy death upon a tree.

MARY.   God have mercy, kings, of your goodness!
  By the guiding of the Godhead hither are ye sent.
The prevision of my sweet Son your ways home redress,
  And ghostly reward you for your present!
        [*As the* KINGS *go away, they say.*]

FIRST REX.   Sir kings, after our promise,
  Home by Herod I must needs go.
SECOND REX.   Now truly brethren, we can no less,
  But I am so for-watched I wot not what to do.
THIRD REX.   Right so am I; wherefore, I you pray,
  Let all us rest us awhile upon this ground.
FIRST REX.   Brethren, your saying is right well unto
    my pay.
  The grace of that sweet child save us all sound!
        [*While they sleep the* ANGEL *appears.*]

ANGEL.   King of Taurus, Sir Jaspar,
  King of Araby, Sir Balthasar,
Melchior, King of Aginar,
      To you now am I sent.
For dread of Herod, go you west home;
Into those parts when ye come down,
Ye shall be buried with great renown;
  The Holy Ghost thus knowledge hath sent.   [*Exit.*]

FIRST REX.   Awake, sir Kings, I you pray!
  For the voice of an angel I heard in my dream.
SECOND REX.   That is full true that ye do say,
  For he rehearsed our names plain.

THIRD REX.   He bade that we should go down by
    west,
  For dread of Herod's false betray.
FIRST REX.   So for to do it is the best;
  The Child that we have sought guide us the way!

Now farewell, the fairest, of shape so sweet!
And thanked be Jesus of his sond,
That we three together so suddenly should meet,
That dwell so wide and in strange lond,

And here make our presentation
Unto this King's Son, cleansed so clean,
And to his Mother, for our salvation ;
Of much mirth now may we mean,
That we so well have done this oblation.

SECOND REX. Now farewell, Sir Jaspar, brother, to you,
King of Taurus, the most worthy !
Sir Balthasar, also to you I bow,
And I thank you both of your good company
That we together have had.
He that made us to meet on hill,
I thank Him now, and ever I will ;
For now may we go without ill,
And of our offering be full glad.

THIRD REX. Now sith that we must needly go,
For dread of Herod that is so wroth,
Now farewell brother, and brother also,
I take my leave here at you both,
This day on feet.
Now He that made us to meet on plain,
And offer to Mary in her jesayne,
He give us grace in heaven again
All together to meet.

[*They go out, and* HEROD *and his train occupy the pageant.*]

NUNTIUS. Hail King, most worthiest in weed !
Hail, maintainer of courtesy through all this world
wide !
Hail, the most mightiest that ever bestrode a steed !
Hail, most manfullest man in armour man to abide !
Hail in thine honour !
These three kings that forth were sent,
And should have come again before thee here present,
Another way, lord, home they went,
Contrary to thine honour.

HEROD. Another way! Out! out! out!
  Hath those false traitors done me this deed?
I stamp! I stare! I look all about!
  Might I them take I should them burn at a gleed!
I rend! I raw! and now run I wood!
Ah! that these villain traitors hath marred this my
    mood!
  They shall be hanged if I may come them to!
  Here Herod rages in the pageant and in the street also.

Eh! and that kerne of Bethlehem, he shall be
    dead,
  And thus shall I fordo his prophecy.

How say you, sir Knights? is not this the best rede,
That all young children for this should be dead,
    With sword to be slain?
Then shall I Herod live in lede
And all folk me doubt and drede,
  And offer to me both gold, riches and meed;
    Thereto will they be full fain.

FIRST MILES. My lord king, Herod by name,
  Thy words against my will shall be;
To see so many young children die is shame,
  Thesefore counsel thereto gettest thou none of me.

SECOND MILES. Well said, fellow, my truth I plight.
  Sir King, perceive right well you may,
So great a murder to see of young fruit
  Will make a rising in thine own country.

HEROD. A rising? Out! out! out!
    [*There Herod rages again and then saith thus :*]

Out! villain wretches, haro upon you I cry!
  My will utterly look that it be wrought,
Or upon a gallows both you shall die,
  By Mahound most mightiest, that me dear hath
    bought.

FIRST MILES. Now, cruel Herod, sith we shall do this
      deed,
   Your will needfully in this realm must be wrought;
All the children of that age die they must need;
   Now with all my might they shall be upsought.

SECOND MILES. And I will swear here upon your
      bright swerd,
   All the children that I find, slain they shall be;
That make many a mother to weep and be full sore
      aferd,
   In our armour bright when they us see.

HEROD. Now you have sworn, forth that ye go,
   And my will that ye work both by day and night,
And then will I for fain trip like a doe;
   But when they be dead I warn you bring them before
      my sight.
[HEROD *and his train go away, and* JOSEPH *and* MARY
      are, while asleep, addressed by an ANGEL.]

ANGEL. Mary and Joseph, to you, I say,
   Sweet word from the Father I bring you full right;
Out of Bethlehem into Egypt forth go ye the way,
   And with you take the King, full of might,
      For dread of Herod's rede!
JOSEPH. Arise up, Mary, hastily and soon;
   Our Lord's will needs must be done,
      Like as the angel us bade.

MARY. Meekly, Joseph, mine own spouse,
   Toward that country let us repair;
At Egypt to some kind of house,
   God grant us His grace safe to come there!
*Here the women come in with their children, singing
      them ; and* MARY *and* JOSEPH *go away clean.*

FIRST WOMAN. I lull my child, wondrously sweet,
And in mine arms I do it keep,
   Because that it should not cry.
SECOND WOMAN. That Babe that is born in Bethlehem,
      so meek,
   He save my child and me from villainy!

THIRD WOMAN. Be still, be still, my little child!
That Lord of lords save both thee and me!
For Herod hath sworn with wordes wild
    That all young children slain they shall be.

FIRST MILES. Say ye, whither, wives, whither are ye
    away?
What bear you in your arms needs must we see.
If they be man-children, die they must this day,
    For at Herod's will all thing must be.

SECOND MILES. And I in hands once them hent,
    Them for to slay nought will I spare;
We must fulfil Herod's commandement,
    Else be we as traitors and cast all in care.

FIRST WOMAN. Sir knights, of your courtesy,
This day shame not your chivalry,
But on my child have pity
    For my sake in this stead;
For a simple slaughter it were to slo
Or to work such a child woe,
That can neither speak nor go,
    Nor never harm did.

SECOND WOMAN. He that slays my child in sight,
If that my strokes on him may light,
Be he squire or knight,
    I hold him but lost.
See, thou false losenger,
A stroke shalt thou bear me here,
    And spare for no cost.

THIRD WOMAN. Sit he never so high in saddle,
But I shall make his brains addle,
And here with my pot-ladle
    With him will I fight.
I shall lay on him as though I wood were,
With this same womanly gear;
There shall no man steer,
    Whether that he be king or knight.

FIRST MILES.   Who heard ever such a cry
  Of women that their children have lost?
And greatly rebuking chivalry
  Throughout this realm in every coast,
  Which many a man's life is like to cost;
For this great wreak that here is done
I fear much vengeance thereof will come.

SECOND MILES.   Eh! brother, such tales may we not
  tell;
  Wherefore to the king let us go,
For he is like to bear the peril,
  Which was the causer that we did so.
  Yet must they all be brought him to,
With wains and waggons fully freight;
I trow there will be a careful sight.
               [*They go to* HEROD.]

FIRST MILES.   Lo! Herod, King, here mayest thou see
  How many thousands that we have slain.
SECOND MILES.   And needs thy will fulfilled must be;
  There may no man say there-again.
                [*Enter* NUNTIUS.]

NUNTIUS   Herod, King, I shall thee tell
  All thy deeds is come to nought;
This child is gone into Egypt to dwell.
  Lo! sir, in thine own land what wonders ben wrought!

HEROD.   Into Egypt? alas for woe!
  Longer in land here I cannot abide;
Saddle my palfrey, for in haste will I go,
  After yonder traitors now will I ride,
    Them for to slo.
  Now all men hie fast
  Into Egypt in haste!
  All that country will I taste
    Till I may come them to.

Finis ludi de tailors and shearmen.

This matter newly corrected by Robert Croo, the 14th day of March, finished in the year of our Lord God 1534, then being mayor Master Palmer; also Masters of the said Fellowship, Hugh Corbett, Randal Pinkard, and John Baggeley.

These songs belong to the Tailors' and Shearmen's Pageant. The first and the last the shepherds sing, and the second or middlemost the women sing.

Thomas Mawdycke, die decimo tertio Maii, anno domini millesimo quingentesimo nonagesimo primo. Praetor fuit civitatis Conventriae D. Matthaeus Richardson, tunc consules Johannis Whitehead et Thomas Cravener.

SONG 1.

As I out rode this enderes night,
Of three jolly shepherds I saw a sight,
And all about their fold a star shone bright;
   They sang terli, terlow;
  So merrily the shepherds their pipes can blow.

SONG 2.

Lully, lullay, thou little tiny child,
By by, lully, lullay, thou little tiny child
  By by, lully, lullay!

O sisters two,
How may we do,
  For to preserve this day
This poor youngling,
For whom we do sing
  By by, lully, lullay?

Herod the King,
In his raging,
   Charged he hath this day
His men of might,
In his own sight
   All young children to slay,—

That woe is me,
Poor child for thee,
   And ever mourn, and may,
For thy parting,
Neither say nor sing
   By by, lully, lullay.

SONG 3.

Down from heaven, from heaven so high,
Of angels there came a great company,
With mirth and joy and great solemnity,
   They sang terli, terlow,
So merrily the shepherds their pipes can blow.

Everyman.

[From JOHN SKOT's Editions,
c. 1525.]

Everyman.

[From John Skot's Editions, c. 1525.]

Here beginneth a treatise how the High Father of Heaven sendeth
Death to summon every creature to come and give a count of their
lives in this world, and is in manner of a moral play.

MESSENGER.　I pray you all give your audience,
And hear this matter with reverence,
　　By figure a moral play.
'The summoning of Everyman' called it is,
That of our lives and ending shows
　　How transitory we be all day.
This matter is wondrous precious,
But the intent of it is more gracious
　　And sweet to bear away.
This story saith 'man, in the beginning
Look well, and take good heed to the ending,
　　Be you never so gay;
Ye think sin in the beginning full sweet,
Which in the end causeth thy soul to weep,
　　When the body lieth in clay.'
Here shall you see how fellowship and jollity,
Both strength, pleasure, and beauty,
　　Will fade from thee as flower in May;
For ye shall hear how our heaven king
Calleth every man to a general reckoning:
　　Give audience, and hear what he will say.

GOD SPEAKETH.

GOD.　I perceive here in my majesty
How that all creatures be to me unkind,
Living without dread in worldly prosperity.
Of ghostly sight the people be so blind,

Drownèd in sin, they know me not for their God ;
In worldly riches is all their mind.
They fear not my righteousness, that sharp rod ;
   My law that I showed, when I for them died,
They forget clean, and shedding of my blood so red.
I hanged between two thieves, it cannot be denied,
To get them life, I suffered to be dead ;
I healed their feet—with thorns hurt was my head—
I could do no more than I did, truly.
And now I see the people do clean forsake me ;
They use the seven deadly sins damnable ;
As pride, covetise, wrath, and lechery,
Now in the world be made commendable ;
And thus they leave of angels the heavenly company.
Every man liveth so after his own pleasure,
And yet of their life they be not sure.
I see the more that I them forbear
The worse they are from year to year.
All that liveth appaireth fast,
Therefore I will in all the haste
Have a reckoning of every man's person,
For, and I leave the people thus alone
In their life and wicked tempests,
Verily they will become much worse than beasts,
For now one would by envy another up eat ;
Charity they all do clean forget.
I hoped well that every man
In my glory should make his mansion,
And thereto I had them all elect,
But now I see that, like traitors deject,
They thank me not for the pleasure that I to them meant,
Nor yet for their being that I them have lent.
I proffered the people great multitude of mercy,
And few there be that asketh it heartily ;
They be so cumbered with worldly riches
That needs on them I must do justice,
On every man living without fear.
Where **art** thou, Death, thou mighty messenger?

DEATH.   Almighty God, I am here at your will,
Your commandement to fulfil.

GOD. Go thou to Everyman
And show him, in my name,
A pilgrimage he must on him take,
Which he in no wise may escape ;
And that he bring with him a sure reckoning,
Without delay or any tarrying.

DEATH. Lord, I will in the world go run over all,
And truly outsearch both great and small,
Everyman I will beset that liveth beastly,
Out of God's laws, and dreadeth not folly.
He that loveth riches I will strike with my dart,
His sight to blind, and from heaven depart,
Except that alms-deeds be his good friend,
In hell for to dwell, world without end.
Lo, yonder I see Everyman walking !
Full little he thinketh on my coming !
His mind is on fleshly lusts, and his treasure,
And great pain it shall cause him to endure
Before the Lord, heaven king.
Everyman, stand still ! whither art thou going
Thus gaily ? Hast thou thy Maker forgot ?

EVERYMAN. Why askest thou ?
Wouldest thou wot ?

DEATH. Yea, sir, I will show you :
In great haste I am sent to thee,
From God out of his Majesty.

EVERYMAN. What ! sent to me ?

DEATH. Yea, certainly.
Though thou hast forgot Him here,
He thinketh on thee in the heavenly sphere,
As, or we depart, thou shalt know.

EVERYMAN. What desireth God of me ?

DEATH. That shall I shew thee :
A reckoning he will needs have,
Without any longer respite.

EVERYMAN.   To give a reckoning longer leisure I crave ;
This blind matter troubleth my wit.

DEATH.   On thee thou must take a long journey,
Therefore thy book of count with thee thou bring—
For turn again thou cannot by no way—
And look thou be sure of thy reckoning ;
For before God shalt thou answer, and shew
Thy many bad deeds, and good but a few—
How thou hast sped thy life, and in what wise—
Before the chief Lord of Paradise.
Have ado that we were in that way,
For wot thou well thou shalt make none attorney.

EVERYMAN.   Full unready I am such reckoning to give,
I know thee not ; what messenger art thou ?

DEATH.   I am Death, that no man dreadeth,
For every man I rest, and none spareth ;
For it is God's commandement
That all to me should be obedient.

EVERYMAN.   O Death, thou comest when I had thee
     least in mind !
In thy power it lieth me to save ;
Yet of my good will I give thee, if ye will be kind,
Yea, a thousand pound shalt thou have,
And defer this matter till another day.

DEATH.   Everyman, it may not be by no way :
I set not by gold, silver, nor riches,
Ne by pope, emperor, king, duke, ne princes ;
For, and I would receive giftes great,
All the world I might get—
All my custom is clean contrary ;
I give thee no respite ; come hence and not tarry.

EVERYMAN.   Alas ! shall I have no longer respite ?
I may say Death giveth no warning.
To think on thee it maketh my heart sick,
For all unready is my book of reckoning.

But twelve years, and I might have abiding,
My counting book I would make so clear
That my reckoning I should not need to fear;
Wherefore, Death, I pray thee for God's mercy,
Spare me, till I be provided of remedy.

DEATH.   Thee availeth not to cry, weep, and pray,
But haste thee lightly that thou were gone the journey,
And prove thy friendes if thou can;
For wot you well the tide abideth no man,
And in the world each living creature,
For Adam's sin, must die of Nature.

EVERYMAN.   Death, if I should this pilgrimage take,
And my reckoning surely make,
Show me, for saint charity,
Should I not come again shortly?

DEATH.   No, Everyman; and thou be once there,
Thou must never more come here,
Trust me, verily!

EVERYMAN.   Gracious God, in high seat celestial,
Have mercy on me in this most need!
Shall I have no company, from this vale terrestrial,
Of mine acquaintance, that way me to lead?

DEATH.   Yea, if any be so hardy
That would go with thee, and bear thee company.
Hie thee that thou were gone to God's Magnificence
Thy reckoning to give before His presence!
What! weenest thou thy life is given thee,
And thy worldly goods also?

EVERYMAN.   I had weened so, verily!

DEATH.   Nay, nay! it was but lent thee;
For as soon as thou art gone
Another a while shall have it, and then go therefrom
Even as thou hast done.
Everyman, thou art mad! that hast thy wittes five,
And here on earth will not amend thy life!
For suddenly I do come!

EVERYMAN.   Oh, wretched caitiff! whither shall I
     flee,
That I might scape this endless sorrow?
Now, gentle Death, spare me till to-morrow,
That I may amend me
With good advisement.

DEATH.   Nay, thereto I will not consent,
Nor no man will I respite,
But to the heart suddenly I shall smite,
Without any advisement.
And now out of sight I will me hie;
See thou make thee ready shortly,
For thou may'st say this is the day
That no man living may scape away.

EVERYMAN.   Alas! I may well weep with sighes
     deep!
Now have I no manner of company
To help me in my journey, and me to keep;
And also my writing is full unready.
How shall I do now for to excuse me?
I would to God I had never be gete!
To my soul a great profit it had be,
For now I fear pains huge and great.
The time passeth—Lord, help, that all wrought!
For though I mourn it availeth nought;
The day passeth and is almost ago—
I wot not well what to do—
To whom were I best my complaint to make?
What and I to Fellowship thereof spake,
And showed him of this sudden chance?
For in him is all mine affiance.
We have in the world, so many a day,
Been good friends in sport and play;
I see him yonder certainly!
I trust that he will bear me company;
Therefore to him will I speak to ease my sorrow:
Well met, good Fellowship, and good morrow!

FELLOWSHIP *speaketh.*

FELLOW.   Everyman, good morrow! by this day,
Sir, why lookest thou so piteously?
If anything be amiss, I pray thee, me say,
That I may help to remedy.

EVERYMAN.   Yea, good Fellowship, yea,
I am in great jeopardy!

FELLOW.   My true friend, show to me your mind;
I will not forsake thee unto my life's end—
In the way of good company.

EVERYMAN.   That is well spoken, and lovingly!

FELLOW.   Sir, I must needs know your heaviness;
I have pity to see you in any distress!
If any have you wronged, ye shall revengèd be,
Though I on the ground be slain for thee,
Though that I know before that I should die!

EVERYMAN.   Verily, Fellowship, gramercy!

FELLOW.   Tush! by thy thanks I set not a straw!
Show me your grief, and say no more.

EVERYMAN.   If I my heart should to you break,
And then you to turn your mind from me,
And would not me comfort, when you hear me speak,
Then should I ten times sorrier be.

FELLOW.   Sir, I say as I will do in deed.

EVERYMAN.   Then be you a good friend at need!
I have found you true here before.

FELLOW.   And so ye shall evermore;
For in faith, and thou go to hell
I will not forsake thee by the way!

EVERYMAN.   Ye speak like a good friend; I believe
   you well;
I shall deserve it, and I may.

FELLOW. I speak of no deserving, by this day !
For he that will say, and nothing do,
Is not worthy with good company to go ;
Therefore show me the grief of your mind,
As to your friend most loving and kind.

EVERYMAN. I shall show you how it is :
Commanded I am to go a journey—
A long way, hard and dangerous—
And give a strait count, without delay,
Before the high judge Adonay ;
Wherefore, I pray you, bear me company
As ye have promised, in this journey.

FELLOW. That is matter indeed ! promise is duty ;
But and I should take such a voyage on me,
I know it well it should be to my pain ;
Also it maketh me afeard, certain.
But let us take counsel here as we can,
For your words would fear a strong man.

EVERYMAN. Why ! ye said if I had need,
Ye would me never forsake, quick ne dead,
Though it were to hell, truly !

FELLOW. So I said, certainly ;
But such pleasures be set aside, the sooth to say,
And also, if we took such a journey,
When should we come again ?

EVERYMAN. Nay, never again till the Day of Doom.

FELLOW. In faith, then will not I come there ;
Who hath you these tidings brought ?

EVERYMAN. Indeed, Death was with me here.

FELLOW. Now, by God that all hath bought,
If Death were the messenger,
For no man that is living to-day
I will not go that loathsome journey,
Not for the father that begat me !

EVERYMAN. Ye promised me otherwise, pardie!

FELLOW. I wot well I said so, truly,
And yet if thou wilt eat and drink and make good cheer,
Or haunt to women, that lusty company,
I would not forsake you while the day is clear,
Trust me verily!

EVERYMAN. Yea, thereto ye would be ready,
To go to mirth, solace, and play;
Your mind to folly will sooner apply
Than to bear me company in my long journey.

FELLOW. Nay, in good faith, I will not that way,
But and thou wilt murder, or any man kill,
In that I will help thee with a good will.

EVERYMAN. Oh, that is a simple advice, indeed!
Gentle fellow, help me in my necessity!
We have loved long, and now I need,
And now, gentle Fellowship, remember me.

FELLOW. Whether ye have loved me or no,
By Saint John I will not with thee go!

EVERYMAN. Yet, I pray thee, take the labour and do so
   much for me
To bring me forward, for saint charity,
And comfort me till I come without the town.

FELLOW. Nay, and thou would give me a new gown
I will not one foot with thee go;
But and thou had tarried I would not ha' left thee so.
And as now, God speed thee in thy journey!
For from thee I will depart as fast as I may.

EVERYMAN. Whither away, Fellowship? wilt thou forsake me?

FELLOW. Yea, by my fay; to God I betake thee!

EVERYMAN. Farewell, good Fellowship! for thee my
heart is sore.

Adieu! for I shall never see thee no more.

FELLOW.   In faith, Everyman, farewell now at the end!
For you I will remember that parting is mourning.

EVERYMAN.   Alack! shall we thus depart indeed?
Oh Lady, help! without any more comfort,
Lo! Fellowship forsaketh me in my most need.
For help in this world whither shall I resort?
Fellowship here before with me would merry make,
And now little sorrow for me doth he take.
It is said, in prosperity men friends may find,
Which in adversity be full unkind
Now whither for succour shall I flee,
Sith that Fellowship hath forsaken me?
To my kinnesmen I will, truly,
Praying them to help me in my necessity.
I believe that they will do so,
For kind will creep where it may not go.
I will go say, for yonder I see them go:
Where be ye now, my friends and kinnesmen?

KINDRED.   Here be we now at your commandement:
Cousin, I pray you, show us your intent
In any wise, and do not spare.

COUSIN.   Yea, Everyman, and us to declare
If ye be disposed to go any whither,
For wot ye well, we will live and die together.

KINDRED.   In wealth and woe we will with you hold,
For over his kin a man may be bold.

EVERYMAN.   Gramercy! my friends and kinsmen kind:
Now shall I show you the grief of my mind.
I was commanded by a messenger,
That is a high king's chief officer;
He bade me go a pilgrimage to my pain,
But I know well I shall never come again.
Also I must give reckoning strait,
For I have a great enemy that hath me in wait,
Which intendeth me for to hinder.

KINDRED. What account is that which ye must render?
That would I know.

EVERYMAN. Of all my works I must show,
How I have lived and my dayes spent ;
Also of ill deeds that I have used
In my time, sith life was me lent,
And of all virtues that I have refused ;
Therefore, I pray you, go thither with me,
To help to make mine account, for saint charity!

COUSIN. What! to go thither? is that the matter?
Nay, Everyman, I had liefer fast, bread and water,
All this five year and more.

EVERYMAN. Alas, that ever I was born!
For now shall I never be merry
If that you forsake me.

KINDRED. Ah, sir, what! ye be a merry man!
Take good heart to you, and make no moan ;
But one thing I warn you—by Saint Anne,
As for me, ye shall go alone!

EVERYMAN. My cousin, will you not with me go?

COUSIN. No, by our Lady! I have the cramp in my
toe!
Trust not to me, for so God me speed,
I will deceive you in your most need!

KINDRED. It availeth not us to 'tice;
Ye shall have my maid, with all my heart!
She loveth to go to feasts, there to be nice,
And to dance, and abroad to start ;
I will give her leave to help you in that journey,
If that you and she may agree.

EVERYMAN. Now show me the very effect of your mind :
Will you go with me or abide behind?

KINDRED. Abide behind? Yea, that will I, and I may,
Therefore farewell, till another day!

EVERYMAN. How should I be merry or glad?
For fair promises men to me do make,
But when I have most need they me forsake.
I am deceived—that maketh me sad.

COUSIN. Cousin Everyman, farewell now!
For verily I will not go with you.
Also of my own an unready reckoning
I have to account, therefore I make tarrying.
Now God keep thee! for now I go.

EVERYMAN. Ah, Jesus! is all come hereto?
Lo! fair words maketh fools fain!
They promise, and nothing will do, certain!
My kinnesmen promised me faithfully
For to abide with me steadfastly,
And now fast away do they flee;
Even so Fellowship promised me.
What friend were best me of to provide?
I lose my time here longer to abide.
Yet in my mind a thing there is—
All my life I have loved riches;
If that my Good now help me might,
It would make my heart full light.
I will speak to him in this distress:
Where art thou, my Goods and Riches?

GOODS. Who calleth me? Everyman? what! hast thou
    haste?
I lie here in corners, trussed and piled so high,
And in chests I am locked full fast,
Also sacked in bags—thou mayst see with thine eye—
I cannot stir; in packs low I lie.
What would ye have? lightly me say.

EVERYMAN. Come hither, Good, in all the haste thou
    may,
For of counsel I must desire thee.

GOODS. Sir, and ye in the world have trouble or adver-
    sity,
Then can I help you to remedy shortly.

EVERYMAN.   It is another disease that grieveth me;
In this world it is not—I tell so—
I am sent for, another way to go,
To give a strait account general
Before the highest Jupiter of all.
And all my life I have had joy and pleasure in thee,
Therefore, I pray thee, go with me;
For peradventure thou mayest, before God Almighty,
My reckoning help to clean and purify;
For it is said, ever among,
That money maketh all right that is wrong.

GOODS.   Nay, Everyman, I sing another song!
I follow no man in such voyages,
For and I went with thee,
Thou should'st fare much the worse for me;
For because on me thou did set thy mind,
Thy reckoning I have made blotted and blind,
That thine account thou cannot make truly,
And that hast thou for the love of me.

EVERYMAN.   That would grieve me full sore,
When I should come to that fearful answer.
Up! let us go thither together!

GOODS.   Nay, not so! I am too brittle, I may not
  endure;
I will follow no man one foot, be thou sure.

EVERYMAN.   Alas! I have thee loved, and had great
  pleasure
All my life's days on good and treasure.

GOODS.   That is to thy damnation, without leasing,
For my love is contrary to the love everlasting;
But if thou had me loved moderately, during,
As to the poor to give part for me,
Then shouldest thou not in this dolour be,
Nor in this great sorrow and care.

EVERYMAN.   Lo now! I was deceived or I was ware!
And all I may wyte my spending of time.

T   12

GOODS.   What! weenest thou that I am thine?

EVERYMAN.   I had weened so.

GOODS.   Nay, Everyman, I say no!
As for a while I was lent thee,
A season thou hast had me in prosperity.
My conditions is man's soul to kill;
If I save one, a thousand I do spill.
Weenest thou that I will follow thee
From this world? nay, verily!

EVERYMAN.   I had weened otherwise.

GOODS.   Therefore to thy soul Good is a thief;
For when thou art dead, this is my guise—
Another to deceive, in the same wise
As I have done thee, and all to his soul's reprief.

EVERYMAN.   Oh false Good, cursed thou be!
Thou traitor to God, thou hast deceived me
And caught me in thy snare!

GOODS.   Marry! thou brought thyself in care,
Whereof I am glad;
I must needs laugh, I cannot be sad.

EVERYMAN.   Ah, Good, thou hast had my heartly love!
I gave thee that which should be the Lord's above.
But wilt thou not go with me indeed?
I pray thee truth to say.

GOODS.   No, so God me speed!
Therefore farewell, and have good day!

EVERYMAN.   Oh, to whom shall I make my moan,
For to go with me in that heavy journey?
First Fellowship, he said he would with me go—
His wordes were very pleasant and gay—
But afterward he left me alone;
Then spake I to my kinsmen, all in despair,
And also they gave me wordes fair—

They lacked no fair speaking—
But all forsake me in the ending.
Then went I to my Goods, that I loved best,
In hope to have comfort, but there had I least,
For my Goods sharply did me tell
That he bringeth many in hell.
Then of myself I was ashamed,
And so I am worthy to be blamed:
Thus may I well myself hate.
Of whom shall I now counsel take?
I think that I shall never speed
Till that I go to my Good Deed,
But alas! she is so weak
That she can neither go nor speak,
Yet will I venture on her now:
My Good Deeds, where be you?

GOOD DEEDS. Here I lie, cold in the ground;
Thy sins have me so sore bound
That I cannot stir.

EVERYMAN. Oh, Good Deeds, I stand in fear!
I must you pray of counsel,
For help now should come right well.

GOOD DEEDS. Everyman, I have understanding
That thou art summoned account to make
Before Messias, of Jerusalem King;
And you do by me, that journey with you will I take.

EVERYMAN. Therefore I come to you, my moan to make;
I pray thee to go with me.

GOOD DEEDS. I would full fain, but I cannot stand,
verily!

EVERYMAN. Why? is there anything on you fall?

GOOD DEEDS. Yea, sir; I may thank you of all.
If ye had perfectly cheered me,
Your book of account full ready now had be.

Look! the books of your workes and deedes eke,
Behold how they lie under the feet,
To your soules heaviness!

EVERYMAN.   Our Lord Jesus helpe me!
For one letter herein can I not see.

GOOD DEEDS.   There is a blind reckoning in time of distress.

EVERYMAN.   Good Deeds, I pray you help me in this need,
Or else I am for ever damned indeed;
Therefore help me to make my reckoning
Before the Redeemer of all thing,
That King is, and was, and ever shall.

GOOD DEEDS.   Everyman, I am sorry of your fall,
And fain would I help you, and I were able.

EVERYMAN.   Good Deeds, your counsel I pray you give me.

GOOD DEEDS.   That shall I do, verily!
Though that on my feet I may not go,
I have a sister, that shall with you also,
Called Knowledge, which shall with you abide,
To help you to make that dreadful reckoning.

KNOWLEDGE.   Everyman, I will go with thee and be thy guide,
In thy most need to go by thy side.

EVERYMAN.   In good condition I am now in everything
And am wholly content with this good thing:
Thanked be God, my Creator!

GOOD DEEDS.   And when he hath brought thee there
Where thou shalt heal thee of thy smart,
Then go thou with thy reckoning and thy good deeds together,
For to make thee joyful at the heart,
Before the Blessed Trinity.

EVERYMAN. My good Deeds, I thank thee heartily;
I am well content, certainly,
With your wordes sweet.

KNOWLEDGE. Now go we thither, lovingly,
To confession, that cleansing river.

EVERYMAN. For joy I weep! I would we were there!
But I pray you to instruct me by intellection,
Where dwelleth that holy virtue, Confession?

KNOWLEDGE. In the house of salvation;
We shall find him, in that place,
That shall us comfort, by God's grace.
Lo! this is Confession; kneel down and ask mercy,
For he is in good conceit with God Almighty.

EVERYMAN. Oh glorious fountain, that all uncleanness
    doth clarify,
Wash from me the spots of vices unclean,
That on me no sin may be seen!
I come with Knowledge, for my redemption,
Redeemed with heart, and full of contrition;
For I am commanded a pilgrimage to take,
And great accounts before God to make.
Now I pray you, Shrift, mother of salvation,
Help my Good Deeds, for my piteous exclamation!

CONFESSION. I know your sorrow well, Everyman;
Because with Knowledge ye come to me
I will you comfort, as well as I can,
And a precious jewel I will give thee,
Called penance, voider of adversity;
Therewith shall your body chastised be,
With abstinence, and perseverance in God's service.
Here shall you receive that scourge of me
Which is penance strong, that ye must endure,
To remember thy Saviour was scourged for thee
With sharp scourges, and suffered it patiently.
So must thou, or thou scape that painful pilgrimage:
Knowledge, keep him in this voyage,

And by that time Good Deeds will be with thee ;
But in any wise be sure of mercy—
For your time draweth fast—and ye will saved be ;
Ask God mercy and He will grant, truly.
When with the scourge of penance man doth him bind,
The oil of forgiveness then shall he find.

EVERYMAN.   Thanked be God for His gracious work !
For now I will my penance begin :
This hath rejoiced and lighted my heart,
Though the knots be painful and hard within.

KNOWLEDGE.   Everyman, your penance look that ye
    fulfil,
What pain that ever it to you be,
And Knowledge will give you counsel at will,
How your accounts ye shall make clearly.

EVERYMAN.   Oh eternal God ! Oh heavenly figure !
O way of righteousness !   Oh goodly vision !
Which descended down in a virgin pure,
Because He would every man to redeem,
Which Adam forfeited by his disobedience ;
Oh blessed Godhead elect and high divine,
Forgive me my grievous offence !
Here I cry thee mercy in this presence.
Oh Ghostly treasure ! O Ransomer and Redeemer
Of all the world !   Hope and Conductor !
Mirror of joy and Founder of mercy,
Which illumineth heaven and earth thereby,
Hear my clamorous complaint, though it late be !
Receive my prayers, of thy benignity !
Though I be a sinner most abominable,
Yet let my name be written in Moses' table !
Oh Mary ! pray to the Maker of all thing,
Me for to help at my ending !
And save me from the power of my enemy,
For death assaileth me strongly ;
And, Lady, that I may by means of thy prayer,
Of thy Son's glory to be partaker,
By the means of His Passion, I it crave :

I beseech you, help my soul to save!
Knowledge, give me the scourge of penance;
My flesh therewith shall give a quittance—
I will now begin, if God give me grace.

KNOWLEDGE.   Everyman, God give you time and
    space!
Thus I bequeath you in the hands of our Saviour;
Thus may you make your reckoning sure.

EVERYMAN.   In the name of the Holy Trinity,
My body sore punished shall be!
Take this, body, for the sin of the flesh,
Also thou delightest to go gay and fresh,
And in way of damnation thou did me bring,
Therefore suffer now strokes and punishing!
Now of penance I will wade the water clear,
To save me from hell and from the fire.

GOOD DEEDS.   I thank God, now I can walk and go!
I am delivered of my sickness and woe;
Therefore with Everyman I will go, and not spare;
His good works I will help him to declare.

KNOWLEDGE.   Now, Everyman, be merry and glad!
Your Good Deeds do come, ye may not be sad.
Now is your Good Deeds whole and sound,
Going upright upon the ground.

EVERYMAN.   My heart is light, and shall be evermore:
Now will I smite faster than I did before.

GOOD DEEDS.   Everyman, pilgrim, my special friend,
Blessed be thou without end!
For thee is prepared the eternal glory.
Ye have me made whole and sound,
Therefore I will abide with thee in every stound.

EVERYMAN.   Welcome, my Good Deeds! now I hear
    thy voice
I weep for very sweetness of love.

KNOWLEDGE. Be no more sad, but ever more rejoice ;
God seeth thy living in His throne above.
Put on this garment to thy behove,
Which with your tears is now all wet,
Lest before God it be unsweet
When you to your journey's end come shall.

EVERYMAN. Gentle Knowledge, what do ye it call?

KNOWLEDGE. It is the garment of sorrow—
From pain it will you borrow—
Contrition it is,
That getteth forgiveness,
It pleaseth God passing well.

GOOD DEEDS. Everyman, will you wear it for your heal?

EVERYMAN. Now blessed be Jesu, Mary's Son !
For now have I on true contrition ;
And let us go now without tarrying.
Good Deeds, have we clear our reckoning?

GOOD DEEDS. Yea, indeed, I have it here.

EVERYMAN. Then I trust we need not fear.
Now friends, let us not part in twain.

KINDRED. Nay, Everyman, that will we not, certain !

GOOD DEEDS. Yet must thou lead with thee
Three persons of great might.

EVERYMAN. Who should they be?

GOOD DEEDS. Discretion and Strength they hight,
And thy Beauty may not abide behind.

KNOWLEDGE. Also ye must call to mind
Your five wits, as for your councillors.

GOOD DEEDS. You must have them ready at all hours.

EVERYMAN. How shall I get them hither?

KINDRED. You must call them all together,
And they will hear you, incontinent.

EVERYMAN. My friends, come hither and be present!
Discretion, Strength, my Five Wits, and Beauty!

BEAUTY. Here are your will me be ready;
What would ye that we should do?

GOOD DEEDS. That ye would with Everyman go,
And help him in his pilgrimage.
Advise you—will ye with him or not, in that voyage?

STRENGTH. We will bring him all thither,
To his help and comfort, ye may believe me.

DISCRETION. So will we go with him all together.

EVERYMAN. Almighty God, loved may thou be!
I give thee laud that I have hither brought
Strength, Discretion, Beauty, and Five Wits,—lack I
    nought—
And my Good Deeds, with Knowledge clear,
All be in company at my will here;
I desire no more to my business.

STRENGTH. And I, Strength, will stand by you in
    distress,
Though thou wouldest in battle fight on the ground.

FIVE WITS. And though it were through the world
    round,
We will not depart, for sweet nor sour.

BEAUTY. No more will I, unto death's hour,
Whatsoever thereof befall.

DISCRETION. Everyman, advise you first of all;
Go with a good advisement and deliberation.
We all give you virtuous monition.

EVERYMAN.   That all shall be well.
My friendes, hearken what I will tell:
I pray God reward you in His heavenly sphere!
Now hearken, all that be here,
For I will make my testament
Here before you all present.
In alms half my goods I will give with my handes twain
In the way of charity, with good intent;
And the other half still shall remain
In quiet, to be returned there it ought to be.
This I do in despite of the fiend of hell,
To go quite out of his peril,
Ever after and this day.

KNOWLEDGE.   Everyman, hearken what I say:
Go to priesthood, I you advise,
And receive of him, in any wise,
The Holy Sacrament and ointment together;
Then shortly see ye turn again hither:
We will all abide you here.

FIVE WITS.   Yea, Everyman, hie you that ye ready were
There is no emperor, king, duke, ne baron,
That of God hath commission,
As hath the least priest in the world being;
For of the Blessed Sacraments, pure and benign,
He beareth the keys and thereof hath he cure;
For man's redemption it is ever sure,
Which God, for our soul's medicine,
Gave us out of his heart with great pain.
Here in this transitory life, for thee and me,
The Blessed Sacraments Seven there be;
Baptism, Confirmation, with Priesthood good,
And the Sacrament of God's precious flesh and blood;
Marriage, the Holy Extreme Unction, and Penance.
These seven be good to have in remembrance,
Gracious sacraments of high divinity.

EVERYMAN.   Fain would I receive that Holy Body,
And meekly to my ghostly father I will go.

FIVE WITS.   Everyman, that is the best that ye can do :
God will you to salvation bring,
For good priesthood exceedeth all other thing.
To us holy scripture they do teach,
And converteth man from sin, heaven to reach.
God hath to them more power given
Than to any angel that is in heaven.
With five words he may consecrate,
God's body in flesh and blood to make,
And handleth his maker between his hands.
The priest bindeth and unbindeth all bands
Both in earth and in heaven.
Thou ministers all the sacraments seven—
Though we kiss thy feet thou were worthy—
Thou art surgeon that cureth sin deadly.
No remedy we find under God
But all only priesthood.
Everyman, God gave priests that dignity,
And setteth them in his stead, among us to be ;
Thus be they above angels in degree.

KNOWLEDGE.   If priests be good, it is so surely ;
But when Jesus hung on the cross with great smart,
There he gave, out of his blessed heart,
The same sacrament, in great torment ;
He sold them not to us, that Lord omnipotent :
Therefore Saint Peter the Apostle doth say,
That Jesus' curse hath all they
Which God their Saviour do buy or sell,
Or they for any money do take or tell.
Sinful priests giveth the sinners example bad ;
Their children sitteth by other men's fires, I have
   heard,
And some haunteth women's company,
With unclean life, as lusts of lechery :
These be with sin made blind.

FIVE WITS.   I trust to God no such may we find !
Therefore let us priesthood honour,
And follow their doctrine for our souls' succour.

We be their sheep, and they shepherds be,
By whom we all be kept in surety.
Peace! for yonder I see Everyman come,
Which hath made true satisfaction.

GOOD DEEDS.   Me-thinketh it is he indeed.

EVERYMAN.   Now Jesus Christ be your alder speed!
I have received the Sacrament for my redemption,
And thou, mine Extreme Unction:
Blessed be all they that counselled me to take it!
And now, friends, let us go without longer respite—
I thank God that ye have tarried so long—
Now set, each of you, on this rod your hand,
And shortly follow me:
I go before there I would be; God be our guide!

STRENGTH.   Everyman, we will not from you go
Till ye have gone this voyage long.

DISCRETION.   I, Discretion, will bide by you also.

KNOWLEDGE.   And though this pilgrimage be never so
   strong,
I will never part you from.
Everyman, I will be as sure by thee
As ever I did by Judas Macchabe.

EVERYMAN.   Alas! I am so faint I may not stand!
My limbs under me do fold.
Friends, let us not turn again to this land,
Not for all the worldes gold;
For into this cave must I creep,
And turn to the earth, and there to sleep.

BEAUTY.   What! into this grave, alas!?

EVERYMAN.   Yea, there shall you consume, more and
   less.

BEAUTY.   And what! should I smother here?

EVERYMAN. Yea, by my faith, and never more appear.
In this world live no more we shall.
But in heaven, before the highest Lord of all.

BEAUTY. I cross out all this—adieu, by Saint John!
I take my cap in my lap and am gone.

EVERYMAN. What, Beauty! whither will ye?

BEAUTY. Peace! I am deaf! I look not behind me!
Not and thou would give me all the gold in thy chest.

EVERYMAN. Alas! whereto may I trust?
Beauty goeth fast away and from me;
She promised with me to live and die.

STRENGTH. Everyman, I will thee also forsake and
deny;
Thy game liketh me not at all.

EVERYMAN. Why! then ye will forsake me all!
Sweet Strength, tarry a little space.

STRENGTH. Nay, sir, by the Rood of Grace!
I will hie me from thee fast,
Though thou weep till thy heart brast.

EVERYMAN. Ye would ever bide by me, ye said.

STRENGTH. Yea, I have you far enough conveyed:
Ye be old enough, I understand,
Your pilgrimage to take on hand—
I repent me that I hither came.

EVERYMAN. Strength, you to displease I am to blame;
Will you break promise, that is debt?

STRENGTH. In faith I care not.
Thou art but a fool to complain—
You spend your speech and waste your brain—
Go, thrust thee into the ground!

EVERYMAN. I had weened surer I should you have, found:
He that trusteth in his Strength,
She him deceiveth at the length.
Both Strength and Beauty forsaketh me,
Yet they promised me, fair and lovingly.

DISCRETION. Everyman, I will after Strength be gone;
As for me, I will leave you alone.

EVERYMAN. Why Discretion, will ye forsake me?

DISCRETION. Yea, in faith, I will go from thee,
For when Strength goeth before
I follow after, evermore.

EVERYMAN. Yet I pray thee, for the love of the Trinity
Look in my grave once piteously!

DISCRETION. Nay, so nigh I will not come!
Farewell, everyone!

EVERYMAN. Oh, all thing faileth save God alone—
Beauty, Strength, and Discretion—
For when Death bloweth his blast
They all run from me full fast.

FIVE WITS. Everyman, of thee now my leave I take;
I will follow the others, for here I thee forsake.

EVERYMAN. Alas! then may I wail and weep.
For I took you for my best friend!

FIVE WITS. I will no longer thee keep;
Now farewell, and there an end!

EVERYMAN. Oh Jesus, help! all hath forsaken me.

GOOD DEEDS. Nay, Everyman, I will bide with the;
I will not forsake thee, indeed—
Thou shalt find me a good friend at need.

EVERYMAN.   Gramercy, Good Deeds! now may I true
    friends see!
They have forsaken me, everyone;
I loved them better than my Good Deeds alone.
Knowledge will ye forsake me also?

KNOWLEDGE.   Yea, Everyman, when ye to death do go,
But not yet, for no manner of danger.

EVERYMAN.   Gramercy, Knowledge with all my heart!

KNOWLEDGE.   Nay, yet I will not from hence depart
Till I see where ye shall become.

EVERYMAN.   Me-thinketh, alas, that I must be gone
To make my reckoning, and my debtes pay,
For I see my time is nigh spent away.
Take example, all ye that this do hear or see,
How they that I loved best do forsake me,
Except my Good Deeds, that bideth truly.

GOOD DEEDS.   All earthly thing is but vanity:
Beauty, Strength, and Discretion do man forsake—
Foolish friends and kinsmen that fair spake—
All fleeth save Good Deeds, and that am I.

EVERYMAN.   Have mercy on me, God most mighty!
And stand by me, thou mother and maid, Holy Mary!

GOOD DEEDS.   Fear not, I will speak for thee.

EVERYMAN.   Here I cry God mercy!

GOOD DEEDS.   Short our end and minish our pain!
Let us go and never come again.

EVERYMAN.   Into thy hands, Lord, my soul I commend!
Receive it, Lord, that it be not lost:
As thou me boughtest so me defend,
And save me from the fiendes boast,
That I may appear with that blessed host
That shall be savèd at the Doom,
(In manus tuas) of mightes most,
For ever (commendo spiritum meum).

KNOWLEDGE.　Now hath he suffered that we all shall
　　endure;
The Good Deeds shall make all sure.
Now hath he made ending—
Me-thinketh that I hear angels sing,
And make great joy and melody,
Where Everyman's soul shall received be.

ANGEL.　Come excellent elect spouse to Jesu!
Here above thou shalt go
Because of thy singular virtue.
Now thy soul is taken thy body fro,
Thy reckoning is crystal clear.
Now shalt thou into the heavenly sphere,
Unto the which all ye shall come
That liveth well, before the day of Doom.

DOCTOR.　This memorial men may have in mind:
Ye hearears, take it of worth, old and young,
And forsake pride, for he deceiveth you in the end;
And remember beauty, five wits, strength and discretion,
They all at the last do every man forsake,
Save his good deeds, there doth he take.
But beware!　for and they be small,
Before God he hath no help at all.
None excuse may be there for every man,
Alas!　how shall he do then?
For after death amends may no man make.
For then mercy and pity doth him forsake.
If his reckoning be not clear when he do come,
God will say (ite maledicti in ignem eternum)
And he that hath his account whole and sound,
High in heaven he shall be crowned.
Unto the which place God bring us all thither,
That we may live, body and soul, together.
Thereto help the Trinity!
Say ye, for Saint Charity,
　　　　　　　　　Amen!

Pleadings in
A Theatrical Lawsuit.
Temp. H ENRY VIII.

[From the Records of the Court of
Requests.]

Pleadings in a Theatrical Lawsuit.

From the Records of the Court of Requests.

John Rastell *v.* Henry Walton.

I

Umbly complaineth unto your gracious Highness your poor orator and humble subject John Rastell, that where your said orator delivered to one Henry Walton certain parcels of stuff and goods to the value of 20 marks, safely to keep to the use of your said orator, that is to say, a player's garment of green sarcenet lined with red tuke and with roman letters stitched upon it of blue and red sarcenet, and another garment paned with blue and green sarcenet lined with red buckram, and another garment paned likewise and lined as the other, with a cape furred with white cats, and another garment paned with yellow, green, blue, and red sarcenet, and lined with red buckram. Another garment for a priest to play in, of red Say, and a garment of red and green Say, paned and guarded with gold skins, and fustians of Naples black, and sleeved with red, green, yellow, and blue sarcenet. And another garment, spangled, of blue satin of Bruges, and lined with green sarcenet. Also two old short garments, paned of satin Bruges and of sarcenet of divers colours in the bodies. Also a woman's garment of green and blue sarcenet, chequered and lined with red buckram, also two caps of yellow and red sarcenet, and two curtains of green and yellow sarcenet. Also two long broad pieces of blue linen cloth, with lyre in them. Also three pieces of open silvered linen cloths; also one

long broad piece of red buckram. Which said stuff and
goods the said Walton promised to deliver again to your
said orator, whensoever he should be by your said orator
thereto required. Which said stuff and goods, after the
said delivery to him made, the said Walton occupied at his
pleasure, by the space of half a year and more, during the
time that your said orator was in the parts beyond the sea,
in France. After whose coming home your said orator
demanded of the said Walton relivery of the said stuff and
goods, to whom the said Walton answered and said that
he would bring him home the said goods and stuff, yet
that notwithstanding he brought to him no part thereof, but
drove him forth from time to time, by the space of two or
three weeks, during which time the said Walton, unknown
to your said orator, which was every day continually in the
said city, and constantly in company with the said Walton,
craftily, falsely, by the subtle advice and counsel of a
clerk of the Mayor's Court in the City of London, and
by a Sergeant of the same Court, entered a false feigned
plaint, put in bill in the said Court, against your said orator,
supposing that your said orator should owe to the said
Walton 40 shillings stirling, wherein indeed your said orator
owed him never a penny, and by the custom of the said
City made attachment of the said goods and stuff being
in his own hands, and caused that one John Wilkinson,
plasterer, and one Thomas Curtis, were assigned to be
pricers ; which Wilkinson, at the request and desire of the
said Henry, priced the said goods and stuff but to the value
of 35s. 9d., which goods and stuff at that time were well
worth 20 marks and above. Upon which pricement the
said Henry had judgement to recover the said goods and
stuff, for the which your said orator can never have remedy
by course of the common law ; and though your said orator
within the year did put in surety to answer to the said plaint
and bill, and to disprove the said action, yet your said orator
could never, nor shall never by the order of the common
law, there recover again the said stuff and goods, but shall
recover no more for them but only the sum wherefor they
were priced, which is but 35s. 9d. as is before said ; and so
hath and shall, by such falsehood, subtlety, and design of
the said Walton, and of the said Wilkinson and Curtis

which were pricers, lose 11 or 12 pounds or above, and is without remedy therefore for ever, except your gracious Highness be showed to him in this behalf. In consideration whereof it may please your Grace and your most honourable Council to command one of your officers of arms to go to the said Henry Walton and to the said John Wilkinson and Thomas Curtis, and to command them in your name to appear before your Grace and your honourable Council at Westminster, there to answer to the premises and there to be directed according to right and good conscience ; and your said orator and subject shall daily pray for the preservation of your Royal estate, long to endure.

(Signed) JOHANNES RASTELL.

II

The answer of HENRY WALTON *to the Bill of Complaint of* JOHN RASTELL *gentleman.*

The said Henry Walton by protestation saith, that the said goods in the bill of complaint of the said John Rastell mentioned, be not of so great value as in his said bill of complaint is supposed. And saith that the said bill of complaint is uncertain, and insufficient in the law to be answered unto, and the matter therein contained feigned and craftily imagined, to the intent to put the said Henry Walton to great costs and expenses. Nevertheless, for answer and declaration of the truth, the said defendant saith that it appeareth by the bill of the said complainant that he hath no cause of action in this honourable court, for it appeareth by his bill of complaint that the said goods be recovered in the King's Court holden before the Mayor and Aldermen of the City of London, according to the custom of the said City. And further, the defendant saith that he brought an action of debt against the said John Rastell of 40s. in the said court; and he, the said Henry Walton, having in his own keeping the said goods in the said bill of complaint supposed, attached them in his own hands, according to the custom of the said City ; which goods were afterwards, by the commandment of the said court, by the said John Wilkinson and Thomas Curtis, were praised at 35s. 9d.   And where the said John Rastell, in his said bill of complaint, saith that the goods aforesaid were praised much under their value, the said Henry Walton saith that they were praised to as much as they at the time of the praisement were worth.   And where the said complainant in his said bill of complaint saith that he oweth not the said defendant the said 40s. and is without remedy, the said Henry Walton will aver that the said John Rastell oweth him the said 40s. And also the said Henry saith that the said John Rastell might have come into the said court, holden before the Mayor and Aldermen aforesaid, within the year and the day according to the custom, and there to have put in sureties, and so to have dissolved the attachment, but hath suffered and s...:. psed his time.   And the said Henry Walton shall aver that the said goods were of no more value than they were priced at, for they were rotten and torn players' garments.   Without that that the said Henry Walton craftily or falsely, and by subtle advice of his counsel, commenced the said action against the said John Rastell, in manner and form as he in his said bill untruly hath alleged. And without that that anything being material or effectual in the said bill, otherwise than in the said answer of the said Henry, is alleged is true.   And in as much as the said goods be lawfully recovered in the King's Court, holden before the Mayor and Aldermen in the City of London aforesaid, being a Court of Record, the which record cannot be undone without errer or attaint, therefore the said Henry Walton prayeth to be dismissed out of this honourable court, with his reasonable costs and expenses for his wrongful vexation, &c.

III.

The replication of JOHN RASTELL to the Answer of HENRY WALTON.

The said John Rastell saith that his said bill is true, and certain, and sufficient to be answered unto, and matter determinable in this honourable court, and will aver every-

thing to be true contained in the said bill of complaint;
and that the said answer is uncertain and insufficient to
be answered unto, and matter feighed and untrue. And
further saith that the said John Rastell, as soon as he had
knowledge that the said Walton had commenced the said
action of debt of 40s. in the said Mayor's Court in London,
the said Rastell came into the said court and there put in
surety to the said action. Whereupon the said Walton
declared against the said Rastell that the said Rastell
should owe to the said Walton 40s., for that that the said
Rastell confessed himself in the said City of London to owe
to the said Walton 40s., to the which the said Rastell
answered and tended his law, according to the custom of
the said City, that he owed nothing to the said Walton
in manner and form as the said Walton against him declared.
Whereby the said Walton perceived that upon the said plea
and tender his said action should be dissolved; demurred
in law upon the same plea, which demurrer, what for lack
that the Recorder of the said City and other Councillors can
have no convenient time to argue the said matter, and also
for lack that the counsel for the said Walton was not ready
when the said matter of law should be argued, the said
matter as yet doth depend there undiscussed. But yet the
said John Rastell saith that if the said matter be discussed
and judged for the said Rastell, as undoubtedly it will be,
yet the said Rastell, by the custom of the said City, shall
never recover again his said goods, nor stuff, but only 35s. 9d.
for the said stuff, so that in the said court he hath no other
remedy nor record to punish the said Walton nor the said
praisers for their said deceit and falsehood in praising
of the said goods and stuff at 35s. 9d., which were worth
at that time 20 marks and above, as in the said bill of complaint is alleged; for the great part of the said goods were
garments of silk and other stuff, fresh and newly made,
with much workmanship done upon them, to the great cost
and charge of your said orator, without that that the said
goods were at the time of the said appraisement of no more
value than they were praised at. And without that that
they were gone rotten and torn players' garments, for the
said Rastell saith that the said Walton hath letten them
out to hire to divers stage-plays and interludes, and hath

received and had for the hire of them since the said praisement of them the sum of 20 nobles and above. And without that that any other thing material or effectual in this said answer alleged necessary to he replied unto is true. All which matters your said orator is ready to prove and aver as this court will award, and prayeth as he prayed in his said bill.

IV.

The parcels confessed by Walton.

In primis. A player's garment of green, lined with red tuke and with Roman letters stitched upon it, of blue and red sarcenet . . . . 8 yds. 22s

FISHPOLE.—*Item.* One other garment, paned with blue and green sarcenet, lined with red buckram . 7 yds. 20s.

FISHPOLE.—*Item.* Another garment, paned likewise, and lined as the other, with a cape furred with white cats . . . 7 yds. 20s.

FISHPOLE.—*Item.* Another garment, paned with yellow, green, red, and blue sarcenet, and lined with old red buckram. 8 yds. 22s.

Item. Another garment, for a priest to play in, of red say . 12 yds. 4s.

Item. A garment of red and green say paned and guarded with gold skins lined with red buckram . . 12 yds. say, and 7 yds. buckram 8s.

Item. A short garment of gold skins and fustian, of Naples black, and sleeved with red, green, yellow, and blue sarcenet . . . .

Item. Another garment, spangled of blue satin of Bruges, and lined with green sarcenet . . . . . 20s. it hath cost Rastell.

Item. Two old short garments, paned of satin of Bruges, and of sarcenet of divers colours in the bodies . . 20s.

Item. A woman's garment, of green and blue sarcenet, checked and lined with red buckram . . . . 24s.

Item. Two caps, of yellow and red sarcenet . . . 3s. 4d.

Item. Two curtains, of green and yellow sarcenet . . 20 yds. 1s.

Item. Two pieces of blue linen cloth with lyre in them . 67 yds. 15s.

Item. Three pieces of old silvered linen cloths . . 10s.

Item. An old remnant of red buckram, that was in a box in my Lord Cardinal's great chamber . . . . 30 yds. 6s. 8d.

Interrogatories for Fishpole.

Im primis.—Whether Fishpole know any of the said garments.

Item. Whether Fishpole made the two long garments of sarcenet down to the ground, and one green gown to the fall of the leg, with wide sleeves of sarcenet, and whether every of them contained not 7 or 8 yards of sarcenet, and whether every of them were not better than 20s. apiece, and whether if such garments were made of new stuff, would not have cost almost twice as much money.

Item. Whether that Fishpole made not a woman's gown of sarcenet of small pieces, and whether it was not worth 20s. and better.

Item. Whether he made not two other garments with wide sleeves of small pieces, and whether they were not worth 20s. or a mark apiece.

Item. How long Fishpole was a-making of them, and whether he had not the while 4d. a day and meat and drink, and whether Rastell's wife hath holp him to sew them.

Item. Whether Walton hath not the same garments lent to him by Rastell, and whether Walton hath not continually this 4 year let them to hire for stage-plays and interludes, above 3 or 4 score times, and what he used to have for a stage-play, and what for an interlude, and how much money he hath won thereby.

Item. What the short spangled garment of blue satin of Bruges was worth, and what every other garment and piece was worth.

V.

Interrogatory ex parte RASTELL.

Item. Whether about 3 or 4 years now past, about which time the King's great banquet was at Greenwich, which this deponent saw, the said garments were occupied there, some in divers stage-plays and interludes, by the letting to hire by Walton, as it was reported, and at that time they were fresh and new, and seemed little the worse for any wearing of them before.

VI.

Depositions for the part of JOHN RASTELL *against* HENRY WALTON.

[*Deposition of* WILLIAM FISHPOLE.]

William Fishpole of London, tailor, of the age of 60 years and above, sworn and examined upon his oath, saith that he made two long gowns down to the ground, of sarcenet, one of them of blue and yellow sarcenet, lined with red tuke or red buckram, whether of the same lining he now remembereth not, and another of green sarcenet, but whether it were lined or not he remembereth not now, which gowns coming to him in pieces contained in every piece 6 ells or thereabouts. And also he saith that if he should have bought out of the mercer's shop, every ell would have cost 6s.; and he saith that every gown was worth 20s. and above. And also he saith that he made a garment for a gallant with wide sleeves, the one side of red and yellow sarcenet, and the other side blue and red lined with red tuke or red buckram, which was a costly garment, better than 20s. And if they had been bought of new stuff it would have cost much more money. And also he saith he made a woman's gown of sarcenet, blue and yellow, as he remembereth, and it was made in quarrels or lozenges, he remembereth not whether, and was a busy work, and Mistress Rastell did help to sew that, and part of the gallant's gown also. And it was lined with red tuke or buckram and garnished with gold skins, as he remembereth, and it was better than 20s. and it was worth a noble the making. And how long he was in making of them he remembereth not, but he had 4d. by the day, meat and drink. And further he saith that he hath heard say, that the said Rastell lent to Walton the said garments, and that he used them in stage-plays. And further he saith that there was a short spangled garment of blue satin of Bruges, and was lined with green sarcenet, which was better than any of the other garments; which he made not, but every one of them, one with another, were better than 20s., and more he knoweth not herein.

(Signed)   per me WILLIAM FISHPOLE.

VII.

[*Deposition of* GEORGE MAYLER.]

George Mayler of London, merchant tailor, of the age of 40 years, sworn and examined upon his oath, saith that he knew the said garments, but how many there be in number he remembereth not, for he hath occupied and played in them by the lending of Walton, and he saith they were worth 20s. apiece and better. And he saith he knoweth well that he lent them out about 20 times to stage-plays in the summer and interludes in the winter, and used to take at a stage-play for them and others, sometimes 40d., sometimes 2s., as they could agree, and at an interlude 8d. for every time. But how many times he perfectly knoweth not, but by estimation 20 times a year in interludes. And he saith that he hath seen the curtains of sarcenet, but how many ells they contained he knoweth not, but it was worth 40d. every ell, and he saith that he had buckram and tuke, but how many yards he knoweth not, but it was better than 2d. a yard; and further he saith that the summer when the King's banquet was at Greenwich, he saw the same garments occupied in divers stage-plays, and occupied part of them himself by the lending of other players that Walton had lent them to hire, which then were fresh and little worse for the wearing; and more he knoweth not.

(Signed)   per me GEORGE MAYLER.

VIII.

[*Deposition of* GEORGE BIRCH.]

George Birch of London, carrier, of the age of 32 years or thereabouts, sworn and examined saith, that he knew well a player's garment lined with red tuke and stitched with Roman letters upon it of blue and red sarcenet; another garment paned with blue and green sarcenet, lined with red buckram, and another garment paned with yellow, green, red, and blue sarcenet, lined with old red buckram; another garment spangled of blue satin of Bruges, lined with green sarcenet, and a woman's gown or garment of green and blue sarcenet, checked and lined with red buckram; in which garments this deponent and his company played in while they remained in the hands of the said Rastell. And he saith that every garment, one with another, were worth 20s., and that Walton did let out the same garments to hire to stage plays and interludes sundry times, but how many times he knoweth not. And further he saith that the common custom is at an interlude 8d. for the garments, and at a stage play as the parties can agree. And he saith if they had been made of new stuff they had been much more worth. And he saith he saw the curtains of sarcenet, but how many ells they were he knoweth not, but every ell was worth 3s. And further he saith that 3 or 4 years past, when the King's banquet was at Greenwich that summer, he saw the said garments played in 3 or 4 times, by the lending of the said Walton, and at that time they seemed fresh and good garments, and more he knoweth not.

(Signed)   per me GEORGE BIRCH.

IX

[*Deposition of* JOHN REDMAN.]

John Redman of London, stationer, of the age of 22 years, sworn and examined upon his oath, saith that he knew the said garments, but how many was of them he remembreth not; and this deponent played in the same divers times when Walton had them, but what they were worth he knoweth not, but they were little worse than new. And this deponent saith that he knoweth that the said Walton divers times lent them out, but what hire he had for them he knoweth not, neither in stage-play nor in interludes; but as to the 6 garments, that is to say 4 gowns of sarcenet, a woman's gown, and a spangled garment, they were good, fresh, and little the worse for the occupying when he knew them first in Walton's hands, and by estimation they were worth 20s. apiece, for they were lined and guarded part with gilt leather; and the curtains of silk were fresh and new; and there were garments of dornyke and saye, which he well remembereth, and more he cannot say.

per me JOHN REDMAN.

X

The interrogatories of HENRY WALTON *against* JOHN RASTELL, *whereupon witnesses to be examined.*

First, whether the said John Rastell did owe any such

sum of money as within the answer of the said Walton is alleged and submitted.

Item.—Whether the said Walton made lawful attachment of such goods as are comprised within the bill of complaint of the said John Rastell.

Item.—Whether the said goods were indifferently appraised by indifferent persons elect and chosen by lawful officers within the City of London to be praisers there.

Item.—What and how much of value the said goods were appraised unto.

Item.—Whether the said goods were lawfully recovered by the custom and law of the said City of London.

Item.—Whether the said goods were delivered unto the above-named Henry Walton by lawful officers of the same City of London.

Item.—Whether the said goods were of any more value or substance than they were praised unto.

Item.—Whether the said goods were fresh and new, as is surmised unjustly by the bill of complaint of the said Rastell.

XI

Depositions for the part of HENRY WALTON *against* JOHN RASTELL.

[*Deposition of* WILLIAM KNIGHT.]

William Knight of London, latten founder, of the age of 56 years, sworn or examined upon his oath, saith that Walton did make of new for stages and stage players as much as by estimation, esteemed by this deponent and William Sayer at 50s. in board, timber, lath, nail, sprig and daubing, which the said Rastell should have paid to the said Walton by their arbitrament, which were chosen indifferently by them both, and then Rastell said it was too much, and afterwards the said Rastell arrested the same Walton, and much business was between them.

And as to the 2nd, 3rd, 4th, 5th, and 6th interrogatories, he knoweth nothing. And as to the 7th and last article, he saith that the said Rastell had certain garments for players, which were made of old sarcenet, but how many he knoweth not, nor he doth not esteem the value of them nor any of them, and more he knoweth not.

(Signed)   per me WILLIAM KNIGHT.

XII.

[*Deposition of* NICHOLAS SAYER.]

Nicholas Sayer of London, skinner, of the age of 49 years or thereabouts, sworn and examined upon his oath, saith that he and William Knight were desired by the said Rastell and Walton, being at the Mitre in Cheap, to view such costs as the said Walton had done in making of stage for player in Rastell's ground beside Finsbury, in timber, board, nail, lath, sprig, and other things. Which they esteemed and judged at 50s. that Rastell should pay to the said Walton, and upon payment of the said 50s. the said Walton to render such garments as he had in his keeping to the said Rastell. And he saith he saw the garments. and there were none of them of new stuff to his know-ledge, nor what the value of them were, and more he knoweth not.

(Signed)   per me NICHOLAS SAYER.

XIII.

[*Deposition of* ROGER TAYLOR.]

Roger Taylor of London, latten founder, of the age of 40 years, sworn and examined upon his oath, he saith he made part of the said players' garments, and some of them were made of saye and some of sarcenet, which were not at that time of new stuff, for they had been occupied in other business, and they were occupied three or four years in playing and disguisings, or they came to the hands of the said Walton, or before any variance was between them for the same; and as to the value of them he cannot esteem nor judge. And more he cannot say herein.

(Signed)   per me ROGER TAYLOR.

XIV.

[*Deposition of* THOMAS CURTIS.]

Thomas Curtis of London, glazier, of the age of 54 years, sworn and examined upon his oath, saith that the said Walton made attachment of 15 playing garments; and thereupon this deponent and one John Wilkinson were commanded by the Mayor's clerk, called John Edmay, to appraise the same garments indifferently. Which the said deponent and John Wilkinson, after their conscience, appraised to the uttermost value of them, and the value or sum amounted unto 35s. 9d., and he and the said Wilkinson delivered a bill thereof to the said clerk of the Mayor's Court; and he thinketh that after the custom of the City of London the said Walton lawfully recovered the same, but how they were delivered to the said Walton he knoweth not. And further he saith, that at the time of the said appraisement the said garments were old and torn, so that then they were not able to be worn nor occupied. And also he saith he would have been loath to have given so much for them as they were appraised at, and more he knoweth not.

The Mark of Thomas Curtis.

XV.

[*Deposition of* JOHN WILKINSON.]

John Wilkinson of London, plasterer, of the age of 33 years or thereabouts, sworn and examined, saith that he was commanded by John Edmay, the Mayor's officer, to appraise certain old playing garments which were broken and torn, some of them of sarcenet and some of saye, and others which he now remembereth not ; and that he and Thomas Curtis appraised the said garments and stuff at 35s. or 36s. 9d., which in his conscience were no better worth, nor he would not have gladly given so much for them, and more he knoweth not.

(Signed)   JOHN WILKINSON.

GLOSSARY

Aldermost, most of all.
Also, so as, so.
Anchor, hermit.
Apaire, appaire, injure, wither.
Appropred, appropriated.
Arette, attribute, account.
Astert, escape.
Avoutry, adultery.
Bain, obedient.
Battles, divisions of an army.
Bear on hand, deceive.
Bedene, bedeen, betimes.
Behote, promise.
Beme, tree.
Betake, beteach, commit.
Blee, countenance.
Blin, departing.
Blinne, cease.
Blyve, quickly.
Borrows, sureties.
Bote, remedy.
Brast, burst.
Brenningly, burningly.
Brere, briar.
Brook, use.
Busk, make ready.
Buxom, obedient, pliant.
Bydene, betimes.
Careful, sorrowful.
Chevice, preserve.
Clap, talk noisily, chatter.
Cleped, called.
Coresed, fit to be a courser [?]
Corser, coffer [?]
Courtepy, short coat.
Covenable, suitable.
Covetise, covetousness.

Crach, crèche, cradle.
Crake, boast.
Curteys, courteous.
Dearworthy, precious.
Deem, judge.
Delibered, deliberated.
Derne, secret, remote.
Dight, make ready.
Digne, worthy.
Discordeth, disagrees.
Dislander, defame.
Dooms, judgments.
Dress, direct.
Eisell, vinegar.
Empechement, hindrance.
Emprised, undertaken.
Encheson, cause.
Enderes-night, former or other night.
Everychone, everyone.
Fand, found.
Farly, marvellous.
Fay, faith.
Fere, companion ; *in-fere*, together.
Fond, find, contrive.
Fone, foon, foes.
Fordo, make nought.
Forlorn, lost.
Forthy, therefore.
Forwhy, because.
Fremd, strange
Frere, frier.
Frese, make ready.
Gabbeth, talks foolishly.
Gent, fair.
Gin, begin.
Gleed, spark.
Grathly, readily.

322

Gree, pleasure.
Groom, man.
Halfendell, half part.
Halk, corner.
Hat, am called.
Hend, courteous.
Hent, seized.
Hight, called.
Hind, servant.
Hipped, hobbled.
Idiots, unskilled persons.
In-fere, together.
i-, participial prefix.
I-pight, pitched.
I-wis, certainly.
Jesen, jesayne, place of childbirth.
Kay, meadow.
Kithe, show.
Knowledge, acknowledge, confess.
Lancegay, lance.
Lang, long.
Leasing, lying.
Leer, cheek.
Lede, following.
Leme, shine.
Lend, stay.
Lere, learn.
Let (1), hinder; (2) cause.
Letting, hindrance.
Lewte, loyalty.
Lithe, listen.
Lo, meadow.
Lore, lost.
Losenger, rascal.
Low, blaze.
Lyre, a kind of stuff.
Mansuete, gentle.
Maugre, despite.
May, maiden.
Meddled, mingled.
Mees, houses.
Mo, more.
Myster, need.
Namely, specially.
Nar, nearer.
Nice, foolish.

No force, no matter.
Nombles, loins of a deer.
Notoyrly, notoriously.
Novels, news.
Okerer, usurer.
Other, or.
Paned, slashed.
Percase, perchance.
Pirie, gust.
Pludde, some kind of kettle.
Postillators, preachers.
Praised, appraised.
Prime, six to nine A.M.
Quarrels, small squares.
Queme, please.
Quere, choir.
Quit, requited.
Race, scratch.
Ray, kind of cloth.
Recheless, careless.
Reprefe, reprief, reproof.
Rown, whisper.
Royaumes, realms.
Salued, saluted.
Saws, sayings.
Say, silk.
Semblable, like.
Shende, harm, spoil.
Sicker, sure; *sikerly*, surely.
Silly, innocent.
Slee, slay.
Slo, slone, slain.
Somedeal, somewhat.
Somers, baggage mules.
Sond, messenger.
Sowning into, tending to.
Spill, destroy.
Starven, die.
Styed, mounted.
Sue, pursue, follow.
Supplye, supplicate.
Stound, space of time.
Sy, saw.
Tayd, tied.
Teen, sorrow.
Thee, thrive.

Tho, then.
Throw, space of time.
Till, to.
Tine, lose.
To-coming, future.
Train, treachery.
Truage, tribute.
Tuke, a dress material.
Tynde, antlers.
Unketh, unknown, strange.
Unneath, *unnethis*, hardly.
Unwieldy, impotent.
Wed, pledge.
Welt, wielded, disposed of.

Werrey, make war on.
Wight, man.
Wight, strong.
Witen, know.
Wonder, wondrous.
Wone, dwell.
Woning wane, dwelling place.
Wood, mad.
Wyte, blame.
Y-, participial prefix.
Yede, *yode*, went.
Y-nocked, notched.
Y-wis, certainly.

Edinburgh : Printed by T. and A. CONSTABLE.